THE CHURCH AS SACRED SPACE IN MIDDLE ENGLISH LITERATURE AND CULTURE

Manchester University Press

Manchester Medieval Literature and Culture publishes monographs and essay collections comprising new research informed by current critical methodologies on the literary cultures of the Middle Ages. We are interested in all periods, from the early Middle Ages through to the late, and we include post-medieval engagements with and representations of the medieval period (or 'medievalism'). 'Literature' is taken in a broad sense, to include the many different medieval genres: imaginative, historical, political, scientific, religious. While we welcome contributions on the diverse cultures of medieval Britain and are happy to receive submissions on Anglo-Norman, Anglo-Latin and Celtic writings, we are also open to work on the Middle Ages in Europe more widely, and beyond.

Titles available in the series

2. *Water and fire: The myth of the Flood in Anglo-Saxon England*
   Daniel Anlezark
3. *Greenery: Ecocritical readings of late medieval English literature*
   Gillian Rudd
4. *Sanctity and pornography in medieval culture: On the verge*
   Bill Burgwinkle and Cary Howie
5. *In strange countries: Middle English literature and its afterlife: Essays in memory of J. J. Anderson*
   David Matthews (ed.)
6. *A knight's legacy: Mandeville and Mandevillian lore in early modern England*
   Ladan Niayesh (ed.)
7. *Rethinking the* South English Legendaries
   Heather Blurton and Jocelyn Wogan-Browne (eds)
8. *Between earth and heaven: Liminality and the Ascension of Christ in Anglo-Saxon literature*
   Johanna Kramer
9. *Transporting Chaucer*
   Helen Barr
10. *Sanctity as literature in late medieval Britain*
    Eva von Contzen and Anke Bernau (eds)
11. *Reading Robin Hood: Content, form and reception in the outlaw myth*
    Stephen Knight
12. *Annotated Chaucer bibliography: 1997–2010*
    Mark Allen and Stephanie Amsel
13. *Roadworks: Medieval roads, medieval Britain*
    Valerie Allen and Ruth Evans (eds)
14. *Love, history and emotion in Chaucer and Shakespeare:* Troilus and Criseyde *and* Troilus and Cressida
    Andrew James Johnston, Russell West-Pavlov and Elisabeth Kempf (eds)
15. *The* Scottish Legendary*: Towards a poetics of hagiographic narration*
    Eva von Contzen
16. *Nonhuman voices in Anglo-Saxon literature and material culture*
    James Paz
17. *The church as sacred space in Middle English literature and culture*
    Laura Varnam

The church as sacred space in Middle English literature and culture

LAURA VARNAM

Manchester University Press

Published by Manchester University Press
Altrincham Street, Manchester M1 7JA

www.manchesteruniversitypress.co.uk

British Library Cataloguing-in-Publication Data
A catalogue record for this book is available from the British Library

ISBN 978 1 7849 9417 4 hardback
ISBN 978 1 5261 4356 3 paperback

First published by Manchester University Press in hardback 2018
This edition published 2019

Typeset by Deanta Global Publishing Services
Chennai, India

Here's the church, here's the steeple,
Open the doors and see all the people.

(Nursery rhyme)

For Mum, Dad, and Teo,
with love.

Contents

Figures

Acknowledgements

This book has been many years in the making and I am more delighted than I can say to see it in print and to write these acknowledgements. I am truly grateful to my family, friends, and colleagues for supporting me throughout this process – I really couldn't have done it with you.

It is difficult to put into words how much I owe to Helen Barr. Helen has been there from the beginning of this project and she has helped me in more ways than I can say, both intellectual and personal. If this book in any way does justice to her fine teaching, wise guidance, and friendship, then I will be most pleased. Her marvellous scholarship has been a shining example of medieval literary study and it has been an incredible privilege to work with her.

I would like to thank my colleagues in 'Team English' at University College, Oxford: Tiffany Stern, Nicholas Halmi, Oliver Clarkson, and Ashley Maher; and in the extended 'Team', Stephanie Dumke and Daniel Grimley. I could not have wished for more supportive colleagues and friends. Tiffany and Nick have been a constant source of encouragement, their scholarship has been an inspiration, and their friendship a true gift.

My students at Univ have been a pleasure to teach. Their enthusiasm, vitality, and sparkle have kept me going and their work has sharpened my own thinking and kept me on my toes. It is an honour to teach such gifted students and to benefit from their intellectual engagement with medieval literature. Discussing everything from Chaucer to Margery Kempe, Harry Potter to Tolkien, with tea and biscuits in hand, could not be a more enjoyable way to spend my time!

My academic debts are many and various. Generous colleagues and friends have offered advice, insight, and feedback throughout this project. Thanks go to Vincent Gillespie, Jenni Nuttall, Laura Kalas Williams, Sarah Salih, Helen Cooper, Marion Turner,

Rachel Delman, Laura Clash, Sandy Murray, Ann Hutchison and James Carley, Gavin and Gill Williams; during my time at the University of Leeds, Catherine Batt and Alfred Hiatt; and during my undergraduate days, Corinne Saunders, whose lectures and tutorials inspired me to pursue medieval literature further. I would like to thank Allan Doig for his comments and guidance on Chapter 1 and Annie Sutherland for her feedback on the same chapter and the introduction, and her support in the early stages of this project. I owe a considerable debt of thanks to my friend Jan Machielsen, who gave me a gentle push when I really needed it, and whose fine work has been a great example to me. I would like to thank everyone at Manchester University Press for supporting this book: the series editors Anke Bernau and David Matthews, the editorial team, and especially the anonymous readers for their invaluable feedback. My friends have also been there every step of the way: Anne Osborne, Stephanie Langin-Hooper, Judith Tings, Beni and Silke Gilich, Ann and David Willmore. Thanks also go to Cathy Shafto and Alicia Spencer-Hall for cheering me on at the finish.

Finally, I would like to thank my family, without whom this book would never have been written. My grandparents, Laura and Ernie ('Tommy'), Nora and Bill, although you're not here to see it, I hope I've done you proud; my brother, Will, whose sense of humour always ensures that I don't take myself too seriously; my Dad, Julian, whose love of Tolkien and history set me on the path to becoming a medievalist; and my Mum, Megan, who probably knows more about the medieval church than she ever imagined possible or indeed desirable. If I could give my Mum an honorary doctorate with this book (on her specialist subject, the Lollards), I would! And finally, my husband, Teo, who has the patience of a saint and never stopped believing that I could finish this book, thank you for putting up with me! I never would have got to the end of this project without the love and support of my family. This book is for all of you.

Abbreviations

EETS	Early English Text Society (1864–)
OS	Original Series (1864–)
ES	Extra Series (1867–1920)
SS	Supplementary Series (1970–)
MED	*Middle English Dictionary*, ed. Hans Kurath and S. M. Kuhn (Ann Arbor: University of Michigan Press; London: Oxford University Press, 1952–) http://quod.lib.umich.edu/m/med/

All of the stained glass windows referred to in this book are available online in *Corpus Vitrearum Medii Aevi* unless otherwise specified: www.cvma.ac.uk/index.html

Introduction: Reading sacred space in late medieval England

In the anonymous fifteenth-century continuation of Chaucer's *Canterbury Tales* known as *The Canterbury Interlude and the Merchant's Tale of Beryn*, the pilgrims finally arrive at the sacred destination of their pilgrimage, Canterbury Cathedral, their terrestrial Jerusalem (Figure 1). The Knight and his companions make for the shrine of St Thomas Becket but the Pardoner, the Miller, and the Host linger in the nave and look around them in wonder at the architecture and the stained glass:

> The Pardoner and the Miller and other lewde sotes
> Sought hemselff in the chirch, right as lewd gotes,
> Pyred fast and poured highe oppon the glase,
> Counterfeting gentilmen, the armes for to blase,
> Diskyveryng fast the peyntour, and for the story mourned
> And ared also – right as rammes horned!
> 'He bereth a balstaff,' quod the toon, 'and els a rakes ende'.
> 'Thow faillest,' quod the Miller, 'thowe hast nat wel thy mynde.
> It is a spere, yf thowe canst se, with a prik tofore
> To bussh adown his enmy and thurh the sholder bore.'
> 'Pese!' quod the Hoost of Southwork. 'Let stond the wyndow glased.
> Goth up and doth yeur offerynge. Ye semeth half amased'.[1]

The Pardoner and his companions gaze 'half amased' upon the stained glass and, perhaps unsurprisingly given their status as the 'lewdest' pilgrims on the road to Canterbury, they are unsuccessful in deciphering the iconography. But crucially, they do try. Even men in a state of sin are conditioned by their pastoral instruction to read the stained glass and to interpret the architecture and symbols that surround them when they enter the medieval cathedral. The church building is at the heart of lay piety and it is a space so marvellous, sacred, and laden with symbolism that even these Canterbury pilgrims cannot help but engage with it and respond.

1 Canterbury Cathedral.

This book is an investigation of the churches of late medieval England. How they were read, constructed, and contested by their communities and how their most important characteristic – their sanctity – was manifested and understood. It is an attempt to stand in the church, as the Canterbury pilgrims did, and by bringing together textual, visual, and material culture, to show how the laity were not only taught to view the church as a sacred space but to contribute to the production of that sanctity. The pilgrims' experiences in the cathedral and at the shrine of Thomas Becket provide a starting point for developing a reading of sacred space that foregrounds the role of lay practice and that is alert to the social and cultural contexts in which sacred space was operating and the debates in which it was entangled. Paul Strohm argues that 'the peculiarity of medieval space involves the extent to which it is already symbolically organised by the meaning-making activities of the many generations that have traversed it'.[2] Consecrated by a ceremony that builds scriptural quotation, liturgical ritual, and communal participation into the very foundations of the building, the church as sacred space is a prime example of a material building and spiritual concept that is already densely laden with meaning. The church was the house of God on earth but in the fourteenth and fifteenth centuries this identity was under considerable scrutiny. Groups such as the Lollards asked whether the church community was better off without the church building, that ornamented distraction grown rich in visual decorations at the expense of the poor and needy. But the legacy of the pastoral care reforms of the Fourth Lateran Council in 1215 saw the church building reinvigorated as a space of teaching and edification. Stained glass windows and wall paintings of pastoral schema such as the Seven Works of Mercy or the Warning against Gossip helped the laity not only to control their behaviour but also to preserve the sanctity of the church by guarding against desecration. Furthermore, increased competition among the parish churches, cathedrals, and pilgrimage sites of medieval England meant that sanctity was increasingly valuable as a form of symbolic capital that could improve a church's social as well as sacred status in the world.

Sacred spaces such as Canterbury Cathedral were a multimedia project and a community concern. They were constructed out of a fusion of architecture, iconography, material culture, and narrative practice. Master builders and artists worked together to create sacred spaces from stone, stained glass and sculpture, and writers and preachers turned to churches, shrines, and miracle sites as symbols of community, places of spiritual edification, and above all, as God's house on earth. This study will bring cultural practices such as preaching, liturgical rituals such as church consecration, the visual arts, and the textual record into conversation with modern theoretical approaches, from theories of space and place to ideas of performance, in order to ask the question, as Mary Carruthers suggests, not only 'what does it mean' but 'what is it good for?'[3] Sacred spaces were constructed in stone, art, language, and embodied performance in order to glorify God and provide a place for worship, but they were also used to edify communities, negotiate social tensions, and debate theological issues. Sacred space was a key tool for medieval communities to represent, understand, and interact with the world around them.

My reading of the church as sacred space demands an interdisciplinary approach and I will have recourse to research from literary studies, history, art history, and a range of theoretical works throughout this book. In the last two decades scholars have increasingly turned to space as a topic for textual analysis and recent work in medieval studies by Keith Lilley, Robert Barrett Jr., and Catherine Clarke's *Mapping Medieval Chester* project team has sought to integrate textual constructions of space with related practices in other media, from maps and buildings to processions and performances.[4] Such approaches ask questions not only about the ways in which medieval communities conceived of and represented the space around them but also how that space was lived and practised, and how it participated in the formation of communal identity. The church as sacred space in particular invites such a methodology, as performance and practice are at the core of sacred space from its inception in the consecration ceremony.

Since Paul Strohm's *Theory and the Premodern Text* in 2000, theoretical approaches to medieval texts have flourished. In the introduction to the 2013 *Handbook of Middle English Studies*, in which scholars brought a range of theories to bear upon literary texts, Marion Turner comments that 'Aristotle, Augustine, and Dante are theorists just as much as Derrida, Foucault, and Žižek. Theory helps us to open texts up and allow them to speak to us.'[5] The fourteenth- and fifteenth-century texts that are my focus in this book are just as theoretical as their modern counterparts. From allegorical readings of church architecture to foundation legends, exempla warning against sacrilege to treatises on the relationship between the material and spiritual church, the medieval writers under discussion are themselves asking theoretical questions. What does the church symbolise, how is sanctity produced and maintained, what is sacrilege, how should we read the painted church? Michel Foucault described the Middle Ages as a space of 'emplacement', foregrounding the 'hierarchic ensemble of places' such as sacred and profane, celestial and terrestrial.[6] In *The Production of Space*, Henri Lefebvre argued that the Middle Ages is 'inhabited, haunted by the church' and he asks 'what would remain of the Church if there were no churches?'[7] This is precisely the question that arises in Middle English debates on the material church in the light of Lollard concerns. How important was the building to the idea of the church? Both medieval and modern texts share an interest in exploring such theoretical issues as the relationship between building and concept, the production of space, and models of spatial hierarchy. Turner concludes that 'theory, in productive relationship with texts, can act as a catalyst, enabling dynamic reading experiences'.[8] To encounter the sacred space of the church in the Middle Ages was a dynamic experience and by drawing upon modern theorists who share a focus on practice, production, and a synthesis between material and intellectual framings of space, I propose a new way of reading and understanding the medieval church in the modern world.

The dynamism of sacred space can be clearly seen in the depiction of the restoration of St Paul's Cathedral in the Middle English miracle narrative *St Erkenwald*:

> Mony a mery mason was made þer to wyrke,
> Harde stones for to hewe wyt eggit toles,
> Mony a grubber in grete þe grounde for to seche
> þat þe fundement on fyrst shuld þe fote halde.
> And as þai makkyde and mynyde a meruayle þai founden
> As ȝet in crafty cronecles is kydde þe memorie.[9]

Here the construction of sacred space is depicted as skilled and joyful physical labour. Merry masons chisel at the stone with specialist tools, men dig deep into the ground to locate the foundations, and as they 'make' and 'mine' they discover a marvel: the uncorrupted body of a pagan judge who speaks to the bishop and the people about his plight as a righteous heathen. This moment in *St Erkenwald* figures the restoration of the church as an energetic and industrious process involving individuals whose collective effort and creativity unearths a marvel in their shared history. The late Middle Ages saw considerable rebuilding work being undertaken in churches and cathedrals across England as communities sought not only to maintain and repair but also to enlarge and elaborate upon their buildings, adding spires or extending porches, installing stained glass windows and populating the nave with devotional images. Sacred space was often a building site and as such occupied a prominent place in the public consciousness as medieval communities came into close contact with the material fabric of their buildings. And at such moments, they looked to their shared sacred history for support and encouragement. Miracles remembered in 'crafty cronecles', such as the one in *St Erkenwald*, were a powerful incentive for communities to honour their sacred spaces. *St Erkenwald*'s use of the alliterative 'makkyde and mynyde' alerts us to the productive relationship between textual and material creation; the Middle

English verb ‘to make’ is used both of material construction and poetic composition.[10] *St Erkenwald* not only records the miraculous, it re-enacts it and brings it to life in the contemporary world. As Sari Katajala-Pelltomaa argues, ‘the recollection of miracles can be seen as an interaction with the sacred’ that strengthens and renews the original moment of sanctity.[11] Such interactions are especially beneficial when a community is rebuilding or restoring its church, as we shall see in *The Book of the Foundation of St Bartholomew's Church* in Chapter 2 of this book.

A truly sacred space, however, relies upon the presence of God as well as human endeavour. In *St Erkenwald*, the miracle of the uncorrupted body and the subsequent miraculous baptism of the pagan judge made God's presence known; at Canterbury Cathedral, it was the miracles of St Thomas Becket. Sacred space is often manifested in the form of miracles, instances of God's supernatural works and intervention in the world. In *The Sacred and Profane*, a study that forms the foundation of my discussion of sanctity in this book, the historian of religion Mircea Eliade argues that in order to be made visible and to operate in the world, sanctity must be made manifest.[12] God's presence is, of course, ubiquitous but a sacred space represents an intensification of that presence, a space in which God is experienced directly through supernatural events or visions. Eliade calls such a manifestation a ‘hierophany’, which he defines as ‘an irruption of the sacred that results in detaching the territory from the surrounding cosmic milieu and making it qualitatively different’.[13] A miracle creates a sacred space by marking out the place in which it occurs as ‘qualitatively different’ to the quotidian space that surrounds it, and such miracles can occur as freely in urban space – in city streets and domestic dwellings – as in ritually consecrated spaces such as the church. My focus in this book is on sacred space because while the church is the cornerstone of the medieval concept of sacred space, sacred outposts can emerge elsewhere as a result of miracles associated with the church. Any space can become sacred if God manifests his power and presence there and, conversely, a consecrated space such as a parish church can become transformed into a profane space if its sanctity is desecrated by sinful behaviour.

Sanctity is not confined to a single place, building, or geographical location – it is fundamentally spacious. As God's house on earth, the church operates as a crucial centre of sanctity but its material objects can travel into the surrounding space and create spaces that are sanctified by association and that reinforce the original source of sanctity by being a site of further miracles. A consecrated host might calm a storm at sea; the sounds of church bells might free a man from prison. Miracles can occur on a pilgrimage route or at a natural spring or well.[14] Even prayers to the saint of a particular church can be efficacious as mentally imagining the space allows devotees to gain access to its sanctity even at a spatial remove. Sacred space is fluid, contagious, and unconstrained by material boundaries. It is flexible, adaptable, and manifests itself in a range of forms and environments.

The characteristic that all sacred spaces share, however, is their intense potency and their ability to organise and redraw the map of the surrounding space. Sacred spaces are magnetic and attractive, and as Eliade argues, they become 'an absolute fixed point, a centre' of orientation.[15] The parish church is one such centre in the local environment and many of the texts under discussion in this book aim to promote and preserve that centrality. When a sacred space is created through miracles, however, a new topography is established as communities gather and regroup around the miracle site, going on pilgrimage to venerate the space and realigning their sacred map to accommodate the new site. Canterbury Cathedral, the 'absolute fixed point' in Chaucer's *Canterbury Tales* and its continuations, was the most popular pilgrimage destination in medieval England and it formed the centre of the sacred map of the country, rather like Jerusalem in medieval *mappa mundi*. Canterbury's centrality in medieval literature and culture makes it a perfect test case for examining how sacred space operates in late medieval England. How might *The Canterbury Interlude*'s recognisable cast of Chaucerian characters read the space and how might they produce, or destabilise, its sanctity?

The Canterbury Interlude: Chaucer's pilgrims in sacred space

The Canterbury Interlude and the Merchant's Tale of Beryn is found in a copy of Chaucer's *Canterbury Tales* known as MS Northumberland 455. The manuscript dates from 1450–70 but the text was composed as much as half a century earlier, perhaps to coincide with the 1420 jubilee of Thomas Becket's martyrdom.[16] The text is anonymous but a Latin couplet at the end of the 'Tale of Beryn' attributes the text to a 'son of the church of St Thomas' (*Filius ecclesie Thome*, 4024). This, coupled with additional evidence, suggests that the author might have been a monk at the cathedral with responsibilities for Becket's shrine.[17] The *Interlude* depicts the pilgrims' arrival in Canterbury, their stay at a pilgrimage hostel called the Checker of the Hoop, and culminates in the fabliau adventures of the Pardoner with Kit the Tapster. Crucially, the text also depicts the pilgrims' experiences in the cathedral (Figure 1) and it gives an insight into the significant urban spaces of the city, such as the city walls. The *Interlude* has most often been analysed by literary critics in terms of its Chaucerian indebtedness but more recently Robert Sturges has argued that rather than assessing the *Interlude*-author as a reader of Chaucer, we should instead examine 'how its author uses Chaucer to serve his contemporary ends' and 'how adaptable Chaucer is to the needs of a later poet concerned with his own cultural circumstances'.[18] For Sturges, the *Interlude* exhibits class and gender anxieties which are played out in the urban space of the city. I would argue that the text also manifests late medieval anxieties surrounding the use and meaning of church buildings and how the laity ought to understand and interact with their sacred confines. The episode has frequently been discussed by art historians as part of the textual evidence for medieval attitudes to the visual arts, attitudes that, as T. A. Heslop puts it, are full of 'ambivalence and contradiction'.[19] Here I want to explore the text's dramatisation of lay engagement with church art and with devotional practice at the sacred destination of their pilgrimage, the shrine of Becket. The *Interlude* marshals a familiar group of characters, about whom the reader shares certain expectations, in order to play into, challenge, and frustrate late medieval approaches to sacred space and its visual codes. Sanctity, as I will argue throughout this book, is dependent upon lay practice for its production and maintenance and in the *Interlude* we are given an opportunity to see that practice in action, and the consequences for sacred space when it is carried out by less than ideal participants.

When the Miller and his companions enter the cathedral and look at the stained glass, they engage in a fourfold process of interpretation that pays very careful attention to its visual codes. To return to the quotation with which I began:

> The Pardoner and the Miller and other lewde sotes
> Sought hemselff in the chirch, right as lewd gotes,
> Pyred fast and poured highe oppon the glase,
> Counterfeting gentilmen, the armes for to blase,
> Diskyveryng fast the peyntour, and for the story mourned
> And ared also – right as rammes horned!
> 'He bereth a balstaff,' quod the toon, 'and els a rakes ende'.
> 'Thow faillest,' quod the Miller, 'thowe hast nat wel thy mynde.

It is a spere, yf thowe canst se, with a prik tofore
To bussh adown his enmy and thurh the sholder bore.'
'Pese!' quod the Hoost of Southwork. 'Let stond the wyndow glased.
Goth up and doth yeur offerynge. Ye semeth half amased.' (147–58)

Firstly, they focus on the visual iconography. They look intently and with purpose ('pyred' and 'poured') in order to discover what the image represents ('diskyveryng fast the peyntour'). Then they 'mourn' (meditate or consider) the 'story' within which the image operates, 'ared' (interpret) the meaning of the image, and finally debate among themselves as to their conclusions. Although the pilgrims are ultimately unsuccessful in their interpretation, as I will discuss further below, their reading practice is systematic and thorough. Indeed, it mirrors the model proposed in the fifteenth-century treatise on the Decalogue, *Dives and Pauper*, in response to Dives' question, 'how shulde I rede in þe book of peynture and of ymagerye?'[20] Phrased in terms of the popular trope that imagery is the book of the laity, Pauper's initial response is to offer an interpretation of the primary Christian symbol, the cross. He urges Dives repeatedly to 'take heid' of different aspects of the image and its meaning: 'take heid' of the crown of thorns and the shedding of Christ's blood 'for to dystroyȝe þe heye synne of pryde'; 'take heid' how Christ's hands are nailed to the cross to 'dystroyȝe þe synne þat Adam and Eue dedyn wyt here hondys' when they took the apple; and so on (p. 83). Leaving aside for a moment that Pauper's example focuses on a purely religious symbol, the *Interlude* pilgrims do 'take heid' of the stained glass and they do try to identify the particular elements of the scene in front of them. Pauper tells Dives that imagery 'sumwhat betokenyȝt in special, sumqhat in comoun and in general' and he explains that 'in special tokene', for example, the Virgin is depicted with a child in her left arm 'in tokene' that she is the mother of God and with a lily or a rose in her right hand 'in tokene' that she is a virgin and the flower of all women (p. 91). The saints, too, have their special symbols: St Peter and his keys, St Paul and his sword, St Katherine and her wheel, St Margaret and her cross and dragon (pp. 91–3). These attributes not only have symbolic meaning – St Peter was given the keys to heaven by Christ, for example – but they also function as cues for narrative recollection. The image of St Margaret reminds the viewer that 'qhanne þe dragoun deuowryd here she blissyd here & be vertue of þe cros þe foul dragoun brast and she cam out of hym heyl and hool' (p. 93). The *Interlude*-pilgrims rack their brains for a narrative with which they can make sense of the Canterbury glass, reminding us that religious imagery often functions as an aid to remembrance rather than a tool for teaching something new.[21] But at this stage of the process, the pilgrims falter and with no authority figure like Pauper to turn to, they begin to quarrel among themselves.

Having moved from the literal meaning to the narrative context, the pilgrims each arrive at an individual interpretation that is judged and negotiated through communal dialogue. This is crucial because reading imagery, and reading sacred space, is a communal and social practice. Each reading by a particular community of readers at a particular time generates its own interpretation, about which there might be dissent and disagreement. The verb of interpretation that the *Interlude*-author uses, 'ared', supports this density of meaning as the verb is used elsewhere in the text of the interpretation of dreams, another mode of representation with deeply symbolic significance that also requires a complex and layered reading process.[22] Michael Camille argues for the similarity between the process of reading text and image, focusing on the role of performance and social dialogue:

> Medieval readers also used books in the ways they used images; in groups, speaking the words out loud, referring back and forth, repeating, returning, even adding to or correcting the unframed continuity of the work. Perception was a performance.[23]

The pilgrims' act of perception here is doubly performative as it is, of course, the narrative construction of the *Interlude*-author. The meaning of sacred space is encoded in the building and its decorations by the church hierarchy, of which the *Interlude*-author is most likely a member, but it is read and interpreted by social groups who may, in the case of the pilgrims, be without the mediating presence of a priest. This leaves the interpretative process dangerously open and unpoliced, and rather than the window contributing to the production of sacred space, it generates confusion and argument. While it is unlikely that the *Interlude*-author, as a Canterbury monk, would have any sympathy with the Lollard position on imagery, the text's dramatization of the pilgrims' misinterpretation does raise similar concerns about the efficacy of visual representation as a stand-alone teaching tool.[24]

The pilgrims' disagreement in the *Interlude* centres upon the implement that the figure in the window is holding and it unsettles the easy equivalence between 'tokene' and narrative that Pauper rehearsed. The relationship between sign and signified is not straightforward here:

> 'He bereth a balstaff,' quod the toon, 'and els a rakes ende.'
> 'Thou faillest,' quod the Miller, 'thowe hast nat wel thy mynde.
> It is a spere, yf thowe canst se, with a prik tofore
> To bussh adown his enmy and thurh the sholder bore.' (153–6)

It is significant that the Miller is portrayed in debate with a nameless pilgrim here ('quod the toon') as it demonstrates that the cathedral is a space for all, not just the known. This nameless pilgrim suggests that the figure in the window is bearing a staff or rake but the Miller forcefully disagrees, proposing instead that the man carries a spear. John Bowers suggests that the image that might have provoked such controversy could be the twelfth-century panel from the Ancestors of Christ window, featuring Adam tilling the earth:

> It would be appropriate if the image causing such confusion in interpretation – a man with a staff? or rake? or spear? – were the panel originally in the north window, opposite the main southwest entrance, showing Adam delving the earth since the Miller and his friends so clearly belong to the unregenerated class of the Old Adam.[25]

The pilgrims' inability to recognise the image could be a sign of their sin and an indication to the reader that while they might be able to enter the symbolic Jerusalem on their terrestrial pilgrimage, the heavenly Jerusalem is currently out of reach. Madeline Caviness argues that many of the images in the cathedral, most notably the typological windows, are particularly challenging and that they were directed at the monks of the cathedral rather than the general populous. Many of the images are 'bookish and esoteric' and Caviness suggests that 'the typological windows were less a poor man's Bible than an elaborate display of twelfth-century theology which could only be fully understood by the literate'.[26] The ability to successfully read the visual codes of sacred space was determined in large part by education and literacy, and by the status of the particular foundation. Canterbury Cathedral served multiple purposes: it was part of the Benedictine monastery, the seat of the archbishop of Canterbury, and a major pilgrimage site, and as such its visual iconography was seen by multiple audiences. The Canterbury pilgrims may not have been the target audience for the typological windows and as such their inability to read the image is understandable. When they reached Becket's shrine in the Trinity Chapel, however, they would have seen the miracle windows that depicted pilgrims just such as themselves, visiting the shrine and encountering the saint; images that were deliberately designed for their edification and to validate their journey to the shrine.

But as Helen Barr has recently pointed out, the 'identity of the stick-like object over which the pilgrims squabble is never revealed'.[27] Indeed, Barr asserts that it is not 'possible conclusively to identify the window in question':

> There are numerous windows in Trinity Chapel which feature such an implement: either as a weapon, pilgrim staff or St Thomas's pastoral staff. With no localisation of the window, what the pilgrims see has the potential to figure an implement that has a range of significances from healing to injury across the whole social spectrum.[28]

Without a clear referent for the window, although it is tempting for us to judge the pilgrims' reading practice as ineffectual, we cannot be sure on what grounds they are wrong. Their interpretation might also be affected not only by their location in the cathedral but by their spatial positioning. Michael Camille comments wryly that if the image is the figure of Adam from the twelfth-century Ancestors of Christ, the windows were 'far above them, both spatially and cognitively'.[29] The *Interlude*-author does note that they 'poured highe' upon the glass in order to see it and when the Miller disagrees with his fellow pilgrim's interpretation, he comments 'yf thowe canst se', which suggests that their confused interpretation could be a result of the window's location inhibiting a clear view of its iconography. Any analysis of sacred space should take account of its physical coordinates and be aware that the lived, practised experience of sacred space is shaped by the access that different groups have to the space, both physical and visual, but also in terms of social status and knowledge. On a basic level, the laity were excluded from the most sacred space of the church, the chancel, and their knowledge of religious narratives was to a large extent dependent upon the education they received from their parish priest. The *Interlude* makes the status of the Miller and his companions abundantly clear when he repeats the Middle English word for uneducated twice in the space of as many lines: 'The Pardoner and the Miller and other *lewde* sotes/Sought hemselff in the chirch, right as *lewd* gotes' (147–8, italics mine). Lay education was a major concern following the decrees of the Fourth Lateran Council, and in the third chapter of this book I will analyse the didactic materials used by priests to teach the laity the meaning of sacred space and their responsibility for its continued maintenance. What is additionally important for our understanding of *The Canterbury Interlude*, however, is the status of the church as a pilgrimage site. While pilgrimage to Thomas Becket was hugely popular in medieval England, the fact remains that Canterbury Cathedral was an unfamiliar space to most pilgrims. It was not their local parish church, with its recognisable visual codes, a space with which parishioners were encouraged to develop a personal, emotional relationship based on loyalty and familiarity over an extended period of time. The *Interlude*-pilgrims are encountering unknown imagery in a new and awe-inspiring space. It is perhaps to be expected that they fail in their first attempt to read it.

The disagreement between the pilgrims is expressed with considerable vehemence, however. The Miller declares: 'Thow faillest! Thowe has not wel thy mynde!' (154). Sacred space is important, it is worth arguing about, and it demands an interpretative response. But it also provides an opportunity for individuals to assert themselves within the group and to establish their social superiority. Chaucer himself recognised this in the *General Prologue* to *The Canterbury Tales* when he describes the Wife of Bath's behaviour in church. She has to be the first to make her offering, otherwise she is 'out of alle charitee' and on a Sunday, her headdress is so elaborate that the narrator swears 'they weyeden ten pound'.[30] The Wife's appearance at church is primarily a social performance here. The narrator also relates her marital history with reference to the church, 'housbondes at chirche dore she hadde fyve', and while this refers to the tradition of marriages taking place in the church porch, it reminds us that sacred space is also social space, even amorous space.[31] We might recall the parish clerk Absolon in *The Miller's Tale* in this context who, when 'sensynge the wyves of the parisshe faste' on a holy day, 'many a lovely look on hem he caste/And namely on this carpenteris wyf.'[32] The pastoral care texts that will be the focus of Chapter 3 demonstrate that sacred space never operated apart from social and secular concerns. As Katherine French has shown, the 'centrality of the parish church' in the lives of medieval communities was not purely due to its status as a sacred space. The church was used by its parishioners for a variety of other legitimate purposes: 'business, legal settlements, sociability, and entertainment, in addition to worship' brought parishioners to the church.[33] The laity may have been warned against gossip and amorous encounters in the nave, and fairs and games in the churchyard, but this did not mean that they did not take place. In fact, the very proliferation of pastoral material addressing such activities suggests that they were a regular facet of parish life in the church.

The social status of the pilgrims is foregrounded by the *Interlude* when the Miller and his companions attempt to read the heraldic symbols in the stained glass, 'counterfeting gentilmen, the armes for to blase' (150).[34] There is clear social comedy here, as the Miller and Pardoner assume an air of nobility in order to pretend that they can read the armorial bearings in the glass, but this incident also foregrounds the way in which sacred space was used to display and negotiate power structures. Monarchs, nobles, and increasingly, the middle classes were aware of the power that could be conferred by the establishment of a visual identity in sacred space.[35] Social display in sacred space came in for considerable criticism, however. The Lollards foregrounded the consequences for the poor when money was donated to church decorations rather than charitable works of mercy and in *Piers Plowman*, Langland's narrator declares:

> God to alle good folk swich gravynge defendeth [forbids]
> To writen in wyndowes of hir wel dedes
> — An aventure pride be peynted there, and pomp of the world.[36]

Support for the material church as a sign of the 'pomp of the world' will be discussed in my final chapter and here in the *Interlude*, the pilgrims' undisciplined gaze wanders from the depiction of biblical subjects that contribute to the sanctity of the space to the ostentatiously social display of their superiors. The pilgrims place the social at the centre of their vision and God and his saints are relegated to the margins. In the pilgrims' defence, however, this secularity is already present in the windows; they are merely responding to the heraldry that is displayed before them. The secular and the sacred are inextricably linked in the late Middle Ages.

While the Miller and Pardoner might not be able to 'blase' the heraldry in the stained glass, they do place value on another form of visual display available at the cathedral: pilgrimage badges. After the visit to Becket's shrine and 'other places of holynes' in the cathedral, the *Interlude*-author tells us:

> Then, as manere and custom is, signes there they boughte,
> For men of contre shuld know whom they had soughte.
> Ech man set his sylver in such thing as they liked.
> And in the meenwhile, the Miller had i-piked

His bosom ful of signes of Caunterbury broches,
Huch the Pardoner and he pryvely in hir pouches
They put hem afterward, that noon of hem it wist,
Save the Sompnour seid somewhat and seyd to hem, 'List,
Halff part!' quod he pryvely, rownyng on hir ere. (171–9)

The badges advertise to 'men of contre' that the pilgrims have visited the shrine of St Thomas. Such souvenirs enabled the visitor both to take a symbolic token of the shrine back home with them and to use that token to construct a competitive devotional identity in relation to their neighbours. The more pilgrimage badges you have collected, the more sacred spaces you have visited, and therefore the more 'pious' you are in relation to your neighbours. The Miller and the Pardoner's strategy of stuffing their pockets with 'Caunterbury broches', however, demonstrates an insistently material and earthbound approach to pilgrimage. The Canterbury badge, some of which were in the shape of St Thomas's shrine, is a 'sign' of the space in which the pilgrims have made their devotions (175); it could even become a contact relic if it came into physical contact with the shrine.[37] But the Miller does not exchange his 'sylver' for one badge (173), he steals a pocketful of badges that he and the Pardoner attempt to conceal 'pryvely' (176). The Pardoner's profession, and confession of avarice in his prologue in *The Canterbury Tales*, may give us reason to believe that he will attempt to sell on the badges for his own profit, reducing their sacred significance to monetary value and personal gain.

While it is not surprising to see this behaviour if we think back to Chaucer's *Tales*, we might not expect to encounter theft in the cathedral if we consider the authorship of the *Interlude*. Peter Brown suggests that the author might be one of the monks 'charged with custodial duties' at the shrine of Becket and that the text's mention of the pilgrims' gifts of silver brooches and rings (134) reflects the author's concern for the shrine's income.[38] By stealing pilgrimage badges, the Miller and Pardoner are depriving the cathedral of crucial income, but even more gravely, they are committing the sin of sacrilege. As the Parson's sermon on the Seven Deadly Sins in *The Canterbury Tales* reminds us, stealing from holy church constitutes sacrilege and a devout reader of the *Interlude* would recognise that the pilgrims' behaviour constitutes a violation not only of appropriate pilgrimage practice but of sacred space itself.[39] An individual's personal virtue or vice was brought into sharp focus by an encounter with sacred space. In sermon exempla, the presence of the unrepentant or the immoral often caused sacred space to respond to the threat of desecration by violently ejecting such sinners or publicly revealing their shame. Sacred space functions as a moral barometer with an individual's spiritual condition being revealed through their proximity to the physical building. Although the Miller remains unpunished for his behaviour in the *Interlude*, the narrator shows his awareness of this trope when he has Kit the Tapster describe her dream to the Pardoner:

> How I was in a chirch when it was al i-massed
> And was in my devocioune tyl service was al doon,
> Tyll the preest and the clerk boystly bad me goon
> And put me out of the chirch with an eger mode. (102–5)

Kit dreams that she is ejected from the church by a priest and clerk with 'eger mode' (angrily) and this implies that she is an immoral character deserving of censure. The author goes on to comment that he will narrate her trickery of the Pardoner 'thoughe it be no grete holynes for to prech this ilk matere' (119); the use of 'prech' and 'holynes' here ironically compounds her sinful behaviour. Medieval rituals of penance often required sinners to be barred from the church, to safeguard both the space and its community from desecration. As Barbara Hanawalt and Michel Kobialka note in *Medieval Practices of Space*, 'spatial distance' is often used as a 'healing device for conflict'.[40] The moral disruption that the sinner poses is avoided by their spatial remove and in this episode in the *Interlude*, the author excludes Kit from the dream-church. When we then witness the behaviour of the Pardoner and Miller some sixty lines after the author's depiction of Kit, our moral judgement is encouraged. When the 'lewd' pilgrims enter the cathedral, the narrator comments that they 'sought hemselff in the chirch' (148), and the verb 'sought' has a telling ambiguity here. They 'place or assemble' themselves in the church but they are also expected to seek for themselves and to map out an identity, both individually and as part of the Christian community.[41] Sacred space intensifies an individual's identity and forces them to place themselves in relation to its sacred confines, spatially, socially, and most importantly, spiritually.

Placement within space also comes to the fore when the pilgrims enter the cathedral. The church door is a liminal space that was often used in medieval ritual to purify and reconfigure the community; the 'churching' of women, for example, took place at the door, as did rituals of penance in which the sinful were ejected and the repentant welcomed back into the community.[42] When the pilgrims reach the door of the cathedral, they enter according to their position within the three estates:

> Then atte chirch dorr the curtesy gan to ryse,
> Tyl the Knyght of gentilnes that knewe righte wele the guyse
> Put forth the prelates, the Person and his fere.
> A monk that toke the spryngill with a manly cher
> And did as the maner is, moilled al hir pates,
> Everich after other, righte as they were of states.
> The Frere feynded fetously the spryngil for to hold
> To spryng oppon the remnaunt, that for his cope he nold
> Have lafft that occupacioune in that holy plase,
> So longed his holy conscience to se the Nonnes fase! (135–44)

The Knight ushers the churchmen of the party into the cathedral first, as befits his status at the top of the social hierarchy and the ecclesiastical status of the prelates. The pilgrims then follow 'righte as they were of states' but the Friar clashes over the sprinkling of the holy water with one of the Canterbury monks. It is appropriate that the monk should bless the pilgrims as they enter the cathedral, which is under the jurisdiction of the monastery, but the Friar attempts to usurp this office in order to see the Nun's face. The irony of his 'holy conscience' in comparison with 'that holy plase' is pointed here; a central church practice is being performed at the threshold to sacred space without the holiness that should attend it.

The competition between the monk and friar reflects the conflict between the monastic and mendicant orders more generally in this period. Anti-fraternal satire was widespread throughout the Middle Ages and in the *Interlude*, as Bowers put it, 'we should not be surprised by such snide references from a monk-poet with an institutional bias against the mendicant orders'.[43] The Canterbury monk who greets the pilgrims at the shrine of Becket is, of course, a 'goodly monke' and he does his institutional duty by teaching the pilgrims about the holy relics that they encounter there (167). Rivalry between monks, mendicants, and parish priests played a significant role in the promotion of sacred space in this period. There was considerable competition for the attention, devotions, and financial support of the laity from wandering friars and great sites of pilgrimage such as Canterbury or Walsingham, and the local parish church often made use of its sanctity as a key resource for self-promotion. The sanctity of a site was a powerful way to attract the laity and this was often advertised in terms of the miracles that had taken place there. The more sacred a space, the more likely it was to attract visitors, and as I have already noted, it is possible that the *Interlude* itself was composed to advertise the shrine and bolster its reputation on the occasion of the 1420 jubilee of Becket's martyrdom. Brown notes that at least one Canterbury monk was making use of texts to promote the benefits of pilgrimage to the shrine at this time, penning a Latin poem that was not only 'pinned to a prominent position' within the cathedral but also attached to the door of St Paul's Cathedral.[44] Competition between sacred spaces is an important theme in my second chapter, focusing on the relationship between St Bartholomew the Great in London and its neighbours, both local and international. Texts play a crucial role in the promotion of sanctity and here the depiction of the Canterbury pilgrims encourages readers to follow in their footsteps. As Brown states, the *Interlude* would have been 'capable not only of entertaining but creating the pleasing impression among listeners that by visiting Canterbury they would become nothing less than Chaucer's pilgrims incarnate, enacting his fiction, enjoying the jokes and bonhomie and playing out the appropriate roles. In the course of doing so, they would bring the *Canterbury Tales* to fruition by arriving in the city and visiting the shrine.'[45]

The Chaucerian context, coupled with the 'lewd' pilgrims' argument over the meaning of the stained glass, foregrounds the importance of narrative practice in the construction and maintenance of sacred space. The pilgrims' argument is in many ways a particularly Chaucerian response. Reading sacred space generates the telling of competitive tales and sacred space can accommodate and sustain multiple readings simultaneously, even if the Miller's decidedly un-sacred interpretation of the man with the spear to 'bussh adown his enmy' suggests that not all readings should be equally valid (156). Telling tales in a Chaucerian context is a social affair. The tales that the pilgrims tell establish and negotiate their position in the social hierarchy. The tales and treatises that I will examine in this book also establish relationships between communities and their churches, individuals and their own salvation, and explore the consequences for sacred space when they do so. Secular tales are often seen as antithetical to devout practice and a distraction from spiritual duties such as church attendance. In *The Canterbury Tales*, Chaucer's Parson delivers a sermon on the Seven Deadly Sins, telling the Host in no uncertain terms: 'Thou getest fable noon ytoold for me.'[46] Although as we shall see in

Chapter 3 of this book, sermons and penitential handbooks relied heavily upon tales and fables to achieve their didactic ends. In his criticism of pilgrimage, the Lollard William Thorpe castigates those who, like the Canterbury group, bring with them men and women who can sing 'rowtinge songis' and play bagpipes like the Miller to entertain them on the journey, concluding that 'if þese men and wymmen ben a moneþe oute in her pilgrimage, manye of hem an half ȝeere aftir schulen be greete ianglers, tale tellers and lyeris'.[47] For Thorpe, pilgrimage fostered jangling and sins of the tongue. When the Miller and his companions enter the cathedral in the *Interlude*, they are unable to entirely rid themselves of the habit of telling competitive tales. In *Dives and Pauper*, lay fondness for tales is even more problematic: Pauper claims that the laity would rather 'heryn a tale or a song of Robyn Hood or of som rybaudye þan to heryn messe or matynys' (p. 189). But this dichotomy is in fact misleading. As Katherine French has shown, even tales of outlaws could benefit the church as there is evidence that Robin Hood revels were performed for parish fundraising, in one instance funding the restoration of the community's image of St George.[48] Just as sacred and secular imagery exist side by side in the visual art of the church, the relationship between sacred space and tale-telling can be productive as well as potentially disruptive.

In the *Interlude*, the tussle between the monk and the friar, and the disagreements between the 'lewd' pilgrims, shows that the authority to control, access and define sacred space was contested and not necessarily equally distributed. Sacred spaces were always at stake as their sanctity conferred power and prestige on those who controlled them. The verbal and visual motifs which construct sacred space thus represent a vocabulary of desire, possession and ownership as they enable a community or individual to stake a claim to their sacred space. As we have seen with the Miller and his companions, those claims were often contradictory and competitive, and each utterance has a performative role in transforming the space according to the desires of the speaker. The group that had the most influence over the construction and interpretation of sacred space was, of course, the ecclesiastical hierarchy. They structured the laity's experience of sacred space in the liturgy and taught them how to behave within it. In the medieval church, the relationship between the clergy and laity was represented by their access to sacred space. The laity were housed in the nave and were responsible for its upkeep, but the most sacred space of the church, the chancel, was restricted to the clergy. The language that was used to construct the sacred was also the domain of the literate ecclesiastical hierarchy and this is especially important to remember when analysing textual depictions of sacred space such as the *Interlude*. The language used to describe the stained glass windows is not in fact the Miller's, it belongs to the Canterbury monk who composed the text, and it is not surprising therefore to find the pilgrims at a loss to interpret its sanctity when they are depicted without a firm ecclesiastical lead. The absence of authoritative guidance leads to an absence of sanctity.

The representation of sacred space can be understood further through the concepts of *langue* and *parole* in the field of linguistics. *Langue*, as formulated by Saussure, is defined as the system of language that every member of society shares. All the sacred spaces discussed in this book share a number of major image clusters that function as a form of *langue* or a lexicon of sanctity: the 'House of God' and the 'Gate of Heaven' (Genesis, 28.17), for example, the cruciform church imitating the body of Christ on the cross, or the church as an image of Jerusalem. Every sacred space draws upon these shared motifs to some degree but each construction of sacred space also establishes a particular identity in the local environment that we might think of as a form of *parole*, or an individual's language use. In the *Interlude*, the cathedral is understood universally as the 'House of God' but more specifically, it is also the house of Becket, and indeed the Canterbury monk's house. Norman Fairclough comments that while Saussure's formulation assumes that 'everyone in a language community has equal access to and command of its langue', 'in reality access to and command of standard languages are unequal'.[49] This can be seen clearly in the responses of the pilgrims in the *Interlude* which resonate with a larger picture of competition for control over sacred space in the period. The majority of the texts that I will discuss in this book are produced by the ecclesiastical hierarchy and they attempt to provide a script for the laity to understand, produce and safeguard sacred space. But it is important to remember that the depiction of lay practice that we encounter does not necessarily originate with, or is under the control of, the laity themselves. In the final chapter of this book, I will turn to the Lollard texts that aim to wrest back control for the devout layperson by showing how the true church is the devotional community and that the material building and its decorations not only hinder lay practice but destroy the hopes of the poor and needy. The author of the *Interlude* is no Lollard but his depiction of a lay audience unable to engage with the stained glass windows successfully chimes uncomfortably with Lollard critiques of church decoration.

Despite the 'lewd' pilgrims failing to read the stained glass, we do find a model of positive pilgrimage practice in the *Interlude*. The Knight and his companions make straight for the shrine, 'to do that they were com fore' (146), and the Host holds up this behaviour as a good example when he intervenes to restore order to the pilgrim company:

> 'Pese!' quod the Hoost of Southwork. 'Let stond the wyndow glased.
> Goth up and doth yeur offerynge. Ye semeth half amased.
> Sith ye be in company of honest men and good,
> Worcheth somwhat after, and let the kynd of brode
> Pas for a tyme. I hold it for the best,
> For who doth after company may lyve the bet in rest.' (157–62)

The Host encourages the pilgrims to make their offerings to the shrine and to follow the example of the 'honest men and good' within their company. He does suggest that this will require them to 'let the kynde of brode/Pas for a tyme', by which he means that they should forsake the behaviour natural to their kind, implying that good Christian behaviour does not come instinctively to them.[50] But the pilgrims are able to adapt their behaviour effectively, as the following passage demonstrates:

> Then passed they forth boystly, goglyng with hir hedes,
> Kneled adown tofore the shryne, and hertlich hir bedes
> They preyd to Seynt Thomas, in such wise as they couth.
> And sith the holy relikes ech man with his mowth
> Kissed, as a goodly monke the names told and taught.
> And sith to other places of holynes they raughte,
> And were in hir devocioun tyl service were al doon,
> And sith they drowgh to dynerward, as it drew to noon. (163–70)

Initially the pilgrims are overwhelmed by the space – they are 'goglyng with hir hedes' (163) as they make their way to the shrine, reinforcing the Host's opinion that they 'semeth half amased' (158). Marvel is a characteristic response to the sacred, encouraging veneration and impressing upon the viewer that the space really is the house of God on earth, but in conjunction with their 'boystly' or boisterous manner here, the emphasis seems to be more upon their earthbound behaviour rather than the heavenly potential of their surroundings. Nevertheless, when they reach the shrine, the pilgrims perform the appropriate devotional gestures. They kneel, pray, and with the assistance of the cathedral monk, they kiss each of the relics in turn. This devotional performance is crucial to the production of sacred space. The pilgrims' veneration generates and reinforces the sanctity of the shrine. Located in the Trinity Chapel, the shrine was surrounded by stained glass depicting pilgrims and miracles at the shrine. The *Interlude*-pilgrims become part of this community of believers when they perform their devotions, mirroring the pilgrims in the glass whose presence testifies to the great sanctity of the saint and his shrine. Visual art and devotional practice mutually reinforce the production of sacred space.

What is additionally important about the pilgrims' behaviour at the shrine is the manner in which they make their prayers: 'hertlich hir bedes/They preyd to Seynt Thomas, in such wise as they couth' (164–5). The *Interlude*-author qualifies their prayers by saying 'in such wise as they couth', but crucially, they all pray 'hertlich', devoutly or with heart. And this emotional performance is not hindered by their lack of knowledge or their social status, as we saw in their attempt to read the stained glass. Their prayers are heartfelt and this could not be more important for the production of a sacred space that is truly valued both by the people and by God himself. In *Dives and Pauper*, Pauper explains that 'God takyth mor hede to a manys herte þan to his ȝifte and mor to his deuocioun þan to his dede' (p. 188) and a major theme in the third and fourth chapters of this book is the importance of emotional engagement if sacred space is to remain a living presence in the community. The pastoral care texts that I will analyse aim to create a relationship between the people and their parish churches based on affection, loyalty and familiarity, and this kind of relationship starts with 'hertlich' prayer and devotion, as modelled by the *Interlude*-pilgrims.

Once the visit to the shrine is complete, the pilgrims naturally leave the cathedral and the focus of the *Interlude* shifts to the urban space around the cathedral. The relationship between the 'contre' and the shrine is important as it establishes Canterbury as a central space on the devotional map. The miracles that St Thomas performed at his shrine establish the cathedral as an 'absolute fixed point, a centre', to return to Eliade's definition of the hierophany.[51] While the cathedral is the pilgrims' destination and therefore the dominant space in their journey, the *Interlude* also places the cathedral in a dynamic relationship with the urban space of the city. Sacred spaces are always constructed with reference to the other spaces that surround them, both literal and symbolic, from the oppositional relationship with profane space established by the consecration ceremony to the competitive relationship with other churches found in texts such as *The Book of the Foundation of St Bartholomew's Church*. In the *Interlude*, the walls, the tavern and the road to Canterbury itself enable us to further map the sacred meaning of the cathedral and to consider how sacred space fits into the lived experience of medieval pilgrimage and the space of the city.[52]

The Knight and the Squire visit the city walls and inspect their defensive capabilities:

> The Knyght with his meyné went to se the wall
> And the wardes of the town, as to a knyght befall,
> Devising ententiflich the strengthes al about,
> And apoynted to his sone the perell and the dout
> For shot of arblast and of bowe, and eke for shot of gonne,
> Unto the wardes of the town, and how it myght be wone.
> And al defence therageyn, after his entent,
> He declared compendiously. (237–44)

The Knight examines the defensive strength of the walls, including their resistance to gunfire, and the violence of this imagery of attack reminds us of the Miller's image of the man with his spear ready to 'bussh adown his enmy' in the stained glass (156). The cathedral is the fixed point from which the rest of the city radiates outwards, and the city walls protect and enclose the city and its sacred space from such attacks, in this period particularly from the French. Robert Sturges comments that in the late Middle Ages 'as cities became more closely identified with their bishops, representations [of the city] focused more on the spiritual protection afforded by their religious spaces, such as the cathedral', than on the city walls.[53] In Canterbury, the walls and cathedral shared a material connection as when the walls were rebuilt between 1378 and 1409, the architect was Henry Yevele who was also responsible for rebuilding the nave in the cathedral.[54] Both the city and its sacred space were enclosed by the architecture of the master builder. Imagery of enclosure resonates with the concept of sacred space as it draws upon the paradigm of anchoritic enclosure, a practice which protects and contains the holy individual from external threat and attack.[55] The walls of the church served a similar purpose in the consecration ceremony, materialising the boundary between sacred and secular space and establishing a clear demarcation. In the *Interlude*, the cathedral sits within the city walls like the enclosed anchorite, teaching and protecting the laity in return for their spiritual and financial support.

The pilgrimage hostel, the Checker of the Hoop, also has a material relationship with the cathedral because the building and its land was not only owned by the cathedral, it was specifically constructed by the cathedral authorities to support the pilgrimage trade.[56] In the literature of pastoral care, the tavern was often figured as the devil's chapel or devil's temple; indeed, in one Middle English treatise, the tavern's patrons are personifications of the Seven Deadly Sins.[57] We can see this trope at the beginning of Chaucer's *Pardoner's Tale*:

> In Flaundres whilom was a compaignye
> Of yonge folk that haunteden folye,
> As riot, hasard, stywes, and tavernes,
> Where as with harpes, lutes, and gyternes
> They daunce and pleyen at dees, bothe day and nyght,
> And eten also and drynken over hir myght,
> Thurgh which they doon the devel sacrifise
> Withinne that develes temple in cursed wise,
> By superfluytee abhomynable.
> Hir othes been so grete and so dampnable
> That it is grisly for to heere hem swere.
> Oure blissed Lordes body they totere—
> Hem thoughte that Jewes rente hym noght ynough—
> And ech of hem at otheres synne lough.
> And right anon thanne comen tombesteres
> Fetys and smale, and yonge frutesteres,
> Syngeres with harpes, baudes, wafereres,
> Whiche been the verray develes officeres
> To kyndle and blowe the fyr of lecherye,
> That is annexed unto glotonye.[58]

The tavern is the 'develes temple' in which overindulgence and the vices of dancing, dicing and swearing are the 'develes sacrifise'. Swearing by Christ's body was commonly understood to torture him anew; in a medieval wall painting at Broughton, Buckinghamshire, for example, an image of the pietà is surrounded by men holding Christ's body parts, from his heart to his hands and feet, in a macabre visual representation of the consequences of swearing.[59] The dancing girls, musicians and bawds in the inn are the 'verray develes officeres' and the medieval audience of the *Interlude* may have had this imagery in mind when they encountered Kit the tapster at the Checker of the Hoop, especially as the text goes on to narrate the Pardoner's misadventures in her company. Such depictions locate profane space outside the church but are nevertheless constructed with reference to ecclesiastical ritual and imagery. The language of temples, officers and sin keeps the tavern's holy counterpart in mind and also reminds us that what makes the tavern a profane space is sinful practice. Just as the cathedral sustains secular and sacred meanings according to the behaviour of the pilgrims, the pilgrimage hostel has the potential to be a profane house of vice or a wholesome lodging place, depending upon the actions of its inhabitants.

The Pardoner's 'compaignye / Of yonge folk' in the tavern reminds us of the 'fressh feleship' of pilgrims on the road to Canterbury at the beginning of the *Interlude*:

> When all this fressh feleship were com to Caunterbury,
> As ye have herd tofore, with tales glad and mery,
> Som of sotill centence, of vertu and of lore,
> And som of other myrthes for hem that hold no store
> Of wisdom, ne of holynes, ne of chivalry,
> Nether vertuouse matere, but to foly
> Leyd wit and lustes all, to such japes
> As Hurlewaynes meyné in every hegg that capes
> Thurh unstabill mynde, ryght as the leves grene
> Stonden ageyn the weder. (1–10)

On the surface, this depiction of the pilgrims recalls the tales of 'sentence' and 'solaas' requested by Harry Bailey in the *General Prologue*, but on closer inspection, the *Interlude*-author is already signalling a profane turn of events.[60] As a reader of Chaucer, the author and his audience would be aware of the connotations of the word 'fressh' and its repeated use by the Merchant to describe May in his tale.[61] The use of 'fressh' to describe the pilgrims as they finally arrive in Canterbury suggests that the 'feleship', and its holy purpose, may have become stale. The author goes on to declare that some of the pilgrims have set their minds to such japes as Harlequin's company performed behind the hedges when green leaves fight against the weather. Hurlewain or Harlequin appears to have been a goblin-like spirit whose band of demons pursued wild hunts in the woods, and here the pilgrims are imagined as spirited pranksters hiding in the hedgerows outside the city walls, rather like the Green Men of folklore.[62] The *Interlude*-author uses this imagery to unsettle the boundary between sacred and profane, secular and ecclesiastical spacc, because here Harlequin's men enter the cathedral. They are not confined to a country road, or shut out and safely contained within their own devil's chapel like the 'yonge compaignie' of *The Pardoner's Tale*. The sacred can only be defined in relation to the profane and the secular, and in order to be continually visible within the landscape, the sacred must be challenged and forced to manifest itself anew. Lay practice has the power to desecrate and to reinforce sanctity and, as I will show, once established, sacred space is tested and paradoxically strengthened by contact with the profane. By allowing the profane to enter the cathedral, or to take place within its own jurisdiction if we think of Kit plying her trade on the cathedral's own land, sacred space can contain, neutralise and profit from that threat. A Green Man in the cathedral was a much safer proposition than a Green Man lurking on the roadside. But for the *Interlude*-author, this resolution in favour of the sacred never fully takes place. The pilgrims leave the sacred safety of the cathedral and the narrative focus turns firmly to the tavern and the profane antics of the Pardoner and Kit the Tapster.

Reading the pilgrims' experiences in *The Canterbury Interlude* demonstrates that sacred space was debated, challenged, promoted and above all experienced as a powerful, living force in medieval England. It enabled communities to constitute meaning and to both affirm and test their social, political and theological values. Buildings that were intended for the glory of God often provided an opportunity for the negotiation of social identity as priests and pilgrims, monks and merchants, interacted with their sacred confines. In the chapters that follow, sacred space emerges as a prominent concern in late medieval England. It is produced through a fusion of text, architecture, and performance and it exists in a dynamic relationship with profane space and the socio-political environment. Sacred space is 'the House of God' and the 'Gate of Heaven' (Genesis, 28.17), but as Christ declared in the gospels, 'in my Father's house there are many mansions' (John, 14.2) and within the landscape of medieval England, there are many sacred spaces and many debates concerning their use and meaning.

My first chapter will examine the church consecration ceremony and the paradigm that it sets up for the construction and interpretation of sacred space. The performance of the liturgical ritual unites building, community, and scripture, purifying and consecrating the space as an ideal location for the communal worship of God. Having sketched out the ritual construction of sacred space common to all churches, I will then turn to a particular production of space in Chapter 2, St Bartholomew the Great, in Smithfield, London, as established in the Middle English translation of the church's foundation legend, *The Book of the Foundation of St Bartholomew's Church*. The Middle English text was translated during the 'Great Restoration' of the church at the turn of the fifteenth century and my analysis will show how the foundation legend's catalogue of miracles presents St Bartholomew's as a highly competitive sacred space in medieval London and beyond. The sanctity of *The Book* is performative. It is made manifest by miracles and re-enacted by the narration of those miracles in the foundation legend. As the texts in my third chapter make clear, however, the sacred space at the heart of *The Book of the Foundation* is idealised. Always potent and efficacious, never under threat, the community at St Bartholomew's can say with confidence that 'trewly, God is yn this place'.[63] But the local parish church, the centre of everyday life and pastoral education, is a place of precarious sanctity, dependent on a congregation whose sin can transform sacred space into profane space in the twinkling of an eye.

The literature of pastoral care and the visual art of the medieval parish church will form the basis of my third chapter in which I will argue that the profane challenge posed by lay misbehaviour paradoxically strengthens sacred space. Devils and demons, such as the fiendish scribe Tutivillus, appear in the church to assist priests in detecting sinful conduct and to cleanse the church of profane contamination such as the bodies of the unrepentant dead. The sermon exempla of John Mirk's *Festial*, the *Alphabet of Tales*, and Robert Mannyng's *Handlyng Synne* depict a sacred space teetering on the edge of collapse but marshalling all its didactic resources to combat and exploit profane challenges. These challenges are often met with violent punishment and I will also argue for the integral relationship between violence and the sacred, with recourse to Rene Girard's theory, both in the violent expulsion of sinners from the church but also in the presence of Christ's blood in both visual and textual exempla. The blood of the saviour consecrates sacred space and holds the laity accountable for their sins. This chapter also reassesses the relationship between church art and sermon exempla in order to argue for a symbiotic relationship that presents the church, and its devotional objects, as a living, breathing actor in the drama of salvation. The performance of narrative exempla animates the visual depictions of angels, devils and saints in the church who come to life to protect and fight for their sacred spaces.

The material architecture of the church is crucial to its sanctity. If it is not constructed virtuously, the church will literally fall down. But for some medieval readers, dismantling the material church was a desirable goal rather than a potential tragedy, however. In my final chapter, I will examine the debate over the relationship between the church building and its community in orthodox and Lollard texts. The allegorical reading of church architecture established by William of Durandus's *Rationale divinorum officiorum* regained traction in the fifteenth century and I will discuss the Middle English translation of Durandus called *What the Church Betokeneth* in the light of the Lollard critique of the material church. Where Durandus's allegorical schema gave each member of the community a secure place in the material church, polemical Lollard texts such as *The Lanterne of Liȝt* aimed to divorce the building from the people, presenting the church as an elaborate distraction that not only disrupted worship but harmed the poor by draining the community's financial resources. In *Pierce the Ploughman's Crede* we see the 'curious' and 'crafty' church made flesh as the narrator visits the great churches of the friars in the vain hope of learning his Creed but instead encounters only greed, pride and sterile materiality. All is not lost for sacred space, however. I will conclude by showing how the medieval churches of fifteenth-century England represented an 'architecture of the heart' for their parishioners.[64] In the great age of church building and restoration, parish communities invested in their churches both spiritually and materially. They cared deeply for their local sacred spaces and performed their devotions, like the Canterbury pilgrims, 'hertlich' or with heart, so much so that Dives is able to assert confidently to Pauper that 'God is in no lond so wel seruyd in holy chyrche ne so mychil worchepyd in holy chyrche as he is in þis lond, for so many fayre chirches [...] is in non oþir lond as in þis lond' (p. 188). England's fair churches truly were the house of God on earth for their devoted lay communities.

Notes

1 *The Canterbury Interlude* in *The Canterbury Tales: Fifteenth Century Continuations and Additions*, ed. John M. Bowers (Kalamazoo: Medieval Institute Publications, 1992), pp. 60–79, lines 147–58. All subsequent quotations refer to this edition by line number.

2 Paul Strohm, *Theory and the Premodern Text* (Minneapolis: University of Minnesota Press, 2000), p. 4.

3 Mary Carruthers, *The Craft of Thought: Meditation, Rhetoric, and the Making of Images, 400–1200* (Cambridge: Cambridge University Press, 1998; paperback 2000), p. 111.
4 Keith Lilley, *City and Cosmos: The Medieval World in Urban Form* (London: Reaktion, 2009); Robert Barrett Jr., *Against All England: Regional Identity and Cheshire Writing, 1195–1656* (Notre Dame: University of Notre Dame Press, 2009); Catherine Clarke, 'Mapping medieval Chester: place and identity in an English borderland city c.1200–1500', see www.medievalchester.ac.uk [accessed 29 September 2016].
5 Marion Turner, 'Introduction', in Marion Turner (ed.), *A Handbook of Middle English Studies* (Chichester: Wiley-Blackwell, 2013), pp. 1–11, p. 3.
6 Michel Foucault, 'Of other spaces', trans. Jay Miskowiec, *Diacritics* 18 (1986), 22–7, p. 22.
7 Henri Lefebvre, *The Production of Space*, trans. Donald Nicholson Smith (Oxford: Blackwell, 1991), pp. 255 and 44.
8 Turner, 'Introduction', p. 2.
9 *St Erkenwald*, ed. Clifford Peterson (University Park, PA: University of Pennsylvania Press, 1977), lines 33–88.
10 *MED* 'maken' (v.1) 2, 3 and 5.
11 Sari Katajala-Peltomaa, *Gender, Miracles, and Daily Life: The Evidence of Fourteenth Century Canonization Processes* (Turnhout: Brepols, 2009), p. 267.
12 Mircea Eliade, *The Sacred and Profane: The Nature of Religion*, trans. Willard R. Trask (Orlando: Harcourt, 1987), p. 11.
13 Eliade, *The Sacred and Profane*, p. 26.
14 On the sanctification of the natural landscape, see Alexandra Walsham, *The Reformation of the Landscape: Religion, Identity, and Memory in Early Modern Britain and Ireland* (Oxford: Oxford University Press, 2011), pp. 49–66.
15 Eliade, *The Sacred and Profane*, p. 21.
16 *Canterbury Tales: Fifteenth-Century Continuations*, ed. Bowers, p. 57. Peter Brown summarises the arguments for the dating in 'Journey's end: the prologue to the tale of Beryn', in Julia Boffey and Janet Cowen (eds), *Chaucer and Fifteenth-Century Poetry* (London: Centre for Late Antique and Medieval Studies, King's College, 1991), pp. 143–74, pp. 150–3.
17 See Brown, 'Journey's end', pp. 148–50.
18 Robert Sturges, 'The pardoner in Canterbury: class, gender, and urban space in "The prologue to the tale of Beryn"', *College Literature*, 33 (2006), 52–76, p. 53.
19 T. A. Heslop, 'Attitudes to the visual arts: the evidence from written sources', in Jonathan Alexander and Paul Binski (eds), *The Age of Chivalry: Art in Plantagenet England 1200–1400* (London: Royal Academy of Arts, 1987), pp. 26–32, p. 32.

20 *Dives and Pauper*, ed. Priscilla Barnum, EETS OS 275 (London: Oxford University Press, 1976), vol. I, p. 83. All subsequent quotations refer to this edition and volume by page number.
21 See Lawrence G. Duggan, 'Was art really the "book of the illiterate?"', in Marielle Hageman and Marco Mostert (eds), *Reading Images and Texts: Medieval Images and Texts as Forms of Communication: Papers from the Third Utrecht Symposium on Medieval Literary, Utrecht, 7–9 December 2000* (Turnhout: Brepols, 2005), pp. 63–107, pp. 95–6.
22 Line 99. Compare line 289 in Chaucer's *The Book of the Duchess*, in Geoffrey Chaucer, *The Riverside Chaucer*, ed. Larry D. Benson et al. (Oxford: Oxford University Press, 1987; paperback 1988), p. 334.
23 Michael Camille, 'The language of images in medieval England 1200–1400', in Alexander and Binski (eds), *The Age of Chivalry*, pp. 33–40, p. 33.
24 I discuss the Lollard attitude to visual decoration in the church in Chapter 4.
25 *Canterbury Tales: Fifteenth-Century Continuations*, ed. Bowers, p. 167.
26 Madeline Harrison Caviness, *The Early Stained Glass of Canterbury Cathedral: c.1175–1220* (Princeton: Princeton University Press, 1997), p. 102.
27 Helen Barr, *Transporting Chaucer* (Manchester: Manchester University Press, 2014), p. 34.
28 Barr, *Transporting Chaucer*, p. 34.
29 Michael Camille, '"When Adam delved": labouring on the land in medieval art', in Del Sweeney (ed.), *Agriculture in the Middle Ages: Technology, Practice, and Representation* (University Park, PA: University of Pennsylvania Press, 1995), pp. 247–76, p. 247.
30 *The Riverside Chaucer*, p. 30, lines 452 and 454, respectively.
31 *Ibid.*, p. 30, line 460. 'So openlyche at the chyrche dore/Lete hem eyther wedde othere', in *Instructions for Parish Priests by John Myrc*, ed. Edward Peacock, EETS OS 31 (London: Trübner, 1868), p. 7, lines 206–7.
32 *The Riverside Chaucer*, p. 70, lines 3341–3.
33 Katherine L. French, *The People of the Parish: Life in a Late Medieval Diocese* (Philadelphia: University of Pennsylvania Press, 2001), p. 2.
34 *MED* 'blasen' (v.3) b) 'to identify armorial bearings'. See Ann Payne, 'Medieval heraldry', in Alexander and Binski (eds), *The Age of Chivalry*, pp. 55–9.
35 See for example Paul Binski's discussion of Richard II in *Westminster Abbey and the Plantagenets: Kingship and the Representation of Power 1200–1400* (London: Yale University Press, 1995), pp. 175–206.
36 William Langland, *The Vision of Piers Plowman: A Complete Edition of the B Text*, ed. A. V. C. Schmidt (London: Dent, 1978), p. 36, lines 64–6.
37 See Sarah Blick, 'Reconstructing the shrine of St Thomas Becket, Canterbury cathedral', in Sarah Blick and Rita Tekippe (eds), *Art and*

Archaeology of Late Medieval Pilgrimage in Northern Europe and the British Isles (Leiden: Brill, 2005), pp. 405–41.

38 Brown, 'Journey's end', pp. 148–50. Brown also suggests that this might be a reason for the stained glass receiving 'special attention' because 'income at the shrine was used for the upkeep of the windows in the shrine precincts', p. 150.

39 'Espiritueel thefte is sacrilege; that is to seyn, hurtynge of hooly thynges, or of thynges sacred to Crist, in two maneres: by reson of the hooly place, as chirches or chirche-hawes [churchyards], for which every vileyns synne that men doon in swiche places may be cleped sacrilege', *The Parson's Tale*, in *The Riverside Chaucer*, p. 315.

40 Barbara Hanawalt and Michel Kobialka, 'Introduction' in Barbara Hanawalt and Michel Kobialka (eds), *Medieval Practices of Space* (Minneapolis: University of Minnesota Press, 2000), pp. ix-viii, p. xiv.

41 *MED* 'sorten' (v.2) 2. Cf. line 235, 'sorted hem togider righte as hir lustes lay'.

42 See for example Gail McMurray Gibson, 'Blessing from sun and moon: churching as women's theatre', in Barbara A. Hanawalt and David Wallace (eds), *Bodies and Disciplines: Intersections of Literature and History in Fifteenth-Century England* (Minneapolis: University of Minnesota Press, 1996), pp. 139–54.

43 *Canterbury Tales: Fifteenth-Century Continuations*, ed. Bowers, p. 171.

44 Brown, 'Journey's end', p. 152.

45 *Ibid.*, p. 153.

46 *The Riverside Chaucer*, p. 287, line 31.

47 *The Testimony of William Thorpe* in *Two Wycliffite Texts*, ed. Anne Hudson, EETS OS 301 (Oxford: Oxford University Press, 1993), pp. 24–93, p. 64.

48 French, *People of the Parish*, pp. 130–2.

49 Norman Fairclough, *Language and Power* (London: Longman, 1989), p. 21.

50 *MED* 'brod' (n.2), 2a) 'kind of'.

51 Eliade, *The Sacred and Profane*, p. 21.

52 On city identity see Jonathan Hsy, 'City', in Turner (ed.), *Handbook of Middle English Studies*, pp. 315–29.

53 Sturges, 'The pardoner in Canterbury', p. 54.

54 Christopher Wilson, 'Yevele, Henry (d. 1400)', *Oxford Dictionary of National Biography*, Oxford University Press, 2004: www.oxforddnb.com/view/article/30220 [accessed 20 October 2014].

55 For further discussion of the relationship between enclosure and city walls, see Laura Varnam, 'Sanctity and the city: sacred space in *The Life of St Werburgh*', in Catherine A. M. Clarke (ed.), *Mapping the Medieval City: Space, Place, and Identity in Chester c.1200–1500* (Cardiff: University of Wales Press, 2010), pp. 114–30, pp. 127–8.

56 *Canterbury Tales: Fifteenth-Century Continuations*, ed. Bowers, pp. 213–4.

57 *A Middle English Treatise on the Ten Commandments: From St John's College, Oxford, MS 94 1420–1434*, ed. James Finch Royster (University of Chicago, 1910–11), pp. 21–2.
58 *The Riverside Chaucer*, p. 196, lines 463–82.
59 See http://paintedchurch.org/brougbsw.htm [accessed 12 September 2016].
60 *The Riverside Chaucer*, p. 36, line 798.
61 *Ibid.*, for example pp. 160–1, lines 1782, 1822, 1858 and 1871.
62 *Canterbury Tales: Fifteenth-Century Continuations*, ed. Bowers, p. 165.
63 *The Book of the Foundation of St Bartholomew's Church*, ed. Norman Moore, EETS OS 163 (Oxford: Oxford University Press, 1923), p. 32.
64 The phrase comes from Shelley Hornstein, *Losing Site: Architecture, Memory, and Place* (Farnham: Ashgate, 2011), p. 3. I will discuss this theory in more detail in Chapter 4.

1

The church consecration ceremony and the construction of sacred space

The church consecration ceremony was the chief ritual expression of sanctity in the Middle Ages, and the symbolism and practice that the ceremony established were the foundation for all subsequent encounters with sacred space. Despite this fact, surprisingly little research has been done on the ceremony. The most illuminating recent studies are Dawn Marie Hayes's discussion in *Body and Sacred Place in Medieval Europe* and Brian Repsher's *The Rite of Church Dedication in the Early Medieval Era*.[1] Repsher's monograph also includes a translation of the Carolingian *Ordo ad benedicandam ecclesiam*, which he describes as the fullest expression of the consecration ceremony and its significance, and the immediate source of the twelfth- and thirteenth-century Roman Pontificals.[2] My discussion of the ceremony in this chapter will be drawn primarily from the influential description and interpretation in William of Durandus's *Rationale officiorum divinorum*, but I will also have recourse to the *Ordo* and to sermons for the dedication of churches, principally that of Jacobus de Voragine in the *Legenda Aurea* and two Middle English examples, from John Mirk's *Festial* and the *Speculum Sacerdotale*.[3] The consecration ceremony remained virtually unchanged through the later Middle Ages and there is neither the room here nor the need to provide a liturgical history; rather my aim is to draw out the major strategies and performative practices through which the ritual created and shaped the medieval understanding of sacred space.[4] Writers such as Durandus established what Hayes calls a 'learned concept' of sacred space, and this is crucial for understanding a community's subsequent sacred practice.[5] The themes, images, and methods of construction delineated here will, therefore, be a touchstone throughout this book.

The meaning and purpose of the consecration ceremony

In his sermon for the dedication of a church, Jacobus de Voragine declares that there are five purposes behind the consecration ceremony:

> The first is to drive out the devil and his power [...] Secondly, the church is consecrated in order that those who take refuge in it in may be saved. [...] The third purpose is that prayers offered in the church be surely heard. [...] The fourth reason for the consecration of the church is to provide a place where praises may be rendered to God. [...] Fifthly, the church is consecrated so that the sacraments may be administered there.[6]

The practice of consecration ensured that the church truly was God's house on earth and that his eyes and ears would have attendance upon the building and its congregation (1 Kings, 8.29; 2 Chronicles, 6.40). The consecration ceremony enabled the community to 'communicate with and about' the divine.[7] It facilitated access to God but it also constructed a space in which the congregation could represent, understand, and talk about God among themselves. The consecration of a church was simultaneously the consecration of a new community and an opportunity to establish social order, focalised through a building that was the centre of the social world. Brian Repsher asserts that the liturgy was the place where 'society was made, restored, and nourished towards moral perfection', and the consecration ceremony ensured that the liturgy could be performed, and society sustained, within a sacred space.[8]

For most late medieval communities, the consecration ceremony had not been performed in living memory, but traces of the ritual and its meaning remained. Many parishioners would have witnessed the ceremony for the reconciliation of a church, for example, which closely mirrored the original consecration rite, and was often required as a result of violent bloodshed in the church, as Daniel Thiery has shown.[9] Parishioners may also have been aware of the need to consecrate newly acquired items of church plate and vestments, and the altars of chapels added to the church.[10] More importantly, on the annual feast day of the consecration, the dedication sermon would have specifically reminded the congregation of the continued relevance of the original ceremony to their experience of sacred space. The potency of consecrated space was frequently employed in the literature of pastoral care as a deterrent for lay misbehaviour. 'O Lord, what this place is gretely to be a-dredde! For the place is holy', declares the *Speculum Sacerdotale* dedication sermon, instilling a fear of the place because of its great sanctity.[11] The physical imprint of the ceremony was often still visible both inside and outside the church, as consecration crosses on the walls reminded parishioners that the material fabric of the building had been anointed and set apart.[12] The ceremony established a paradigm for constructing and encountering sacred space that left traces in the visual, textual, and material culture of the medieval church.

In his influential interpretation of the church and its symbolism, the thirteenth-century *Rationale divinorum officiorum*, William of Durandus identified three types of Christian space: sacred space (*sacra*), holy space (*sancta*), and religious space (*religiosa*).[13] He distinguished between these categories as follows:

> Those that are sacred have been dedicated in a ceremony by the hands of a bishop, and are sanctified by God [...] Holy places are those that have immunity or privileges, and they are assigned to the servants and ministers of churches; places which, lest anyone presume to violate them, or seek a legal remedy or special privilege to violate them, carry the threat of certain punishment. Among these places is the atrium of churches, and in some regions, cloisters, within which are the dwellings of the canons; in these places, anyone fleeing from a crime, if he is received there, is given protection [...] Religious places are those where an intact human cadaver, or at least a head, is buried.[14]

The distinction rests upon the way in which the space is constructed and its subsequent use. Christian bodies are buried in religious places, holy places have certain privileges and are used by ministers of the church, and sacred spaces are ritually consecrated by a bishop and, most importantly, they are sanctified by God. Durandus explains later in the *Rationale* that the bishop alone is able to consecrate the church because he 'bears the figure and image' of Christ, who dedicates the church spiritually while the bishop consecrates the building physically.[15] Without God, Christ, and his representative, the bishop, sacred space cannot exist.

As I discussed in my introduction, Mircea Eliade defines sacred space as 'qualitatively different' to the quotidian space that surrounds it, and the ritual of consecration both constructs and accentuates that difference.[16] Jonathan Z. Smith argues that 'ritual is, above all, an assertion of difference', and the consecration ceremony demonstrates the singularity of the church building publicly.[17] The consecration itself consists of a ritual performance centred upon the physical structure of the church. The building is a fundamental requirement for constructing sanctity because it acts as a visible sign and concrete embodiment of the sacred. As Emile Durkheim puts it, 'collective ideals can only be manifested [...] by being concretely realised in material objects that can be seen by all, understood by all, and represented to all minds'.[18] The church building becomes the material sign of sacred space, but a sacred space cannot be sustained by architecture alone; it requires performance in order to be actualised within the material frame. Performance theory can usefully sharpen our understanding of the way in which the ceremony produces sacred space as it directs our attention to the ability of ritual to constitute rather than merely express meaning.[19] As Richard Schechner argues, performative rituals not only 'symbolise', they 'actualise' a change in space.[20] The act of performing the consecration ceremony transforms the material building and its coordinates into a sacred space.

The ritual of consecration is characterised by what Manfred Pfister calls 'multimediality': it is made up 'not only of verbal but also acoustic and visual codes. It is a synaesthetic text.'[21] The consecration ceremony 'activates all the channels of the human senses', employing visual display, liturgical recitation, ritual censing, gesture, procession, and collective response to construct sacred space.[22] This multimediality contributes to the efficacy of the ritual because of the powerful emotive effect that it has on the participants and its consequent ability to function as a tool for social cohesion. Lawrence Sullivan suggests that the 'symbolic experience of the unity of the senses enables a culture to entertain itself with the idea of the unity of meaning'.[23] The multisensory experience of the consecration ceremony enables it to be emotionally effective and to produce a holistic experience that unites the community in a harmony worthy of heaven itself. The ritual also exploits the ability of sensory practices to represent God. The candles emit the light of divinity and the incense pervades the space with the presence of God. Sensory experience is thus heightened and sounds, sights, and smells take on sacred significance as they bring participants closer to God.

One of the most important elements of this multimediality is the use of movement and the privileging of the body as the instrument for consecration. Evan M. Zuesse argues that ritual centres on the body and that in a ritual context, the body acquires 'prestige' because it facilitates 'a much stronger sense of reality than merely mental philosophy or affirmation of faith'.[24] Bodily movement and gesture constructs and accentuates certain meanings within a space. The consecration ceremony begins with the bishop, clergy, and laity processing around the church building three times to demarcate the boundaries of sacred space and to mark out the community's territory. Michel de Certeau argues that space consists of an 'intersection of mobile elements' that are 'actuated by the ensemble of movements deployed within it'.[25] He proposes, with reference to the walker in the city, that the action of moving through a space creates its meaning. The procession in the consecration ceremony draws attention to the building as the centre of sacred space and begins the work of differentiating between sacred and profane space. The physical movement of the body marks out the space as sacred.

The ceremony not only consecrates the material church, however, it also consecrates the individual members of the congregation. In the *Rationale*, Durandus writes that 'truly, whatever is done here visibly, God accomplishes in the soul through an invisible power, which is the true temple of God'.[26] The consecration ceremony 'appropriates the material church and us to God, implying the betrothal to God of the Church and the soul of any of the faithful'.[27] Durandus describes this dual consecration in terms of a marriage union and he suggests that the church which is not consecrated is like a 'girl destined for some man, but not yet dowered, nor with a marriage contract for a carnal union. But in the consecration, she is given a dowry and passes over to her true spouse, Jesus Christ.'[28] The non-consecrated church is dangerously free, uncontrolled, and open to violation. That the building and the people should be consecrated together is fundamental to the construction and maintenance of sacred space. Dawn Marie Hayes argues that 'Christian bodies and church buildings were inextricably joined to the extent that rarely could one exist without the other'.[29] The consecration of the church depended upon human practice but without the maintenance of a sacred body, the sanctity of the church was under continual threat of desecration. The aim of consecration was to produce a Christian body which, through self-regulation, could protect, promote, and continue to practice the sacred space of the church after the consecration ritual had ended. This was achieved through a process that Catherine Bell has theorised as 'ritualisation'.[30]

The goal of any ritual is to be efficacious and for the effects of the ritual to endure. This is achieved through the creation of what Bell terms a 'ritualised social body' which has the ability to 'deploy in the wider social context the schemes internalised in the ritualised environment'.[31] The ceremony instils in the participants knowledge of sacred space that will shape their subsequent behaviour within its confines. Rituals 'define as authoritative certain ways of seeing society', and the consecration ceremony produces a particular way of seeing the sacred space of the church that is dependent upon equating the body of the church, and its sanctity, with the individual's own body.[32] Through participating in the ritual, the congregation is equipped with what Henri Lefebvre calls a 'spatial code':

> A spatial code is not simply a means of reading or interpreting a space: rather it is a means of living in that space, of understanding it, of producing it. As such it brings together verbal signs (words and sentences, along with the meaning invested in them by a signifying process) and non-verbal signs (music, sounds, evocations, architectural constructions).[33]

This code is reinforced by the bishop, who delivers a sermon at the close of the ceremony to explain its significance. Brian Repsher comments that as the ceremony 'consecrated and transformed a people into a new community, it also taught'.[34] The instruction of the faithful in how to interpret and, more importantly, how to behave in sacred space is embedded in its very creation. The bishop's sermon builds the pastoral mission into the foundations of the church and its community. Consecrating sacred space and edifying the community are inseparable activities.

Ritualisation is not a uniform or static state, however. Although the ritual is scripted by the ecclesiastical hierarchy, the responses and levels of understanding of the participants are not necessarily identical. In the fifteenth century, the mystic Margery Kempe's affective response to church ritual was frequently seen as out of place by the other participants, for example.[35] Individual identity, gender, social class, and relationship with others within the community impact upon a participant's level of ritualisation. As Anthony Cohen puts it, although rituals employ a 'commonality of *forms* (ways of behaving)', their 'content (meanings) may vary considerably' among participants.[36] This is compounded because the ritual process also acts as a space for social negotiation and competition, functioning as what Mary Louise Pratt has called a 'contact zone' in which 'peoples geographically and historically separated come into contact with each other and establish ongoing relations'.[37] Pratt's concept is rooted in imperial encounters, which frequently involve 'conditions of coercion, radical inequality, and intractable conflict', but it can be adapted to see the church as a 'contact zone' between heaven and earth in which the relationship between the divine and earthly orders is established and affirmed.[38] The consecration ceremony institutes this contact zone in which a number of groups interact with one another to produce the church community: the ecclesiastical hierarchy and the laity, the earthly congregation and the communion of saints in heaven, mankind and God. This ongoing exchange is dynamic, fluid, and often conflictual as individuals and groups take the opportunity to negotiate their own social identity as part of a wider church community, located in a church building that constitutes the 'contact zone' between heaven and earth.

Brian Repsher argues that the ceremony is a 'recasting of the story of the sacred covenant between God and his people' and that the consecration of a new church is simultaneously the creation of a new community.[39] Ritual is 'an important means through which people experience community', and in the consecration ceremony that community is not just made up of the lay congregation and the clergy, it also reaches out to the heavenly community and to God himself.[40] In the dedication sermon in the *Speculum Sacerdotale*, the author declares of the church: 'In it is the habitacion of God, concourse of angels, reconsiliacion of man, and the lowenes of erþe is in it fellaschipid to the hyenes of heuene'.[41] The word 'fellowship' is crucial here as it unites the earthly and heavenly communities in friendship and harmony.[42] At the beginning of the ceremony the bishop recites the litany, praying that God and his saints assist the clergy and the congregation in the consecration of the church. The living could call upon the holy dead for aid but the earthly congregation also played an important role in ensuring the safe passage of their departed relatives into heaven. The relationship between the living and the dead was played out on a daily basis in the life of the parish church as masses and prayers were offered in order to reduce time in purgatory. Indeed, by the late Middle Ages, Eamon Duffy comments that parish churches were so shaped by beliefs about the afterlife that they had become 'ante-chambers of purgatory'.[43] The church was a space in which individuals could attain fellowship not only with God but also with the departed. Despite the existence of social tensions, the consecration ceremony performed a 'social miracle' by creating an idealised community of unity, mutual support, and spiritual kinship that encompassed the earthly community and those in the afterlife.[44]

Anthony Cohen suggests that ritual not only 'confirms and strengthens social identity', it also enhances 'people's sense of social location'.[45] This creates a feeling of loyalty and local pride in the community and its church. Dedication sermons which celebrate the consecration of the church make frequent use of the deictic 'þis' when explaining the importance of the ceremony.[46] It is 'þis chirche' that is a sacred space; 'þis chirche' to which the local community should pledge their support. Jonathan Z. Smith argues that 'sacrality is, above all, a category of emplacement', and in the consecration ceremony the sanctity which is produced is deliberately anchored to the particular church in question.[47] The performance of the ceremony is site-specific in that the precise movements of the participants are determined by the unique coordinates of the specific church which is being consecrated. A consecrated church can therefore be thought of as a sacred *place* because it has a definite location and a specific set of material coordinates that have been ritually anointed. As Joel Brereton argues, sacred places are 'visible and comprehensible' and therefore they can 'lend concreteness to less visible systems of human relationships and create an identifiable centre of social and political organisation'.[48] The church building becomes the community's 'social visage', as Henri Lefebvre puts it; it is the public symbol of the congregation, and as such it can be used as a tool through which the community can analyse itself.[49] Victor Turner theorises this through the notion of framing:

> To look at itself a society must cut out a piece of itself for inspection. To do this it must set up a frame within which images and symbols of what has been sectioned off can be scrutinized, assessed, and, if need be, remodelled and rearranged. In ritual what is inside the frame is what is often called the 'sacred', what is outside, the 'profane', 'secular', or 'mundane'.[50]

Turner suggests that what is contained within the frame becomes the sacred, and in my final chapter I will argue that as communities begin to place themselves and their devotional lives within the building, the church becomes a symbol of their collective religious identity. The church quite literally stands for the community: its past, present, and future; its material and spiritual incarnations.

The process of consecration falls into three stages and exploits a similar pattern to that detected by Arnold van Gennep in his famous study of rites of passage: detachment, transition, and incorporation.[51] At the beginning of the ritual the church is detached from the territory that surrounds it by processional movement around the walls. The building then undergoes a transitional phase as it is transformed from a profane space to a sacred space through a process of purification and cleansing. This establishes the sanctity of the church in an oppositional but dynamic relationship with the profane space that surrounds it. The sanctity of the space is confirmed and secured with the deposition of the relics in the altar, which then becomes a concentrated sacred zone in the building. The transitional phase is brought to a close with the consecration of liturgical objects. During the final stage of the ceremony the bishop delivers a sermon to the congregation, explaining the significance of what they have witnessed, and performs a mass. This incorporates the building, the people, and their ritual objects into a unified and practised sacred space, bringing together the entire community to worship God in his newly consecrated house on earth. I will now examine these three stages of consecration in turn, focusing in particular on framing, opposition, and material embodiment as key processes in the construction of sacred space.

How to consecrate a church

The process of consecration begins with the detachment of the church from the surrounding space and the community's possession of the building. This begins with the bishop leading the clergy and lay congregation in procession around the walls of the church three times, marking out the boundary and enclosing the space through repeated movement. This procession not only marks out the limits of territory and establishes ownership of the space, it also forms the basis of the sanctity of the church. C. Clifford Flanigan distinguishes between two types of procession: the linear procession in which the movement of a group from one place to another symbolises the attainment of a shared goal, and the circular procession which foregrounds the object at the centre and attributes communal significance to it.[52] A circular procession 'is directed towards some central object of veneration which objectifies and often reifies the values of the community [...] The community gathers around it in order to express and reinforce the larger systems of values which the object symbolises.'[53] The performative veneration of the bishop, clergy, and laity creates a sacred space around and including the material building. The repeated circuit places the church at the centre of the community and presents the building as a symbol of communal values. This is particularly focused on the walls of the building which act as a visible boundary for the space.

Anthony Cohen argues that walls 'encapsulate the identity' of a community and that 'the reality and efficacy of the community's boundary – and, therefore, of the community itself – depends upon its symbolic construction and embellishment'.[54] The construction both of communal identity and of sacred space depends upon the consecration ceremony's ability to distinguish between the sacred and profane, between the community and those who do not belong. The walls of the building act as a visible border between spaces and a protective measure against the incursion of hostile groups. Henri Lefebvre suggests that walls, enclosures, and facades 'serve to define both a *scene* (where something takes place) and an *obscene* area to which everything that cannot or may not happen on the scene is relegated'.[55] The consecration ceremony designates the space which is enclosed by the walls as sacred, the space outside as profane and obscene. Lefebvre recognises, however, that visible boundaries give rise to an 'appearance of separation between spaces where in fact what exists is an ambiguous continuity'.[56] The walls deliberately create the impression of a clear division between sacred and profane which is belied by the everyday life of the church. Ironically, the reliance of sacred space on human practice for its construction makes it prone to desecration and the profane frequently crosses over into the sacred domain as a result of human imperfection.

The interpretation of the three circuits that the bishop makes around the church further nuances our understanding of the precise contours of sacred space. Jacobus de Voragine explains that the three circuits 'denote the three states of those who are to be saved from within the church, namely, the virgins, the continent, and the married':

> These three states are also signified in the arrangement of the church building, as Richard of Saint Victor demonstrates; for the sanctuary denotes the order of the virgins, the choir the order of the continent, and the body of the church the order of the married. The sanctuary is narrower than the choir, and the choir narrower than the body of the church, because the virgins are fewer in number than the continent and these than the married. In like manner the sanctuary is holier than the choir and the choir than the body of the church.[57]

The three circuits correspond to the three areas of the building that embody different concentrations of sanctity. The sanctuary (virgins) is the most sacred space; the chancel (the continent), the next most sacred; and finally, the nave (the married), the least sacred. Levels of bodily purity determine the intensity of sanctity in this model.

Daniel Thiery argues that this division contributed to the laity's 'muddled' understanding of sacred space in the period: how can one area of the church be more sacred than another?[58] The three areas of the building are all sacred but the strength and concentration of that sanctity depends upon the practices performed within them and the agents of those practices. The ordained clergy performed the liturgy and sacraments in the chancel and sanctuary, the laity occupied the nave. Restricting and differentiating spatial access in this way is a major element of ritualisation.[59] Individuals are put in their place in the church. In practice, however, 'most churches', as Eamon Duffy argues, were examples of 'complex space' that were 'based not around a single focal point – the high altar or pulpit – but subdivided into a series of distinct but overlapping enclaves, some more important and private than others, and representing different subgroups and interests in the broader community'.[60]

In the fourteenth and fifteenth centuries, church space began to be appropriated by wealthy nobles and influential local families who founded chantries and adorned the structure with images and stained glass that did as much to promote the earthly patron as the patron saint.[61] The socially aspirant elite could even create private family chapels within the church that asserted their superiority by establishing a sacred space of their own.[62] Spatial differentiation was a major strategy in the church consecration ceremony. But it aimed not only to organise and control sacred space but also to privilege the ecclesiastical hierarchy who performed the ceremony. As I have already mentioned, consecration can only be performed by a bishop because he is Christ's representative and is it through the power of Christ that sacred space is created. The ritual reinforces the sacramental power of the bishop and as such 'constitutes a particular dynamic of social empowerment' in which the bishop is confirmed as the key practitioner for the construction of sacred space.[63] The bishop's unique role is further demonstrated when he performs important parts of the ceremony inside the church with only the deacon present. The anointing of the crosses and the inscription of the alphabet cross are a strictly ecclesiastical affair; during this part of the ceremony, the lay congregation must wait outside the building. This introduces an element of mystery to the consecration rite which impresses its sacred power upon the congregation. As Hans Henrik Lohfert Jørgensen argues, 'the control of what could be seen and heard was a ritual device, serving not just to protect sacred secrets but also to construct the sacred as such'.[64]

The bishop's entry into the church after the procession around the building also serves to construct the church in the image of Jerusalem. Colin Morris comments that 'in the church's observation of place, holiness was determined by what had happened there, by sacred history', and the Holy Land was where the foundational events in Christian sacred history took place.[65] Christ's incarnate presence in Jerusalem created the most sacred of spaces; 'we will adore in the place where his feet stood' declares the Psalms (131.7). In order to create a sacred space elsewhere, in a model in which originary events are the source of sanctity, sacred history must be re-enacted in and mapped on to the new space. The events of Christ's incarnation and their location in Jerusalem are, therefore, a crucial resource in the construction of sacred space and they were invoked visually, architecturally, and most frequently in performance. Morris has detailed the churches in the West which imitated the Holy Sepulchre and garnered the sanctity of Christ's burial place through the architectural reproduction of its church. But this particular kind of material replication was not universally adopted, nor did it need to be as all churches become Jerusalem in ritual performance, an identification which is established in the consecration ceremony. The bishop's entry through the door of the church, for example, re-enacted Christ's entry into Jerusalem on Palm Sunday. This transformed the church into the sacred city and the congregation became citizens of Jerusalem. Such ritual performances function as what Mircea Eliade terms a 'reactualisation of a sacred event that took place in a mythical past, "in the beginning"'.[66] Such a reactualisation was designed to 'reintegrate a primordial situation [...] in which the gods and mythical ancestors were present'.[67] It is not merely a commemoration of sacred history, it is a performance in which the events of sacred time are brought powerfully into the present and the conditions in which the divine had previously appeared are recreated. And this reactualisation is all the more powerful because it does not depend upon specific architectural configurations such as reproduction of the Holy Sepulchre to be effective. It is the ritual re-enactment of events in Christ's life that is key to the church building's successful representation of Jerusalem. The consecration ceremony laid the foundation for the church-as-Jerusalem which subsequent liturgical rituals then developed. The church building came to embody salvation history and as such it could be used to educate the laity in the meaning of the biblical narrative through the emplacement of sacred events at the heart of their own sacred space.

Imagery of Jerusalem is also introduced into the church building through the recitation of antiphons during the ceremony. When the bishop and clergy processed into the church with the relics in the third stage of the ceremony, they recited the following verses:

> The plains of Jerusalem will rejoice and all its villages will sing a canticle of delight. I have sanctified Jerusalem, says the Lord, and I will give a kingdom to my holy ones and a chosen tabernacle, which I prepared in the fragrance of unguent, Alleluia. Alleluia.[68]

The performance of these antiphons enacts Jerusalem's rejoicing; the antiphons are themselves a canticle of delight and a celebration of the church's sacred identity as a holy city. This speech act actualises a change in the space, and the imagery that is used is realised through its ritual pronouncement. Liturgical language and scriptural quotations are a fundamental part of the consecration ceremony. The church becomes a matrix of the sacred word which strengthens the material fabric and provides resources for its symbolic interpretation. As Durandus states, the church is 'walled with the fortifications of the scripture'.[69]

The symbolic significance of Jerusalem is crucial to the consecration of sacred space because not only is the church the house of God on earth, it is also the gate of heaven (Genesis, 28.17). 'Jerusalem' signifies both the terrestrial and celestial city, and imagery of the New Jerusalem from Revelation 21 is similarly employed to sanctify the church in the consecration ritual. The consecration crosses that are inscribed on the walls of the church and are anointed by the bishop during the ceremony are interpreted by the *Ordo* as the jewels which adorn the walls of the New Jerusalem. The *Ordo* states that when the crosses are anointed, the clergy recite 'precious stones, all your walls and the towers of Jerusalem will be built with gems'.[70] In Revelation, 21.19, the 'foundations of the wall of the city were adorned with all manner of precious stones'; the foundation of the heavenly city and the earthly church's sanctity is decorated and glorified with precious stones.[71] Such imagery is made available by the consecration ceremony and can be employed to justify the elaborate and costly decoration of churches. With its jewel-like stained glass and their ornate visual display, the church acts as a window onto the heavenly city that is to come.

The anointing of the consecration crosses is the next major stage of the ceremony. The crosses foreground God's ownership of the building and 'secure the church fabric', acting as a visible and durable sign that consecration has taken place.[72] The crosses are interpreted by Jacobus de Voragine as having multiple meanings:

> The first is to frighten the demons who, having been driven out of the building, see the sign of the cross and are terrified by it, so they do not enter there again [...] The second purpose is to show Christ's triumph, for crosses are his banners and the signs of his victory; so, to make it known that the place is subjugated to Christ's lordship, crosses are painted there. Imperial magnificence is manifested in this way: when a city surrenders, the imperial banner is raised in it [...] Thirdly, these crosses represent the twelve apostles, who brought light to the whole world through faith in Christ crucified.[73]

The crosses are a visual sign to the congregation, and to any devils present, that Christ and his bishop have triumphed over the space and it has been consecrated as God's house. The crosses are to be read differently by different audiences: as a sign of victory to the congregation and as a warning against entry into the space to demons. This multivalency of symbols is characteristic of sacred space: it is accommodating and expansive, and it can sustain multiple meanings simultaneously.

The bishop also inscribes another cross into the building which is traced in ashes across the length and breadth of the pavement, with the Greek alphabet running along one arm of the cross and the Latin alphabet along the other. This spatial enclosure of the church's foundation by the cross has been read by R. W. Muncey as a relic of Roman territory-marking practices, but in addition to encompassing the space of the church within the protective sphere of the cross, the practice is also significant because of its use of text as a marker of sanctity.[74] Madeleine Gray has recently discussed the construction of sacred space through textual inscriptions in church wall paintings. She begins by discussing two consecration crosses discovered in the church of St Saviour in Norwich in which the symbol of the cross is framed by Latin quotations from Genesis 28: '*et aula vocabitur dei* (and it shall be called the hall of God) and *et porta celi* (and the gate of heaven)'.[75] Gray argues that these quotations both 'articulate and remember' the making of sacred space.[76] Such texts, when they are permanently written into the fabric of the building, enable the church to play an active role in the worship of God, 'uttering petition and praise when the congregation is silent or absent'.[77] Although the alphabet cross is traced in impermanent ashes upon the pavement, it embeds the building blocks of textual construction, the very words of God, into the foundation of the church and sanctifies those letters for the use of the congregation. 'Indeed in these few letters', declares Durandus, 'all learning is contained.'[78] When the cross is drawn, the quotation from Genesis, 28.17, which is fundamental to the construction of sacred space, is recited: 'How terrible is this place! There is no other but the house of God and the gate of heaven.' The tracing of the alphabet cross coincides with the naming of the church as the house of God and the creation of its identity as a sacred space. The cross establishes the space as God's house because his identity as 'alpha and omega' is traced on to the pavement.

The use of both the Latin and Greek alphabets is also significant and was interpreted by Durandus as representing unity, community, and faith:

> The alphabet written on the cross represents three things. The first, as some say, is that writing the Greek and Latin letters of the alphabet in the shape of a cross represents the fellowship or union in faith of each people, namely, the Jews and Gentiles, achieved through the cross of Christ [...] Second, writing the alphabet represents the pages of both Testaments which were fulfilled in the cross of Christ [...] Third, it represents the articles of faith, since the pavement of the church is the foundation of our faith.[79]

The cross configuration secures the physical foundation of the church just as it symbolically encompasses the foundation of Christianity.

This first stage of the ceremony sets the church apart as a sacred space, constructs it in the image of Jerusalem, and employs framing and performance to place the church at the centre of the new community. The second stage purifies and cleanses the church, establishing sacred space in opposition to profane space. Mary Douglas has argued for the necessity of the profane in the establishment of the sacred and she states that while 'disorder spoils pattern, it also provides the material of pattern'.[80] The expulsion of demons and the cleansing of the building recognises the profane, demonic, and corrupt at the same time as it rejects them in order to create sacred space. The performative quality of sanctity requires opposition in order for it to be made visible and this stage of the ceremony provides the opportunity for sanctity to be made manifest and its power revealed.

The transitional phase of the ceremony is focused around the church door, a liminal space which marks the boundary between sacred and profane. The purification of the building begins with the expulsion of demons through the door. When the bishop knocks on the door and is admitted by the deacon, he requests that 'there be at the entrance of our humility a rout of demons'.[81] Durandus declares that the 'opening of the church doors is the emptying out of sin', and exemplary narratives in the literature of pastoral care often focus on the church door as the exit, and entrance, for devils and demons.[82] A popular exemplum, derived from Gregory's *Dialogues*, describes the raucous exit of the fiend in the shape of a swine when the church is consecrated. John Mirk's *Festial* explains:

> Whan a chyrch was halowot and relykkus of seyntus broght þidur, sodenly a swyn ran among þe pepules feet hydur and þidur, and so ȝode oute at þe chyrch dore and was seyne no more aftur.[83]

Mirk clarifies that, in this way, 'God schewuth opynly how þe fende be halowing of þe church was dryven oute of þe chyrch'.[84] In the Middle English pastoral care texts that I will discuss in Chapter 3, the expulsion of demons is presented as considerably more violent and noisy than the consecration ceremony would suggest. In the quotation above, Mirk emphasises that God shows 'opynly' the expulsion of the fiend through the spectacle of the swine's exit. The consecration ceremony, on the other hand, aims to demonstrate the ease with which the bishop cleanses the space; demons are not allowed to disrupt the liturgical proceedings and have their protest heard.

The bishop's triumphant entry through the church door and his powerful subjugation of demons also re-enacts Christ breaking down the gates of hell at the harrowing. This imagery is striking because for a moment the church becomes hell, the epitome of profane space. But as soon as the bishop expels the demons and passes through the church doors, this profane symbolism is conquered and subjugated. The entry into the church has both sacred and profane significance; it represents the harrowing of hell and the entry into Jerusalem simultaneously, and as such it functions as what Michel Foucault has called a heterotopia. According to Foucault, the heterotopia is 'capable of juxtaposing in a single space several spaces, several sites that are in themselves incompatible'.[85] For a moment, as the bishop lingers on the threshold to the church, the building represents both Jerusalem and hell. The church is able to sustain multiple meanings and exhibit multiple spatial identities concurrently. Foucault argues that heterotopias 'are formed in the very founding of society' and that they are 'a kind of effectively enacted utopia, in which real sites [...] are simultaneously represented, contested, and inverted'.[86] The consecration ceremony performs the creation of a new community that is placed within a space which is both utopian (it is the house of God and the gate of heaven) and real (it is a particular church in a specific location). The utopian space of God's house is enacted in the newly built church, but in order to construct the sanctity of the space, 'real sites', in this case the profane spaces of the corrupted world and hell itself, must be represented in order that they can be overcome and subjugated. One of the major characteristics of sacred space is its ability to garner the power of those dynamic tensions to bolster its own strength.

In addition to the bishop's expulsion of demons through his entry into the building and his speech, the church is then aspersed with holy water to protect it from the devil. The water itself is blessed so that 'it may repel the devil from the boundary of the just', thus creating a sacred force field around the church.[87] But the water, once consecrated, is also efficacious elsewhere: 'wherever you are poured out or sprinkled, whether in the field or in the home, you will put to flight every phantom and every power of the enemy, so that the Holy Spirit will inhabit this house'.[88] The consecrated water can repel the fiend just as easily in domestic or natural space, but significantly, this purification still aids in the construction of sacred space within the church because it is performed 'so that the Holy Spirit will inhabit *this* house'. This is a continuous theme in *The Book of the Foundation of St Bartholomew's Church*, which I will discuss in Chapter 2. Miracles which are performed outside the church using its material culture strengthen the church's sanctity by association.

Jacobus de Voragine sets out additional reasons for the aspersion of the building:

> The first is to drive out the devil, for the blessed water has the particular power to do this [...] the second purpose is to purify the church itself. All these earthly substances have been corrupted and defiled by sin, and therefore the place itself is sprinkled with the blessed water so that it may be freed, purged, and cleansed of all foulness and uncleanness. [...] The blessed water is used, thirdly, to remove any malediction. From the beginning the earth was accursed with its fruit because its fruit was the means by which man was deceived, but water was not subject to any malediction.[89]

Jacobus associates the defilement of the earth with the fall of Adam, and the purification of the building with holy water therefore brings the physical church back to its Edenic state of perfection.

The church can inhabit prelapsarian innocence because at the moment of consecration it is free from sin. The ritual aspersion of the church is, therefore, a form of baptism.[90] Dawn Marie Hayes suggests that 'the baptism of bodies and the consecration of churches' were often regarded as 'two sides of the same ritual':

> Both separated, cleansed, and strengthened places of worship. The only real difference was the material they effected: baptism was a sacrament of the flesh and consecration a rite of stone.[91]

The sacrament of baptism brings the individual into the community of believers and cleanses them of original sin. The ritual aspersion of the church similarly inducts the building into that spiritual fellowship and banishes the traces of sin. Brian Repsher argues that this baptism is not a one-off solution to the problem of sin, however, as 'understanding the church as a person in need of purification supports the idea that ecclesia is in constant need of repentance'.[92] The church, both as a building and a congregation, must be continually vigilant and alert to the temptation of sin and the need for repentance, and this embeds the clergy's pastoral and sacramental mission into the very foundation of the church.

The next stage of the transitional phase begins with the consecration of the altar, which confirms and secures the sanctity of the space. This process follows a similar pattern to the consecration of the church building: the altar is marked with crosses, aspersed, anointed, and censed, and the bishop makes a circuit around it. The bishop then exits the church and returns with the relics, which he deposits into the altar. The relics give a material embodiment to the sanctity of the church and the altar becomes a constant source of sanctity for the surrounding space. The deposition of the relics is crucial for the creation of the church's unique identity as the particular saint whose relics are chosen becomes the patron saint of the church. The consecration ceremony establishes the space as the house of God, like every other church, but it also inscribes a unique identity for that particular building: the church of St Bartholomew, for example, or the church of St Margaret. The relics are a sign that the church has a heavenly patron who not only possesses the space but who dwells within it and protects it. The deposition itself is reminiscent of funerary rites as the relics which are interred are part of the body of the saint and the altar becomes their tomb. Exemplary narratives which warn against the desecration of churches often mobilise the patron saint as a protector and defender of space, appearing in visions and even in the flesh to banish and punish those who attempt to defile their dwelling place.[93] The saint is the protector and defender of sacred space and even takes up residence in the church.

Veneration of the relics is commended as a way of protecting individuals from hardship and disease. The *Ordo* includes the following prayer for the consecration of the case in which the relics will be housed:

> So for those venerating the merits of the holy ones, for those humbly embracing the relics, against the devil and his angels, against lightening and storms, against hailstorms and various plagues, against corrupt air, against the death of men or animals, against robbers and brigands or the invasions of barbarians and against evil beasts and the most diverse forms of serpents and creeping things, against the wickedest inventions of bad men, you, God, having been placated by the prayers of these same holy ones of yours, extend propitiously the right hand of your unconquered power to drive away noxious things and for the defence of advantageous things always and everywhere.[94]

The saints act as intercessors who encourage God to sweep away natural disasters and protect the church and its people from human evils. The saints' relics not only act as a source of the church's sanctity and a guardian of the church building, they also make the saint present as a resource upon which the congregation can call to protect them in their everyday lives. The mobility of sacred space is greatly enhanced by the saints' presence because although the church functions as their earthly home, saints frequently move out into the surrounding space and perform miracles there. As I will show in Chapter 2, in *The Book of the Foundation of St Bartholomew's Church*, St Bartholomew orbits around the church, performing miracles and creating outposts of the church's sanctity in the city of London.

Once the relics have been deposited the bishop then consecrates the material objects of the church, including the vestments, corporal, paten, chalice, and crosses. Durandus explains that the blessing of ecclesiastical ornaments is 'not done because those things themselves can receive grace, because they are inanimate objects':

> But because grace is known through them, as it were, to men; so that those things that are blessed and consecrated and placed in service of the divine cult, and rendered fitting for it, inspire a much greater reverence.[95]

Just as the material church needed to be cleansed from its inherent corruption as part of the fallen world, so too the objects that will be used in the liturgical practice of the church had to be made suitable for their purpose. Dawn Marie Hayes argues that the consecration of these objects makes them 'sacred in perpetuity', and such objects often feature in Middle English miracle narratives as carriers of the church's sanctity.[96] The official distinction that such objects were 'inanimate' and merely 'rendered suitable' for use in the liturgy by being consecrated did not always transfer into the popular perception of sacred objects, however; crosses in particular were frequently seen as having agency and the ability to generate miracles.[97]

The consecration of liturgical objects is an essential part of the construction of sacred space because without such objects, the sacramental worship of God could not take place and it is this which maintains the space as God's house on earth. The consecration of the church is founded on the expectation that the building will become a working church in which the daily rituals of the liturgical year will be performed. It is through these practices that God's continued presence in the building is ensured and the community that has been formed at the consecration is strengthened and nurtured. The blessing of liturgical objects is a celebration of the working sacred space which the church will become. As I will argue in subsequent chapters, sacred space is in continual need of renewal and it is in the communal worship of God in the liturgy that this renewal takes place.

The consecration ceremony concludes with the bishop performing a mass and preaching to the congregation:

> Thus with all these things finished in order, when he shall have returned again to the door of the church, with silence being established, let the bishop talk to the people concerning ecclesiastical honour and the peace of those coming and leaving, and tithes, and offerings of the churches, and the anniversary dedication of this church. Let him announce to the clergy, as well as to the people, in whose honour the church has been constructed and dedicated, and also the names of the holy ones resting there.[98]

This moment of edification is crucial because it confirms the significance of the ceremony in which the congregation has participated, establishes the church's patronal identity, and encourages the future support of the church, both spiritual and financial. The bishop then performs a mass which incorporates the people, the building, and its material culture, and activates the sanctity of the church. Each subsequent performance of the mass recalls this first ritual and brings the church and its community back to the time of its consecration, the primordial 'in the beginning', as Eliade puts it.[99] The performance of the mass moves seamlessly from the moment of consecration into the daily life of the church and thus extends the sacred time of the consecration ceremony in perpetuity. After the consecration has been completed, it is essential that the church continues to operate in sacred time and as a sacred space just as it did in that original moment of consecration. The importance of retaining and maintaining this state both spatially and temporally can be seen in Durandus's discussion of the instances in which the re-consecration of a church would be necessary. Durandus explains that a church would need to be re-consecrated either because it has been polluted (by homicide, bloodshed, fornication, theft, or the burial of a pagan within its confines) or because the original surface upon which the anointing took place has been damaged.[100] He explains similarly that the re-consecration of the altar would be necessary if the upper surface upon which 'the consecration principally took place' is moved, changed, or broken, or if the seal which encloses the relics is damaged.[101] This suggests that the outer surface of the church and altar are key planes of sanctity and, additionally, that ensuring the church remains intact as it was at the moment of consecration is a primary goal.[102] Durandus continues that re-consecration is also required if 'the whole church, or the greater part of it collapses all at once, and it is repaired from all or some of the stones that fell, mixed with other stones; for the consecration of a church consists, above all, in the anointing of the exterior, and in the joining and the placement of the stones'.[103] The consecration is only valid if the precise configuration of the stonework remains undamaged. The material form of the building is an essential component of and witness to the bishop's consecration of the space. Indeed, consecration could not even take place at all unless the church was 'completely built' and its integrity assured.[104] Each stone must be present and correct. Churches that were entirely rebuilt, such as St Mary's, Sutterton (Lincolnshire), also therefore required re-consecration because the original stonework had been replaced.[105] Durandus does add a caveat, however, that if the building is damaged then the altar does not require re-consecration, and vice versa, 'since the consecration of the altar is one thing, the consecration of the church another'.[106] This is significant for the subsequent maintenance of the church's sanctity because it means that it resides in two distinct places, the building and the altar, and if one is profaned or damaged, at least the other remains to sustain the church's identity as a sacred space.

The consecration ceremony is a ritual performance in which architecture, liturgy, and community work together to create sacred space and each component is crucial to its subsequent maintenance as well as its construction. Just as the building must remain intact, the community must be strong and spiritually inviolate, and the liturgy a continuous presence, praising God within his earthly house. The *Speculum Sacerdotale*'s sermon for the dedication of the church opens by reminding its listeners that the church is both a house of prayer and a house of purification:

> In siche a day ȝe schul haue þe feste of the dedicacion of this chirche, in the whiche place we come and worschepeþ God in, of the whiche þer ben gret sacramentes, for this place is hous of prayinge, hous of sanctificacion.[107]

'Sanctificacion' is the action through which God makes a believer free from sin.[108] The consecration ceremony establishes a sacred space that is free from profane influence and in which the ongoing process of purifying its living stones – the congregation – can take place. The communal, ritual performance of the consecration ceremony builds the congregation into sacred space; the sanctity of the church and the spiritual state of its community are inseparable. As I will show in Chapter 3, however, this inextricable relationship between building and believers means that sacred space is unstable and prone to desecration. The *Speculum*'s sermon, therefore, goes on to urge the congregation that they 'owith [...] to be holy in herte and in body þat ye may be the temples of God': 'therfore let vs kepe clene fro alle fowlynge of flesche and of body that we may worþily worschepe this solempnyte'.[109] Here, 'this solempnyte' is both the festival of the consecration and the place itself. 'This solempnyte' and this church require the congregation to strive for personal holiness in order to ensure that the effects of the consecration ritual remain long after the moment of its performance. The sanctity of the church is an example to the congregation that they must uphold in their personal conduct.

Medieval architecture, as Hans Henrik Lohfert Jørgensen argues, taught the viewer how to see the sacred:

> When gazing through the focused building [the viewer] was able to learn from it how to fix the eyes at the sacred – to see ritually,

> so to speak. The church building acted as a sort of hagioscope on a monumental scale: as a device for making the beholder see the sacred, typically the altar, in an idealised mode of vision.[110]

Jørgensen uses the hagioscope or squint through which a viewer saw the altar of a church as a symbol for the function of church architecture. The form of the building was a lens through which an individual could gaze upon the sacred and learn how to see God. The consecration ceremony is just such a lens. It constructs sacred space 'in an idealised mode of vision', to use Jørgensen's phrase. The space that the ceremony creates is entirely pure, distinct from the profane space which surrounds it, and purged from the inherent corruption of the material world. In practice, however, sacred space was a far more complex entity. The ritualisation that the ceremony aimed to achieve was not always complete and unproblematic, and the ritual did not take account of the socio-political purposes for which sacred space was then, inevitably, used by its community. The consecration ceremony constructed an ideal sacred world in which harmony and unity outweighed conflict and chaos. As Sally Falk Moore and Barbara Myerhoff put it, ritual can make unity 'immediate and real because it is celebrated'.[111]

Henri Lefebvre describes the church as a 'super-coded' structure which 'tends towards the all-embracing presence of the totality'.[112] This totality is both the unity which the consecration ceremony constructs and the totality of God's sacred presence. But as the ceremony also makes clear through its complex symbolism and iconography, sacred space is capable of sustaining and negotiating several meanings simultaneously. Lefebvre states that we should think about architectures as 'architextures': we should 'treat each monument or building viewed in its surroundings and context, in the populated area and associated networks in which it is set down, as part of a particular production of space'.[113] Having explored the paradigm which the consecration ceremony establishes for sacred space, in Chapter 2 I will consider the consecration of a specific church, St Bartholomew the Great in Smithfield, London. I will trace the production of this sacred space through its foundation legend, composed in Latin in the twelfth century and translated into Middle English during the 'Great Restoration' of St Bartholomew's at the turn of the fifteenth century. The text records 'a particular production of space' and an investigation of the 'populated area and associated networks in which it was set down' reveals a sacred space which was mobile, contagious, and intimately connected to the socio-political status of St Bartholomew's and its community in late medieval London. The sanctity of the church was a commodity of great value that the community desperately needed during the time of the 'Great Restoration'. The text maintains that sacred space is the house of God and the gate of heaven but it also demonstrates that it could, additionally, be a place of social performance and competition.

Notes

1 Dawn Marie Hayes, *Body and Sacred Place in Medieval Europe 1100–1389* (London: Routledge, 2003) and Brian Repsher, *The Rite of Church Dedication in the Early Medieval Era* (Lewiston, NY: The Edwin Mellen Press, 1998).
2 Repsher, *Rite of Church Dedication*, p. 33 and p. 25.
3 *The Rationale Divinorum Officiorum of William Durand of Mende: A New Translation of the Prologue and Book One*, trans. Timothy M. Thibodeau (New York: Columbia University Press, 2007); Appendix A, 'An English translation of *Ordo benedicandam ecclesiam*: order to bless a church', in Repsher, *Rite of Church Dedication*, pp. 139–69; Jacobus de Voragine, 'The dedication of a church', in *The Golden Legend: Readings on the Saints*, trans. William Granger Ryan (Princeton: Princeton University Press, 1993), vol. II, pp. 385–95; *John Mirk's Festial*, ed. Susan Powell, EETS OS 335 (Oxford: Oxford University Press, 2011), vol. II, pp. 249–52; and *Speculum Sacerdotale*, ed. Edward H. Weatherly, EETS OS 200 (London: Oxford University Press, 1936), pp. 163–4.
4 Repsher, *Rite of Church Dedication*, p. 23, n. 38.
5 Hayes, *Body and Sacred Place*, p. 3.
6 De Voragine, 'Dedication of a church', p. 385.
7 Joel Brereton, 'Sacred space', in Mircea Eliade (ed.), *The Encyclopedia of Religion* (New York: Macmillan, 1987), vol. 12, pp. 526–35, p. 529.
8 Repsher, *Rite of Church Dedication*, p. 113.
9 Daniel Thiery, 'Welcome to the parish: remove your cap and stop assaulting your neighbour', in Douglas L. Biggs, Sharon D. Michalove and Albert Compton Reeves (eds), *Reputation and Representation in Fifteenth Century Europe* (Leiden: Brill, 2004), pp. 235–65.
10 See Chapter 9, 'Hallowing and vestments', in J. Charles Cox, *Churchwardens' Accounts from the Fourteenth Century to the Close of the Seventeenth Century* (London: Methuen, 1913), pp. 123–37, especially pp. 124–5.
11 *Speculum Sacerdotale*, p. 164.
12 See Roger Rosewell, *Medieval Wall Paintings in English and Welsh Churches* (Woodbridge: Boydell, 2008), pp. 150–2 and Andrew Spicer, '"To show that the place is divine": consecration crosses revisited', in

Krista Kodres and Anu Mänd (eds), *Images and Objects in Ritual Practices in Medieval and Early Modern Northern and Central Europe* (Newcastle-upon-Tyne: Cambridge Scholars Publishing, 2013), pp. 34–52.
13 Durandus, *Rationale*, p. 54.
14 *Ibid.*, pp. 54–5.
15 *Ibid.*, p. 61.
16 Mircea Eliade, *The Sacred and Profane: The Nature of Religion*, trans. Willard R. Trask (Orlando: Harcourt, 1987), p. 15.
17 Jonathan Z. Smith, *To Take Place: Toward Theory in Ritual* (Chicago: University of Chicago Press, 1987), p. 109.
18 Emile Durkheim, *Sociology and Philosophy*, trans. D. F. Pocock (London: Cohen and West, 1953), p. 94.
19 C. Clifford Flanigan, 'The moving subject: medieval liturgical processions in semiotic and cultural perspective', in Kathleen Ashley and Wim Hüsken (eds), *Moving Subjects: Processional Performance in the Middle Ages and the Renaissance* (Amsterdam: Rodopi, 2001), pp. 35–51, p. 38.
20 Richard Schechner, *Performance Theory* (London: Routledge, 2003), p. 127.
21 Manfred Pfister, *The Theory and Analysis of Drama*, trans. John Halliday (Cambridge: Cambridge University Press, 1988), p. 7.
22 Pfister, *Theory and Analysis*, p. 7.
23 Lawrence Sullivan, 'Sound and senses: towards a hermeneutics of performance', *History of Religion*, 26 (1986), 1–33, p. 8.
24 Evan M. Zuesse, 'Ritual', in Eliade (ed.), *Encyclopedia*, pp. 405–22, p. 406.
25 Michel de Certeau, *The Practice of Everyday Life*, trans. Steven Rendall (Berkeley: University of California Press, 1988), pp. 117.
26 Durandus, *Rationale*, p. 63.
27 *Ibid.* cf. Jacobus de Voragine, 'the spiritual temple that we are is consecrated just as the material temple is', de Voragine, 'Dedication of a church', p. 394.
28 *Ibid.*
29 Hayes, *Body and Sacred Place*, p. xv.
30 Catherine Bell, *Ritual Theory, Ritual Practice* (Oxford: Oxford University Press, 2009), p. 101.
31 Bell, *Ritual Theory*, pp. 98–9 and pp. 140–2.
32 Steven Lukes, 'Political ritual and social integration', *Sociology: Journal of the British Sociological Association*, 9 (1975), 289–308, p. 301.
33 Henri Lefebvre, *The Production of Space*, trans. Donald Nicholson Smith (Oxford: Blackwell, 1991), pp. 47–8.
34 Repsher, *Rite of Church Dedication*, p. 66.
35 See for example Chapter 56 of *The Book*, in which Margery is removed to the prior's chapel in St Margaret's parish church because her tears are seen to be disruptive; *The Book of Margery Kempe*, ed. Barry Windeatt (Woodbridge: Brewer, 2004), p. 273.

36 Anthony Cohen, *The Symbolic Construction of Community* (Chichester: Ellis Horwood, 1985), p. 20. Italics original.
37 Mary Louise Pratt, *Imperial Eyes: Travel Writing and Transculturation* (London: Routledge, 1992), p. 6.
38 Pratt, *Imperial Eyes*, p. 6.
39 Repsher, *Rite of Church Dedication*, p. 42.
40 Cohen, *Symbolic Construction of Community*, p. 50.
41 *Speculum Sacerdotale*, p. 163.
42 *MED* 'felaushipen' (v.) 1.
43 Eamon Duffy, 'Religious belief', in Rosemary Horrox and W. Mark Ormrod (eds), *A Social History of England 1200–1500* (Cambridge: Cambridge University Press, 2006), pp. 383–412, p. 309.
44 Miri Rubin, 'Small groups: identity and solidarity in the late middle ages', in Jennifer Kermode (ed.), *Enterprise and Individuals in Fifteenth Century Europe* (Stroud: Alan Sutton, 1991), pp. 132–50, p. 134.
45 Cohen, *Symbolic Construction of Community*, p. 50.
46 I will discuss this in detail in Chapter 3.
47 Smith, *To Take Place*, p. 104.
48 Brereton, 'Sacred space', p. 534.
49 Lefebvre, *The Production of Space*, p. 220.
50 Victor Turner, 'Frame, flow, and reflection: ritual and drama as public liminality', in Michel Benamou and Charles Caramelo (eds), *Performance in Postmodern Culture* (Milwaukee: Center for Twentieth Century Studies, University of Wisconsin-Milwaukee, 1977), pp. 33–55, p. 35.
51 Arnold van Gennep, *The Rites of Passage* (London: Routledge and Kegan Paul, 1960).
52 Flanigan, 'The moving subject', p. 39.
53 *Ibid.*
54 Cohen, *Symbolic Construction of Community*, p. 12 and p. 15.
55 Lefebvre, *The Production of Space* p. 36. Italics original.
56 *Ibid.*, p. 87.
57 De Voragine, 'Dedication of a church', p. 391.
58 Thiery, 'Welcome to the parish', p. 251.
59 Bell, *Ritual Theory*, p. 204.
60 Duffy, 'Religious belief', p. 306. For a further discussion of this issue, see Peter Draper, 'Enclosure and entrances in medieval cathedrals: access and security', in Janet Backhouse (ed.), *The Medieval English Cathedral* (Donington: Shaun Tyas, 2003), pp. 76–88.
61 See Duffy, 'Religious belief', pp. 305–9.
62 Katherine L. French, 'Localized faith: parochial and domestic space', in John H. Arnold (ed.), *The Oxford Handbook of Medieval Christianity* (Oxford: Oxford University Press, 2014), pp. 166–82, p. 175.
63 Bell, *Ritual Theory*, p. 181. Kathleen Ashley argues that procession also has this effect: it does 'more than simply reflect the social structures and ideologies; it actually creates those relations and commitments in

performance'; Kathleen Ashley and Wim Hüsken, 'Introduction: the moving subjects of processional performance', in Ashley and Hüsken (eds), *Moving Subjects*, pp. 7–34, p. 15.

64 Hans Henrik Lohfert Jørgensen, 'Cultic vision – seeing as ritual: visual and liturgical experience in the early Christian and medieval church', in Nils Holger Petersen, Mette Birkedal Bruun, Jeremy Llewellyn and Mette Østrem (eds), *The Appearances of Medieval Rituals: The Play of Construction and Modification* (Turnhout: Brepols, 2004), pp. 173–97, p. 182.

65 Colin Morris, *The Sepulchre of Christ and the Medieval West: From the Beginning to 1600* (Oxford: Oxford University Press, 2005), p. 56.

66 Eliade, *Sacred and Profane*, p. 69.

67 *Ibid.*, p. 91.

68 *Ordo*, p. 165.

69 Durandus, *Rationale*, p. 13.

70 *Ordo*, p. 151.

71 Abbot Suger famously describes the wealth of precious stones embedded in the walls of St Denis in his description of the consecration. See Erwin Panofsky, *Abbot Suger on the Abbey Church of St Denis and its Art Treasures* (Princeton: Princeton University Press, 1979), p. 55 and p. 59.

72 Hayes, *Body and Sacred Place*, p. 15.

73 De Voragine, 'Dedication of a church', p. 392.

74 R. W. Muncey, *A History of the Consecration of Churches and Churchyards* (Cambridge: W. Heffer and Sons, 1930), p. 50.

75 Madeleine Gray, 'Images of words: iconographies of text and the construction of sacred space in medieval church wall painting', in Joseph Sterrett and Peter Thomas (eds), *Sacred Text, Sacred Space: Architectural, Spiritual, and Literary Convergences in England and Wales* (Leiden: Brill, 2011), pp. 15–35, p. 16.

76 Gray, 'Images of words', p. 16.

77 *Ibid.*, p. 34.

78 Durandus, *Rationale*, p. 67.

79 *Ibid.*, p. 67.

80 Mary Douglas, *Purity and Danger: An Analysis of Concepts of Pollution and Taboo* (London: Routledge, 2003), p. 95.

81 *Ordo*, p. 144.

82 Durandus, *Rationale*, p. 66.

83 *John Mirk's Festial*, vol. II, p. 249.

84 *Ibid.*

85 Michel Foucault, 'Of other spaces', trans. Jay Miskowiec, *Diacritics*, 16 (1986), 22–7, p. 25.

86 Foucault, 'Of other spaces', p. 24.

87 *Ordo*, p. 147.

88 *Ibid.*

89 De Voragine, 'Dedication of a church', p. 391.
90 Durandus, *Rationale*, 'in a certain manner the church is itself baptised', p. 63.
91 Hayes, *Body and Sacred Place*, p. 3.
92 Respher, *Rite of Church Dedication*, p. 121.
93 For example, St Erkenwald saves his tomb in St Paul's from fire; see *Supplementary Lives in Some Manuscripts of the Gilte Legende*, ed. Richard Hamer and Vida Russell, EETS OS 315 (Oxford: Oxford University Press, 2000), p. 58. In an exemplum in *The Alphabet of Tales*, saints fight against demons in the church to protect the building from harm; *An Alphabet of Tales*, ed. Mary Macleod Banks, EETS OS 126–7 (London: Kegan Paul, Trench and Trübner, 1904–5), p. 497.
94 *Ordo*, p. 162.
95 Durandus, *Rationale*, p. 99.
96 Hayes, *Body and Sacred Place*, p. 15.
97 I will discuss this further in Chapter 3.
98 *Ordo*, p. 165.
99 Eliade, *The Sacred and Profane*, p. 69 and p. 91.
100 Durandus, *Rationale*, pp. 70–5.
101 *Ibid.*, p. 70.
102 In the rebuilding of St Denis, Abbot Suger even goes so far as to suggest that the original stones should be considered 'relics' because of their consecrated state; Panofsky, *Abbot Suger*, p. 101.
103 Durandus, *Rationale*, p. 70.
104 Repsher, *Rite of Church Dedication*, p. 18.
105 St Mary's, Sutterton, was rebuilt and re-consecrated at the end of the fifteenth century. See Edward Peacock, 'Churchwardens' accounts of Saint Mary's, Sutterton', *Archaeological Journal*, 39 (1882), 53–63, pp. 55–6.
106 Durandus, *Rationale*, p. 70.
107 *Speculum Sacerdotale*, p. 163.
108 *MED* 'sanctificacioun' (n.).
109 *Speculum Sacerdotale*, p. 164.
110 Jørgensen, 'Cultic vision', p. 177.
111 Sally F. Moore and Barbara Myerhoff, 'Secular ritual: forms and meanings', in Sally F. Moore and Barbara G. Myerhoff (eds), *Secular Ritual* (Assen, Netherlands: Van Gorcum, 1977), pp. 3–24, p. 24.
112 Lefebvre, *The Production of Space*, p. 222.
113 *Ibid.*, p. 118.

2

The Book of the Foundation of St Bartholomew's Church: Consecration, restoration, and translation

> So al these thyngis that bene seide or shall be seide, they beholde the ende and consummacioun of this document. For trewly God is yn this place.[1]

This statement appears midway through the Middle English translation of the twelfth-century Latin foundation legend known as *The Book of the Foundation of St Bartholomew's Church*. As a foundation legend, the text's primary aim is to narrate the construction of the church in question: St Bartholomew the Great, in Smithfield, London. And a fundamental part of that process is to establish the church as a sacred space by promoting and performing the church's claims to sanctity. In the case of St Bartholomew's, that sanctity resides in the catalogue of miracles narrated by *The Book*. The relationship between the textual and material church is crucial here. When the quotation above asserts that 'trewly God is yn *this place*', the referent is at once the church itself, the immediate subject of the foundation legend, and the translated document, in need of particular authorisation because of its status as a vernacular text. The use of the deictic 'this' not only unites the textual construction of the church with its material fabric, it brings the reader into close association with both. A relationship of spatial proximity and implied familiarity between reader and church are established which, as we shall see, is essential to *The Book*'s strategy of fostering support, both devotional and financial, for the foundation's attempt to boost its profile and restore the church building during the 'Great Restoration' of the early fifteenth century.

The Middle English translation of *The Book of the Foundation* directly follows a transcription of the original Latin foundation legend in the British Library, MS Cotton Vespasian B IX, dated c. 1400.[2] St Bartholomew the Great was founded in Smithfield, just outside the walls of the city of London, in 1123 by Rahere, who received his instructions from St Bartholomew in a vision and become the first prior, and the Latin foundation legend was composed some fifty years after the building process began. St Bartholomew's was the church of the Augustinian priory and it was closely, although not always harmoniously, associated with St Bartholomew's Hospital through their shared founder, Rahere. The original Latin text was translated into Middle English when the physical church was itself being translated into a new form. During what is now known as the 'Great Restoration' of St Bartholomew's at the beginning of the fifteenth century, the priory church was undergoing a major transformation: the east end of the church was entirely remodelled, the parish chapel was extended, and the monument to the founder, Rahere, was commissioned.[3] Much of this restoration was sponsored by Roger Walden, Bishop of London and favourite of Richard II, and I will argue that it is likely that Walden also instigated the translation of the foundation legend as a parallel activity to his involvement in the material restoration of the church. Walden recognised that the text's promotion of the sanctity of the church could play an important role in the foundation's strategy to re-establish itself as the dominant church and most sacred space in medieval London.

The Middle English translation, which is the focus of this chapter, is Janus-like in its ability to narrate the twelfth-century construction of the church and simultaneously to be of relevance in a socio-political context and built environment in late medieval London that the author of the original Latin text could not have envisaged. The text forms a bridge between the original foundation of the church and its later medieval life, maintaining and re-enacting the sanctity that Rahere's sacred practice established. 'Trewly', God is *still* present 'in this place'. In the liturgical ritual for consecration, discussed in Chapter 1, the inscription of the Greek and Latin alphabet crosses on the pavement of the church not only marked out the space as sacred, it also built textual potential into the very foundations of the material building. In *The Book of the Foundation*, this fundamental synthesis of text and building in the production of sanctity is re-enacted, both in Rahere's construction of the church and in the way in which the foundation legend itself performs a supplementary consecration through the catalogue of miracles that take place in and around the building. The liturgical ritual assigned an important role to textual inscription in the consecration of a church. *The Book of the Foundation* demonstrates the efficacy of texts not only at the moment of their dedication to God, but also in the subsequent working life of the church.

Keeping in mind the themes that the consecration ceremony established, this chapter will examine the paradigm of sacred space constructed in *The Book of the Foundation* and the uses to which that sanctity is put in the socio-political context of early fifteenth-century London. The Middle English foundation legend enables us to examine the 'architexture' of St Bartholomew's, to recall Henri Lefebvre's term: the 'particular production of space' that the text represents and the associated networks in which it operates.[4] It becomes clear that the textual performance of sacred space forms part of a community's 'ensemble of social practices', particularly at a time of socio-political change.[5] Lefebvre's coining of the term 'architexture' is especially useful here because of its felicitous conflation of architecture and text. *The Book of the Foundation* constructs an 'architexture' of St Bartholomew's that is both dependent upon but not constrained by either the material architecture of the church or the original twelfth-century Latin text. Like the sacred space it describes, the foundation legend is fluid, mobile, and a potent resource for community-building.

The Book of the Foundation is especially relevant to this monograph because it is a text that explores the relationship between space and place. Here I am using the definitions of Michel de Certeau, delineated in *The Practice of Everyday Life*. De Certeau argues that place 'implies an indication of stability'; it 'excludes the possibility of two things being in the same location'.[6] Space, on the other hand, is 'composed of intersections of mobile elements' and is 'actuated by the ensemble of movements deployed within it'.[7] Space, therefore, is 'produced by the operations that orient it, situate it, temporalise it, and make it function in a polyvalent unity of conflictual programs or contractual proximities. In short, space is practiced place.'[8] St Bartholomew's, in Smithfield, London, is a 'place'; the presence of the church on that site means that, naturally, no other building can occupy that location. Space, in particular sacred space, as we have seen from the consecration ceremony, is 'actuated by the ensemble of movements deployed within it'. Liturgical consecration transforms place into space and the miracles that take place at St Bartholomew's confirm this transformation. A number of *The Book*'s miracles take place in locations outside the church but they are associated with it in a number of different ways, from the presence of the saint to the prayers of those devoted to the foundation, and as a result the sacred space of St Bartholomew's is extended beyond the material boundaries of the Smithfield buildings. Sacred space is fundamentally spacious and continually produced and re-enacted by human practice.

De Certeau takes his analysis further and argues that one of the ways in which this practice is carried out is through narrative. He declares that every story is a 'travel story – a spatial practice'.[9] Stories, like rituals, 'constantly transform places into spaces or spaces into places'.[10] The story's first function is to 'authorize, or more exactly, to *found*', and narratives often function, therefore, as 'both a renewal and a repetition of the originary founding acts' or a '*recitation*'.[11] *The Book* is precisely such a 'recitation' of Rahere's original founding act, which authorised the church as a sacred space, and a repetition and renewal of the miracles that then confirmed the sanctity of the new foundation. But as de Certeau's use of the language of practice makes clear, this is not a static process. As travel stories, narratives map a journey through the topography that they describe, turning place into space as they do so. For de Certeau, the walker in the city is an analogous case. Through their peregrination, the walker performs a pedestrian speech act, appropriating the topographical system through which they walk, acting out the geographical and material place and, most importantly, establishing relationships between places as a result of their personal mapping. Walking is a 'space of enunciation' in which the walker 'actualises' a series of possible meanings and constitutes, in relation to his position, 'a *here* and a *there*'.[12] *The Book of the Foundation* is itself our walker in the city, our guide through the streets of medieval London, and our navigator in the competitive world of fifteenth-century sacred space. As the pilgrims within the miracle narratives again and again converge upon St Bartholomew's, *The Book* anchors our 'here' in 'this place': the church in medieval Smithfield.

This chapter will begin our peregrination to St Bartholomew's church with the late medieval translation of the foundation legend in the context of the 'Great Restoration' at the beginning of the fifteenth century. Textual and architectural production combine both to reinvigorate the sanctity of St Bartholomew's and to rehabilitate the reputation of Roger Walden in the aftermath of the deposition of his king and patron, Richard II. *The Book*'s depiction of the relationship between church builder and king, in this case Rahere and Henry I, has renewed relevance in the light of the Walden connection, and *The Book* has much to tell us about the socio-political exigencies involved in establishing and maintaining sacred space. I will then turn to the Romanesque church of St Bartholomew the Great, in its twelfth- and fifteenth-century incarnations, and the ways in which the relationship between church, founder and community is crucial to the construction of sanctity. Scriptural and symbolic language is built into the foundations of the material building by Rahere's sacred practice and the church emerges as the very definition of the house of God and the gate of heaven. The miracles which then follow in *The Book* continue to make manifest the church's sanctity as a real presence in the lives of the St Bartholomew's community and beyond. Drawing on Eliade's concept of sacred manifestations, I will show how the miracles produce a sanctity that is mobile, contagious and unrestrained by the material boundaries of St Bartholomew's itself. *The Book* deliberately establishes the church as a sacred centre around which all other sites orbit, analogous to – even surpassing – the position of Jerusalem, the 'symbolic centre of the world', on medieval maps.[13] The final section of this chapter will show how this map places St Bartholomew's in direct competition with its ecclesiastical neighbours. Promoting the sanctity of the church as more potent than that of St Paul's, Westminster Abbey and even Canterbury Cathedral, the text makes clear that St Bartholomew's is not only the most sacred space in medieval London but in the world of Christian pilgrimage. All roads lead to St Bartholomew's and to the confirmation of *The Book*'s assertion that 'trewly God is yn this place'.

The architexture of *The Book of the Foundation*: The great restoration, the book, and the bishop

Henri Lefebvre's concept of 'architexture' proposes that we 'treat each monument or building viewed in its surroundings and context, in the populated area and associated networks in which it is set down, as part of a particular production of space'.[14] The Middle English translation of *The Book of the Foundation* represents a particular reproduction of the space of St Bartholomew the Great, at the turn of the fifteenth century and in the context of a specific moment in its history; what E. A. Webb termed the 'Great Restoration' of the church. If we consider the historical context and socio-political networks in which the translation was produced, it becomes clear that the text was just one part of the 'ensemble of social practices' employed at St Bartholomew's at an important moment of renewal and regeneration.[15] The text embodied and promoted the key aim of the 'Great Restoration' – to regenerate the material fabric of the church and reinvigorate its community – by reminding its audience of the potency and sanctity of the space that they occupied. The Middle English translation encapsulates late medieval attitudes towards and constructions of sacred space and, simultaneously, intersects with its particular historical context in early fifteenth-century London. Communal and individual priorities are negotiated in the text's new life as a vernacular text. The representation of royal-ecclesiastical relations gains new significance in the light of the deposition of Richard II and in the relationship between Roger Walden, intimate of Richard II and prominent ecclesiastical figure, and St Bartholomew's itself. I will propose that Walden was the motivating force, if not the translator himself, of *The Book of the Foundation*, and an examination of Walden's career will show the very real and powerful role that sacred space can play in the authorisation and rehabilitation of private and public reputations. Royal legitimation is a fundamental authorising strategy for the foundation and Walden's relationship with Richard, a monarch who repeatedly appropriated churches and cathedrals as sites of royal power, demonstrates how sanctity could also be exploited for socio-political ends. St Bartholomew's was situated at the heart of a politically charged space in late medieval London and, as my analysis will make clear, sacred space was an important stake in the negotiation and contestation of personal, communal and royal values. Sanctity was an important form of social, as well as spiritual, capital.

The Book of the Foundation of St Bartholomew's Church survives in a single manuscript, c. 1400, now in the British Library Cotton collection, MS Vespasian B IX. It comprises eighty-six vellum leaves, in quires of eight, and contains two versions of the same text. The first forty leaves are a transcription of the original twelfth-century Latin foundation legend and the subsequent thirty-eight are a Middle English translation of that text dating from the period of the manuscript, c. 1400.[16] The manuscript is inscribed on the final page as belonging to the Priory of St Bartholomew's, 'pertinent[is] prioratui eiusdem in Weste Smythfelde', where it resided until the seventeenth century when it came into private hands and eventually became part of the Cotton collection.[17] The Priory of St Bartholomew the Great was founded in 1123 in Smithfield, London, by Rahere and it was closely associated with St Bartholomew's Hospital, also founded by Rahere on a site adjacent to the priory. The text's Latin author is anonymous but is assumed to be one of the Augustinian canons at the priory. In the light of internal evidence, this text is dated 1174–89, fifty years or more after the original foundation.[18] The Middle English translator is also unknown, but following the suggestion of E. A. Webb and the balance of evidence, I will suggest that Roger Walden was responsible for the translation project.[19]

A number of key features of the text must be noted at the outset. The Middle English translation of *The Book* is essentially an accurate translation of the Latin. The narrative sequence is identical. No incidents are omitted and, on the whole, each sentence is faithfully translated. Occasionally a subordinate clause is expanded into a full sentence in the Middle English and a word or two added, but rarely is there more than this level of adaptation (the significant divergence which does occur can be found in Book II, chapter 22 and will be discussed below). The text opens by establishing the character and conversion of the founder, Rahere, and proceeds to depict the process by which he came to build the church in 1123, beginning with his illness and vision of St Bartholomew, and concluding with the securing of the site from Henry I and the building process itself (Book I, chapters 1–11). The remainder of Book I consists of a catalogue of miracles, typically involving healing, employed to authorise and validate the church as a sacred space. Book II opens with a prologue detailing the 'newe solempnyte' and renewal of the church following the death of Rahere in 1140 (p. 31), and offers a nuanced and powerful reading of the nature of sacred space and its relation to God. *The Book* then continues the trajectory of confirmatory miracles during the time of Rahere's successor, Thomas, who was elected in 1141, demonstrating that the sanctity of the church is not limited to the lifetime of the founder. Rahere and St Bartholomew play a central role in the narrative but it is the church itself that emerges as the main character and the focus of the text's energies.

The purpose of *The Book of the Foundation* is to record the founding of the church and the subsequent miracles that took place there, both as a repository of social memory and a relevant means of understanding the present life of the church. Sari Katajala-Peltomaa argues that reminiscence and narration were an 'indispensable part of the miracle process' and that, furthermore, the recollection of miracles can be seen 'as interaction with the sacred': 'the relationship with the intercessor was renewed and strengthened by the repeated narrations of the grace bestowed'.[20] Renewing and strengthening the relationship between the saint and sacred space was especially timely in the context of the fifteenth-century restoration of St Bartholomew's and the prologue to Book I makes the social and spiritual role of the text abundantly clear:

> For Asmooche that the meritory and notable operacyons of famose goode; and deuoute faders yn God sholde be remembred for Instruccion of aftyr cummers, to theyr consolacioun and encres of deuocion, thys Abbreuyat Tretesse shal compendiously expresse and declare the wondreful, and of celestial concel, gracious fundacion of oure hoely placys callyd the Priory of seynt Bartholomew yn Smythfyld, and of the hospital by olde tyme longyng to the same [...] And most specially the gloriouse and excellent myraclys wroghte with-yn them by the Intercessions, suffragys, and meritys of the foresaid benygne, feythfull, and blessid of God Apostyl, Sanct Bartholomy yn-to the laude of almyghty God, and agnicioun [acknowledgement] of his infinite powere. (p. 1)

This passage unites the saint, the foundation and the readers in a mutually beneficial relationship. *The Book* will express and declare the 'wondreful' and 'gracious' foundation of the church and hospital, in particular the 'glorious and excellent myraclys' performed as a result of the saint's intercession, because the 'meritory and notable operacyons' of devout fathers in God such as St Bartholomew should be remembered for the 'instruccion of aftyr cummers' and for the 'encres of deuocion'. The language of wonder and marvel is a characteristic component of the sacred and the prologue depicts the church being founded in the grace and 'celestial concel' of God, as will become clear when I turn to the foundation narrative itself. But the reference to instruction and devotion is also a significant part of the function of *The Book* and the function of the sacred. Katajala-Peltomaa asserts that 'publicity was an essential part of the miracle and the cult. Without publicity miracles could not fulfil their main function, namely, increase the devotion of the faithful.'[21] Increased devotion on the part of the foundation's community would feed back into the church's sanctity because a church that is venerated is a church that is sacred. This is relevant both to the original twelfth-century text and to the Middle English translation. *The Book* not only records the history of the church's foundation, it instructs its multiple audiences in how to recognise its sanctity and how they ought to respond to it. When the prologue declares that the text is for the 'encres of deuocion', the object of that devotional feeling is not made explicit. In Middle English, 'devocioun' encompasses 'the profound religious emotion of awe, reverence, adoration' and also an 'earnestness, devotedness' and a 'desire' to take action.[22] *The Book* aims to harness those emotions in response to the church and, particularly in the context of the early fifteenth century, to direct those earnest desires towards the spiritual and financial support of the 'Great Restoration'.

Christopher Brooke has described *The Book* as a 'sort of prospectus', almost a tourist guide for pilgrims, and he notes that 'many a church, great and small [...] produced such guides or prospectuses in the twelfth century'.[23] In addition to functioning as a guide book, such texts could also be employed for publicity and fundraising purposes, particularly in the case of rebuilding projects. Dawn Marie Hayes explores this possibility in relation to *The Miracles of Our Lady of Chartres* which she argues was composed to aid in the reconstruction of Chartres Cathedral, both materially and spiritually, in the aftermath of the disastrous fire of 1194.[24] Hayes notes that most of the miracles in the text occur within a hundred kilometres of Chartres and concludes that the intended audience was therefore localised. This is also the case in *The Book of the Foundation*, in which a specifically local, yet cosmopolitan, readership is envisaged through the detailed inclusion of the origins of the pilgrims, an issue to which I'll return. Both *The Miracles* and *The Book* validate their respective building projects by encouraging the support of the local laity and of visiting pilgrims. The miracle narratives are a confirmation, and a promise, of sanctity.

What we have, then, in *The Book of the Foundation* is a translated text which presents the miraculous origins of the church and its intensely potent sanctity as a persuasive tool to encourage those engaged in the contemporary 'Great Restoration'. *The Book* is one strand of the community's activity in their regeneration of the material foundations and devotional life of the church. The fourteenth and fifteenth centuries had seen St Bartholomew's boosting its material profile in the public world in a way that clearly presented the church as a competitive force in the religious landscape of medieval London and England more broadly. The extension of the Lady Chapel in the fourteenth century, for example, saw the length of the church extended to 349 ft, more than sufficient to rival the cathedrals at Chester (345 ft), Bristol (325 ft) and Rochester (320 ft).[25] The translation of *The Book of the Foundation* at the beginning of the fifteenth century coincided with building work of an even more extensive and visible kind, however. The east end of the church was entirely remodelled, the parish chapel was extended and the monument to the founder, Rahere, was commissioned. This was a time of considerable material upheaval and it is not surprising that the community at St Bartholomew's turned to a text that depicted their sacred origins and noble history as a source of stability and support. In his work on social memory, Paul Connerton argues that 'our experiences of the present largely depend upon our knowledge of the past' and 'our images of the past commonly serve to legitimate a present social order'.[26] For the community rebuilding their church and encountering their past in a concrete form, the translation of a text explaining the sacred and symbolic import of the tangible foundations would naturally serve to legitimise their efforts.

The changes in the material architecture might also encourage the community, paradoxically, to hang on to that which has not changed, their sacred inheritance from Rahere and the site upon which the foundation is built. E. A. Webb christened the fifteenth-century building work the 'Great Restoration' in his records of the church and inherent within the concept of 'restoration' is a reverence for the past and a concern for its preservation.[27] The tradition of the original foundation conserved within *The Book* gives a sense of dignity and importance to the restoration process and the translation of the textual version of the church parallels the translation of the material building into a new form in a way that is analogous to Rahere's own 'architextual' practice in unifying stones and stories in the consecration of his church. The re-enactment of an idealised time in which the sacred was made manifest in the world relates to Eric Hobsbawm's theory of the 'invention of tradition'. Hobsbawm argues that this discourse tends to be deployed 'when a rapid transformation of society weakens or destroys the social patterns for which "old" traditions have been designed'.[28] One of the striking features of Rahere's construction of the church is the cooperative and accommodating relationship between Rahere and Henry I. This depiction of a moment of stability in ecclesiastical-royal relations, reactivated by the Middle English translation, could not have come a moment too soon, as the end of the fourteenth century saw the deposition and death of Richard II and the Lancastrians' struggle to assert their authority, an authority that was frequently asserted through textual production.[29]

The relationship between the church, the founder and the king brings me to the connection between Roger Walden, *The Book* and St Bartholomew's. The extension of the parish chapel during the 'Great Restoration' was instigated by Walden and the chapel became known as the Walden Chapel. That Walden should add to the parish chapel is significant in that, like the vernacular translation of *The Book*, it aligns him with the lay congregation whose affections and support were so vital to the maintenance of the church's profile in an increasingly competitive devotional landscape. Moreover, in addition to the chapel, Roger Walden also commissioned the monument to the founder Rahere in 1405, which provides further evidence of his interest in a text that narrates the life of the founder.[30] The monument is located at the east end of the church, on the north side of the sanctuary, a position of honour appropriate for the founder, and it features Rahere himself in effigy, hands clasped in prayer, with two figures kneeling with books towards his feet (Figure 2). On the books are inscribed verses from Isaiah, 35.1 and 51.3; the latter declares, 'he will make her wilderness like Eden and her desert like the garden of the Lord'.[31] As I will discuss below, *The Book* presents Rahere sanctifying the wilderness when he cleanses the Smithfield site – previously a marshy place of execution – ready for the building process to begin, but this biblical verse with its associations of regeneration and rebirth are also relevant both to fifteenth-century Smithfield and to Roger

2 The monument to Rahere, St Bartholomew the Great, Smithfield, London. Mike Quinn/Wikimedia Commons/CC BY-SA 2.0.

Walden. Recollecting Rahere's ability to cleanse a space associated with criminals may have been particularly resonant in the period after 1381, when the leader of the Peasant's Revolt, Wat Tyler, was dragged out of St Bartholomew's Hospital and executed. Similarly, in 1401, the first Lollard heresy burning took place in front of the church, unmistakably placing St Bartholomew's at the heart of a politically charged area of medieval London. For Roger Walden, the potential for rehabilitation that Rahere's example offers is both personal and political, as a brief examination of his life and career will demonstrate.

Despite the conclusion of many scholars that he was an 'ecclesiastical non-entity', and the subsequent lack of critical attention to his career aside from casual remarks in histories of Richard II, in the context of St Bartholomew's, Roger Walden emerges as a fascinating and influential figure.[32] Continually advanced by Richard II, Walden rose from parson of Fenny Drayton 1382–5 to Treasurer of Calais in 1387, King's Secretary 1392–5, Lord High Treasurer of England in 1395 and eventually Archbishop of Canterbury in 1397, when he replaced the banished Thomas Arundel.[33] In between, Walden amassed numerous ecclesiastical offices and livings and various prebends, including one at St Paul's in 1397, and clearly discharged his royal appointments with care and efficiency; U. C. Hannam attributes these numerous livings to 'services rendered to the state'.[34] Nigel Saul notes the increase in signet activity during his time as secretary, evidence of intimate involvement with royal business, and he also ascribes the extensive rebuilding of the domestic apartments at Porchester Castle, of which Walden and his brother were governors from 1397, to Richard's favour for him.[35]

Walden's life and career were by no means untouched by controversy, however. His familial origins were unclear and the subject of some debate. He was 'disdained by some contemporaries as of low birth, possibly the son of a butcher' and it may be that he saw himself in *The Book*'s portrayal of Rahere who, at the beginning of the text, although 'richid yn puryte of conscience' and other virtues (p. 1), was 'boryne of lowe lynage' (p. 2) and reduced to frequenting the court and palace with 'iapys and flateryngis' (p. 2) to 'drawe to hym the hertys of many oone' (p. 3).[36] Walden's own preoccupation with origins and, more particularly, a discourse of exile and homecoming, can be detected in the preamble to his will:

> I Roger Walden, by the kindly mercy of God permitting, Bishop of London, undeserving and unworthy, knowing and feeling that the

> continuance of human life, so long as it is *shipwrecked in the raging sea of this world*, is all oftimes tossed by the *whirl of storms*, and in the *exile* to which, for its trial, it is duly exposed, is ever made bare to sorrow and to toil; nor is there an end of its wretchedness until the spirit, an *exile from its native land*, leaves its wretched but too dear place of sojourn and seeks again its native abode where it hopes to enjoy its native land after exile, joy after grief, rest after toil; and whereas for those making their way thither it is necessary first to set their house well in order in accordance with the order the Lord gave to Hezekiah when appointed to die: therefore whilst to me from the Lord there is granted a healthy soundness of reason and memory, I settle, order, and make this my will of my good in the form which follows.[37]

Walden's experience of exile would have been at its most acute when he was imprisoned in the Tower in 1399 for his involvement in the Epiphany plot to restore Richard II to the throne. His sense of being 'tossed by the whirl of storms' and 'shipwrecked in the raging sea of this world' was no doubt exacerbated by court faction and the slurs on his parentage, and in Thomas Walsingham's chronicle, he was again associated with such imagery. According to Walsingham, Walden was 'driven by a changing fortune' and discovered for himself the 'inconstant, uncertain, [and] instable' nature of fortune when he was elevated to and then deprived of the office of Archbishop of Canterbury within two short years.[38] J. H. Wylie even goes so far as to declare that Walden was 'a by-word for the sport of fickle fortune'.[39] In the light of this imagery, the miracles in *The Book of the Foundation* involving rescue from the sea and storms seem peculiarly apt (see pp. 21–2, 38–40 and 43–5). In the Latin original, the same would have been true for the royal and aristocratic audience, as in 1120, just three years prior to the founding of St Bartholomew's, Henry I lost his son and heir, and many of England's young nobility, in the White Ship disaster. The Middle English text is thus able to resonate back in time to the original composition and also be of relevance to contemporary events and individuals never envisaged by the original author.

As Thomas Arundel began the journey which would lead to his constitutions in 1409 and the attempted suppression of vernacular theology, Roger Walden began his own small-scale involvement with Middle English translation and textual production. It was after Walden's loss of the archbishopric of Canterbury that his association with St Bartholomew's began in earnest. According to an anonymous French chronicler, Walden's grandmother was residing at St Bartholomew's in 1399, and indeed we know that he and his brother, John, owned properties within the priory close.[40] After being released from the Tower, at the instigation of Arundel, who also urged his claims for the bishopric of London four years later, Walden went into retirement at St Bartholomew's and became closely involved in the 'Great Restoration'.[41] His commitment to the church is evident as early as 1396, however, when he commissioned the building of the Walden Chapel. That such an individual should show an interest in the Latin foundation legend of the church he was rebuilding is, therefore, entirely understandable. But as he did not have a university education and was, according to Usk's *Chronicle*, 'better versed in military matters and the ways of the world than in church affairs or learning', it is also possible that the translation was commissioned to facilitate his own reading rather than being purely for the benefit of the local and visiting laity.[42] Indeed, the chronicles differ upon this matter of literacy: the *Eulogium* describes him as a 'literate layman' but the *Annales Ricardi Secundi* declare him to be 'illiterate' and 'totally inadequate' for the office of Archbishop.[43] The *Annales*'s accusation could, of course, be politically motivated rather than an accurate appraisal of Walden's abilities. He could have been considered 'illiterate' in the fourteenth century and yet still have possessed a level of Latin sufficient for his episcopal and clerical duties, even if it was not, perhaps, advanced enough to appreciate a text such as *The Book* with ease.

In Walden's will, quoted above, he declared that 'for those making their way thither it is necessary first to set their house well in order in accordance with the order the Lord gave to Hezekiah when appointed to die' (see 2 Kings, 20.1; Isaiah, 38.1). When the Lord told Hezekiah to 'set his house in order', he prayed for deliverance and was granted an extra fifteen years of life. God also promised to deliver his city from the hands of the King of Assyria and to prove his word, God reversed the shadow of the sun by ten degrees. Given Roger Walden's turbulent experiences at the end of the fourteenth century, it is perhaps not surprising that he should turn to the house of God on earth, St Bartholomew's, to set his own house in order. The material extension of the church in the Walden Chapel gives tangible form to his desire to place himself in the protective sanctuary of God's house as the chapel would also have provided prayers for Walden after his death.[44] But the translation of *The Book* brings the narrative of God's miracles to a new audience as evidence of the sanctity of Walden's adopted house. It also places Walden at the heart of the community as the gatekeeper of social memory. As Roger Walden's life came to a close, his wish to rehabilitate his reputation, the need for financial and spiritual support during the 'Great Restoration' and the renewed relevance of *The Book of the Foundation* came together in a nexus of shared need and support.

The preoccupation with social order, particularly associated with a king on the brink of extinction, comes to the fore in the Middle English translation of *The Book*. As I mentioned earlier, the translation is faithful to the original Latin text except for one key deviation. That deviation occurs in Book II, chapter 22 when the translator states:

> The yeir of incarnacioun of oure Lord. M.C. and L^{ti} and nyne of the reigne of kynge Richard the secunde. (p. 58)

The passage should say 'Henry' the second. In his introduction to the text, Norman Moore comments that the scribe's 'slip of the pen' can be used as evidence for the dating of the text as 'nothing is more likely than that a scribe, who had lived with Richard II on the throne, should inadvertently put the name of the reigning king for that of a past sovereign of the same number but a different name'.[45] Moore's choice of the word 'inadvertently' could, however, be obscuring a very real intention on the part of the scribe: the support of contemporary rumours that Richard II was alive and well.[46] This assertion is bold, but not only does the manuscript show no sign of correction, the capital 'R' in Richard is executed with a flourish.[47] Whether deliberate or a fortuitous error, the inclusion of the deposed monarch's name enables the text to include within its frame of reference particular elements of Ricardian activity and, additionally, to bring the events of the text immediately up to the period of translation.[48] In the reign of 'Richard', then, the text continues, 'many tokynnes of vertu were shewyd yn his [Bartholomew's] holy chirche' (pp. 58–9), and as Emma Cownie notes, the best way to boost a saint's cult was to show that the 'saint was active in the world of the living'.[49] Not long after his deposition, of course, the living Richard was no more, but for a brief moment, in the sacred time and sacred space of *The Book of the Foundation*, the monarch whom Roger Walden and many others believed to be the rightful king was resurrected. The disparity between the contemporary Lancastrian rule, under which Walden and other clerics plotted against the king, and the especially harmonious and ordered regime depicted in the Latin original, which shows Rahere and Henry I cooperating in the foundation process, comes to be a poignant reminder of a golden age that had passed away.

At the beginning of *The Book*, when Rahere first consults the barons of London about his vision of St Bartholomew, they declare that 'noone of these myght be parfityd but the kynge were firste I-cowncellid' (p. 9). This is significant not just because the site that the saint proposed for the church rested 'withyn the kingis market' (p. 9), it also supports the authority of the king. As the author states, 'it was not leuefull [lawful] to prynces or other lordys, of there propyr auctoritate eny thyng to mynnysse' of the king's land (p. 9) or indeed his power, as Henry Bolingbroke might have done well to remember. With the help of Bishop Richard de Belmeis, Rahere persuades Henry I to grant him the land and, once the building work has begun, Rahere even convinces the king to assign to St Bartholomew's the same privileges and 'fredommys that his Crowne ys liberttid with', including freedom from customs and, more importantly, from 'all erthly seryuce, power, and subieccion' (p. 16). This independence is significant both financially and symbolically, and is achieved through Rahere's use of the same rhetoric of building that the text's author employs later in *The Book*, namely that the king 'myghte byle to hym-self eternal howse yn heuyn, whyle that he worschippith and defendith the howse of God yn erthe' (p. 16). The king is reminded, as both Roger Walden and Richard II were clearly aware, that the spiritual support and defence of the church on earth will simultaneously contribute to a spiritual edifice in heaven. The monarch's sponsorship and even martial protection are a powerful endorsement of the new foundation, demonstrating that sacred space is not isolated from secular and political modes of life; indeed, it benefits from such interaction. Concepts of ownership and authority are of vital importance to the sustained existence and public profile of the church, and for St Bartholomew's, this strategic layering of authorities begins with the monarch.

Henry I's charter from 1133 is extant and it is worth pausing to note both the full extent of the legal privileges that Rahere's foundation was afforded and the ambiguous rhetoric within which they were delivered. The specific freedoms from secular duties are listed, including considerable tax exemptions as well as complete jurisdiction over criminals within the boundaries of the land, but it is Henry's correlation of the privileges with his own that is particularly notable:

> All the pleases and fines shall belong to *my said canons* in like manner *as they would have been mine* if I were holding the same lands and fees *in my own hands*.

> Now this church with all the things belonging to it, know ye that I have *taken into my own hand, protection and defence* against all men, as being *my demesne chapel*; and that I will it to be free from every earthly authority, *like my crown*.[50]

On the one hand, Henry is *likening* the freedoms of the church to the crown and to his own possessions, but on the other, with phrases such as 'my said canons' and 'my demesne chapel', he is appropriating the church back into his own domain and jurisdiction, despite the rhetoric of protection and defence with which the liberties are proposed. The privileges themselves were, nevertheless, granted and Henry's involvement with the foundation is presented in *The Book* at least as an exemplar of kingly legitimation.

Such generous royal validation reflects well upon Henry himself and he was not the only medieval king to recognise the benefits of ecclesiastical patronage. I have already mentioned Roger Walden's allegiance to Richard II, amply demonstrated by his involvement in the Epiphany plot to restore him to the throne, and if, as I have argued, Walden was responsible for the translation of *The Book*, the scribe's 'slip of the pen' discussed above would accord with his view of the legitimate monarch. The dealings between Rahere and Henry I, and Henry's munificent but not disinterested patronage of the church, would also have intersected with Walden's relationship with Richard. Henri Lefebvre suggests that sacred space is always a 'stake' in the negotiation of power and as Richard's considerable patronage of churches and foundations such as Westminster Abbey, York Minster and others demonstrates, the advantages of claiming that stake were substantial.[51] As a close associate of Richard, and as both Treasurer and King's Secretary, Roger Walden could not have been unaware of the extent to which Richard funded, and exploited, ecclesiastical building projects. Indeed, his involvement with St Bartholomew's could be seen as an attempt to re-style himself after the example of his former king and patron.

Nigel Saul describes Richard II as an 'excessively generous patron of churches' but it is in relation to Westminster Abbey that the fundamental connection between sacred space and royal ideology can be most clearly seen.[52] Paul Binski has charted the evolving relationship between Westminster Abbey and the Plantagenets, arguing that the building represents a 'practical incorporation' of political culture within a sacred space.[53] Binski usefully reminds us that saints' cults, 'even personal ones do not develop in institutional vacuums'.[54] This is particularly evident in the ‘architexture’ of St Bartholomew’s that I have been delineating here. The negotiation of secular and political concerns within ecclesiastical buildings is important to my reading of sacred space. At Westminster, in particular, Richard employed sacred space for his own political purposes. He buried his favourites around the perimeter of St Edward’s shrine and used the glorification of the cult of St Edward to reflect upon his own image, both within the church and in other examples of his visual display, such as the Wilton Diptych.[55] After Richard’s deposition and death, his empty tomb at Westminster became a site symbolic of the Lancastrian’s unlawful occupation of the throne as Richard’s ignominious burial at Langley Abbey ‘prolonged the availability’ of his aura ‘as a source of unease or a locus of desire’, as Paul Strohm puts it.[56] The need for Lancastrian triumph over the symbolic field as well as the martial field is demonstrated by Strohm in his discussion of the Lancastrian ‘language of legitimation’ and the attempts which were made to obliterate the Ricardian imagery of the white hart.[57] That Roger Walden was also aware of the import of symbolic gestures in space is attested by Usk’s *Chronicle* in which he is described as having ‘removed or stripped away’ the arms of Thomas Arundel after his promotion to archbishop and then ‘having his own arms […] sewn onto them’ and displayed.[58] E. A. Webb speculates that the arms of Roger Walden may once have graced the monument to Rahere in St Bartholomew’s itself, suggesting that the design currently in place on one of the shields was part of a redecoration by Sir Stephen Slaney, the Lord Mayor of London, in 1595.[59] Within this context of legitimation and the appropriation of ecclesiastical architecture for personal and public image-making, therefore, *The Book of the Foundation* and its advocate fit effectively.

Roger Walden’s involvement in the ‘Great Restoration’, Ricardian patronage of great churches and Lancastrian attempts to restore social order all form part of the interconnecting web of associations and contexts in which the Middle English translation of *The Book of the Foundation* was produced. The text constitutes a ‘particular production of space’, to return to Lefebvre, but one that is fluid and mobile, with the ability to resonate across time from the twelfth to the fifteenth centuries. The vernacular translation replicates contemporary engagements with sacred space, particularly those associated with the legitimation of royal and social power. And importantly, this is a stable vision of space that does not admit anxiety. Roger Walden might have been tossed upon a sea of fortune but in *The Book of the Foundation*, sailors are always brought safely to shore to give thanks at the altar of St Bartholomew. The Middle English translation's 'slip of the pen' keeps the text poised before the deposition of Richard II, at a time when rightful royal authority had not been overturned. St Bartholomew's is the house of God on earth and God's house has its foundations in a secure socio-political environment.

The 'makynge vp of ther chirche': Textual and physical (re)construction

As a foundation legend, the primary aim of *The Book of the Foundation* is to record the construction of the church, and in doing so, to establish and testify to its sanctity. Throughout this book, I will argue that sacred space is sustained by stories. The textual recollection of the consecration of a church, its miracles and its history is fundamental to the way in which medieval communities interacted with their sacred spaces. If sanctity must be repeatedly made manifest, as Mircea Eliade argued, the production of texts should be considered as one such manifestation that ensures the continued vigour and potency of sacred space in the present moment. *The Book of the Foundation*'s production of space is, moreover, a production of community. An analysis of the text's narration of the foundation process shows how the recollection of the building of the church is also a recollection of the establishment of a new Christian community in medieval London. *The Book of the Foundation* houses the community's social memory within St Bartholomew's church, in the very stones and stories of its construction.

The Book opens with the conversion of the founder, Rahere, and his illness in Rome, a space of authority and sanctity in Christianity. While there, Rahere vows that 'yf helthe God hym wolde grawnte', he will build a 'hospitale yn recreacioun [refreshment, renewal] of poure men' (p. 4).[60] Just as God 'byhelde þe terys of Eȝechie the kynge' (p. 4) – Hezekiah, the king whom God advised to set his house in order – Rahere's prayer for health is answered and he makes the journey home. But the foundation of a hospital is only the beginning of Rahere's mission of 'recreacioun'. Spiritual rejuvenation was an essential counterpart to bodily nourishment, and as he travelled home to London 'in a certayne nyght he sawe a visoun ful of drede and of swetnesse':

> It semyd hym to be bore vp An hye of a certeyne beiste hauynge iiii feete and ii wynggis: and sette hym yn an hye place; and whan

> he from so grete an highnesse wolde inflecte and bowe down his yie to the lower party donward he behelde an horrible pytte whose horryble beholdyng ynpressid in hym, the beholder, grete drede and horroure. For the depnesse of the same pytte was depper than eny man myghte atteyne to see. Therfore he, secrete knowere of his defautes demyd hym self to slyde in-to that cruell a-downcast and therfore, as hym semyd ynwardly he fremyshid, and for drede tremelyd and grete cryes of his moweth procedyd. (pp. 4–5)

In the midst of this terrifying vision, St Bartholomew appears, assuming the appearance of a king. As a 'certayn mane pretendynge in chere the maieste of a kynge of grete bewte and imperiall auctorite', St Bartholomew asks Rahere 'what and howe muche seruyce shuldes thou yeue to hym that yn so grete a perele hath brought help to the' (p. 5)? Rahere answers that 'whatsumeuer myght be of hert and of myghtys diligently shulde I yeue, in recompence to my delyuerer' (p. 5). Rahere pledges his heart and his strength, and his recompense is to build a church. The hospital, which he had already vowed to found, would make restitution for his physical healing but the church would repay his rescue from the terrifying vision of hell with which he had been confronted.

Rahere's vision of the kingly St Bartholomew establishes the divine and authoritative origins of the new foundation. Mary Carruthers suggests that 'major monastic buildings were *expected* to be initiated in the form of a "vision"' and Rahere's experience does just this, drawing on the archetypal temple vision of Ezekiel, chapters 40–8.[61] Like Ezekiel, Rahere is 'bore vp An hye' for his vision (Ezekiel, 40.2), but unlike his biblical counterpart, Rahere is carried there by a beast with four feet and two wings who shows him, not a city or temple, but a vision of hell (pp. 4–5). Luckily for Rahere, St Bartholomew appears to rescue him and in his speech, the saint replaces the vision of hell with a vision of the church that he asks Rahere to found. This verbal description is important because it constructs the church in textual form before it exists in material reality. Carruthers points out that 'it was not lost on medieval exegetes' that Ezekiel's temple was 'a version of the actual temple of Solomon described in 1 Kings Chapter 6' and she examines the monastic contexts in which Ezekiel's vision is invoked, concluding as follows:

> Major buildings were expected to be made in the way of the Ezekiel pattern, first as mental locations, previsualized as schematized

> images in the manner of rhetorical invention, of which the actual stone and wood edifice is the "imitation", just as the poet's words "clothe" the substantive composition of his mind. The mental picture or scheme *precedes* its actualization.[62]

The Book of the Foundation follows this precise pattern. The church is previsualised as a mental location by St Bartholomew before its material imitation is actualised by Rahere. It is worth looking at the apostle's instructions in detail as they build into the foundation of the church the most important tropes of sacred space in the period. St Bartholomew begins by informing Rahere that he has chosen 'a place yn the Subbarbis of Londone, at Smythfeld; wher yn myn name thou shalte founde A Chirche':

> It shall be the house of God. ther shalbe the tabernacle of the lambe, the temple of the Holy Gost. This spirituall howse, almyghty God. shalle ynhabite and halowe yt and glorifie yt: And his yene shall be opyn and his Eerys yntendyng one this howse, nyght and day that the asker yn hit schall resceyue, the seker shall fynde and the rynger or knokker shall entre. (p. 5)

The image of the church that is presented here is constructed out of a group of scriptural quotations that clearly invoke the consecration ritual. As I discussed in my previous chapter, in the consecration ceremony, liturgical practice binds together the physical building and the new congregation to be housed within it through a combination of spatial procession and scriptural quotation. The bishop and priests encircle the church and mark the space out as sacred, and as they do so, they embed key images into the building: the House of God, the Gate of Heaven and the temple of the Holy Ghost, for example. *The Book of the Foundation* might not describe the literal consecration of St Bartholomew's, but here the saint himself performs a textual consecration. The scriptural significance of the ceremony is actualised in the text by the allusions to Ezekiel and St Bartholomew's speech act establishes the identity and sacred potency of the new church.

The most important image here is the church as the 'House of God', drawing upon Genesis 28 in which Jacob had a vision of a ladder leading up to heaven with angels ascending and descending. When Jacob awoke from his vision he declared: 'How terrible is this place! This is no other but the House of God and the Gate of Heaven' (Genesis, 28.17). This passage was the foundational text for the construction of sacred space in the Middle Ages and *The Book of the Foundation* draws more directly on Jacob's declaration in the prologue to Book II when the author sets out a manifesto for sacred space. He states: 'Dredefull, therfore, is this place to the vnderstander, ther is no thyng her els but the howse of God and the gate of heuyn to the belever' (p. 32). *The Book* adapts the quotation, however, adding an important caveat: 'to the vnderstander' and 'to the belever'. This emphasises the importance of both knowledge and faith in the appreciation of sacred space and it reminds us of the text's aim of 'instruccion', set out in the prologue to Book I. It is incumbent upon *The Book* to ensure that its audience become knowledgeable and faithful practitioners of sacred space.

St Bartholomew contributes to the audience's education when he explains that the church will be a 'spirituall howse' that almighty God 'shalle ynhabite and halowe' and glorify (p. 5). And this divine consecration is made manifest in *The Book* by the miracles that take place during the building process.[63] The fourteenth-century priory seal also promoted the apostle's church as God's house as its motto declared *credimus ante Deum proven per Bartholomeum* ('we believe we are brought into the presence of God by Bartholomew').[64] St Bartholomew's church is also represented as the 'Gate of Heaven', the second important epithet from Jacob's dream, and this is because the church acts as an entrance and an access point to God's heavenly house. God will hear those who pray to him within the church and here St Bartholomew conflates two Biblical quotations: 2 Chronicles, 7.15, in which God declares that his eyes shall be open and ears shall attend to those who pray in Solomon's temple (cf. 1 Kings, 8.29), and Christ's words during the Sermon on the Mount when he exhorts the faithful to 'ask, and it shall be given you: seek, and you shall find: knock, and it shall be opened to you' (Matthew, 7.7). *The Book*, however, locates such seeking after God *within* the church of St Bartholomew itself, the 'asker *yn hit* schall resceyue' (p. 5, italics mine). This promotes the benefits of being present in the church and participating in its communal prayers to God; it is here, in St Bartholomew's, that God is listening to mankind. The localisation of sacred space is a crucial strategy in the literature of pastoral care, as I shall argue in Chapter 3, and here St Bartholomew's endorsement of the church establishes the new foundation as a competitive force that is more than worthy of the laity's attention.

The material construction of the church by Rahere is also founded upon scriptural quotation. The building of the church will be aided by the saint; Rahere only need perform his duties diligently and he will receive the required materials, as St Bartholomew explains:

> Nethir of the costis of this bildynge dowte the nowght, onely yeue thy diligence and my parte schalbe to prouyde necessaries, directe, bilde & ende this werke and this place to me accepte with euydent tokenys and signys protecte and defende contynually hyt vndyr the schadowe of my wyngys and therfore of this werke knowe me the maister And thy self onely the mynyster. (p. 6).

Rahere is presented here as the 'mynyster' or earthly founder of the church. St Bartholomew is the 'maister' or architect who guarantees that the building supplies will flow in. The saint is the master builder who will plan and execute the church ('directe, bilde & ende'); he is the supplier of materials ('my part shalbe to prouyde necessaries'), and even the guarantor of site security ('protecte and defende [...] vndyr the schadowe of my wyngys'). St Bartholomew's reference to 'the shadow of my wings' here alludes to the Psalms (e.g. 16.8, 35.8, 62.8, 90.4) and the desire to be under the protection of God. Here, the church and its community will be sheltered under the protection of their patron saint.

The first description of the physical building process occurs after Rahere has secured the support of the bishop of London, Richard Belmeis, for the project and has been granted the king's permission to build the church:

> And aftyr the Apostles word, all necessaryes flowid vnto the hande. The Chirche he made of cumly stoonewerke tabylwyse. And an hospitall howse a litill lenger of from the chirche by hymself he began to edifie. (p. 10)

As St Bartholomew promised, the building materials flow in and Rahere builds his church of 'cumly stoonewerke tabylwyse'. 'Tabylwyse' is unattested elsewhere in Middle English but it appears to mean 'in flat horizontal layers', which presents the church as gradually rising up from the foundations.[65] The word 'cumly' in Middle English means 'of fair appearance' but in a religious context it also means 'noble' or 'holy' and is often used of Christ and the Virgin Mary.[66] This meaning resonates in the context of the church because the building was seen as the symbolic embodiment of the congregation who, spiritually, make up the body of Christ (1 Corinthians, 12.27).[67] Throughout *The Book of the Foundation*, the building process is depicted to maximise its symbolic and spiritual meaning. The textual reconstruction of Rahere's foundation is by no means a detailed and accurate representation of the realities of twelfth-century church building, nor indeed is it meant to be. The miraculous ease with which the church arises from the foundations indicates divine approval of the project and every opportunity is taken by *The Book*'s author to build sacred symbolism into his textual construction.

This can also be seen in the representation of the people of the parish who play a vital role as witnesses to the building process:

> Of this almen grettly were astonyd, boeth of the nouelte of the areysid frame and of the fownder of this newe werke. (p. 13)

The people's reaction to Rahere and his church resonates in both the twelfth- and early fifteenth-century contexts of St Bartholomew's, and may even be a nod to the quality of the architecture itself. The people's astonishment of the 'nouelte of the areysid frame' has occasioned some discussion as to whether this marvel might have an architectural and historical basis beyond its significance as a rhetorical trope of sanctity. Jill Franklin argues that St Bartholomew's may indeed have been a novel building in the twelfth century rather than, as had previously been suggested, merely 'a rather outmoded imitation of Norwich Cathedral'.[68] Franklin comments that the fact that St Bartholomew's had an ambulatory placed it in 'distinctly exalted company' as 'the only other buildings in or near the capital at that time which are likely to have had an ambulatory were highly prestigious'.[69] St Bartholomew's was also architecturally unusual, according to Franklin, due to being 'fully aisled in both presbytery and nave' where contemporary Augustinian churches were constructed to an aisle-less, cruciform plan:

> The decision not to deploy the plan type at Smithfield in 1123 but to opt instead for a church with aisles, ambulatory, and distinctive radiating chapels represented a marked departure from contemporary Augustinian practice.[70]

Franklin goes on to propose, more tentatively, that the 'frame' of the church might have given rise to particular astonishment because of its unique solution to the architecture of the crossing. The reinforced piers in the westernmost part of the presbytery 'may have been designed', Franklin argues, 'as supports for weighty or lofty structures rising above them':

> In other words, they may have been intended as the basis for a quartet of towers, flanking the presbytery and the nave at the four points where these meet the transept arms. This theory generates a configuration at the crossing which might well have impressed twelfth-century bystanders at Smithfield, for it would have been unparalleled in England.[71]

There is, Franklin admits, no surviving archaeological evidence for such a feature, but E. A. Webb, who compiled the records of St Bartholomew's, argues that a central tower was planned for in the twelfth century.[72] Franklin also notes that there is precedent for church towers being timber-framed with a masonry base, which might explain the reinforced bays in the presbytery and the lack of further archaeological evidence of the tower itself.[73]

The people's astonishment at the novelty of the church resonates even more strongly with the fifteenth-century context of the 'Great Restoration' at St Bartholomew's, however, as the major remodelling of the east end and Lady Chapel would have had a significant visual impact as people walked around medieval Smithfield and entered the church from the Cloth Fair on the northern side of the close. As I've already mentioned, after the extension of the Lady Chapel in the fourteenth century, the length of the church was already considerable and the construction of the Walden Chapel in the 1390s would have had a direct impact upon the parish as it was an extension of the chapel that housed the parish altar in the northern transept of the church. Marvel is an important response to the sacred and the community's amazement at the building process depicts even the material framework of the church as miraculous.

If we consider *The Book*'s remark about novelty in its immediate context, however, the author goes on to exclaim: 'Whoe wolde trowe this place with so sodayn A clensyng to be purgid and ther to be sette vp the tokenys of crosse!' (p. 13). This refers to the conditions of the Smithfield site which, as the *Book* describes it, was 'as a maryce dunge and fenny with water almost euerytyme habowndynge' (p. 12). In addition to the boggy conditions, the site also has a profane history as a place of execution, 'the Iubeit or galowys of thevys' (p. 12). Rahere's cleansing of the site therefore needs to work on both the literal and symbolic level. He not only needs to stabilise the ground if he is to build a great church upon such marshy foundations but he must also purge the space of its association with the execution of criminals, part of the ritual purification that the consecration ceremony effects. Rahere's association with the sanctification of the wilderness was foregrounded on the 1405 monument erected during the 'Great Restoration', featuring the quote from Isaiah, 51.3 ('He will make her wilderness like Eden and her desert like the garden of the Lord'), but in *The Book*, the site is not only a physical wilderness, it is a spiritual desert that will need a miracle to transform it into a sacred space. Indeed, *The Book*'s author declares:

> Who schulde nat mervel þer to be haunttid the mysterie of our lordys body and precious blode where was sumtyme schewid owte the blode of gentyly and hethyn peple! (p. 14)

Bloodshed causes desecration and it was specifically prohibited in the church, so it is essential that Rahere cleanse the site before he built his church.[74] Moreover, this is not Christian blood that has been spilt, it is the blood of 'gentyly and hethyn peple'. The Christianisation of a pagan site might remind us of Gregory the Great's recommendation that the most effective way to convert the people was to consecrate their sacred spaces to the Christian God.[75] But the site of St Bartholomew's has been a site of pagan bloodshed, and as the narrator forcefully exclaims, the only blood which will now be shed on the site is Christ's blood in the Eucharist, washing away the sins of humanity as well as the sinful past of earthly space. The presence of the marshy water and the blood of the guilty at the site combines as a profane precursor to the water and blood that issued from Christ's side at the crucifixion and that will be ritually reproduced by the sacraments of baptism and the Eucharist in the new church. Indeed, the opening description of the Smithfield site as housing 'a galowys of thevys' would have triggered an association with the crucifixion in the mind of a medieval reader, given the presence of the thieves with Christ at Calvary (Luke, 23.33), even before it is made explicit by *The Book*'s author:

> O cryst, these ben thy workys that of thyn excellent vertu and synguler pyte, makyst of vnclene clene and chesist the feble of the worlde to confownde the myghty [...] the whiche golgotha, the place of opyne abhominacioun madist a seyntwary of prayer and a solempne tokyne or sygne of deuocioun. (p. 14)

Christ transformed Golgotha from a place of 'opyne abhominacioun' to 'a seyntwary of prayer' and Rahere's conversion of the Smithfield site will do the same. The sacramental reading of the physical landscape enables the space to be resurrected and reborn like Christ himself, and as Christian believers hope to be in the future through their participation in church ritual. St Bartholomew's church becomes Christ-like as it functions as a conduit of salvation through the imitation of Christ's experience on Calvary. Mircea Eliade argues that a common strategy in the construction of sacred space is the 'reactualization of a sacred event that took place in a mythical past', and here the cleansing of the site at St Bartholomew's reactualises Christ's death and resurrection at Calvary.[76] As Colin Morris has shown, imitation of the Holy Sepulchre in the material architecture of the church was an available strategy in the medieval West, but here the imitation of the holy spaces of Jerusalem is performed in the textual allusions of *The Book*.[77]

Once the Smithfield site has been reborn in Christ, Rahere begins the process of recruiting workers for his building project. The virtue of both the geographical location for the church and the community who will establish it are crucial if the material building is to become a sacred space. Rahere begins by feigning 'the cheyr of an ydiotte' and hiding the 'secretnesse of his soule' (p. 13). 'The moore secretely he wroght, the moore wysely he dyd his werke' and eventually he gathers a 'felaschipe of children and seruantis' to work with him on the project. Once the 'grete frame' of the church has been erected, he reveals himself and begins to preach to the people. Rahere's pretence that he is an 'ydiotte' aligns him with the trope of the holy fool and his fellowship of children and servants builds an ideal congregation into the fabric of the building from its foundation. This would encourage the participation of all the people in the parish, not only during the twelfth-century construction of the church but also the fifteenth-century restoration. *The Book of the Foundation* promotes an image of the church as a sacred space that serves and is served by its parishioners, rather than a purely monastic space that is set aside from the world. The focus on the laity is especially important because it is from lay parishioners and pilgrims to the church that the Augustinian canons, outward looking in their commitment to pastoral care, would gain both their spiritual reputation in the local community and their financial support.[78] E. A. Webb notes that, as tenants of the priory close, the parishioners, who included Roger Walden, 'materially increased the revenue of their house'; their physical presence on church land sustained the foundation's very existence.[79]

When Rahere reveals himself, he begins to preach 'by dyuerse chirches' and exhorts the people to 'folowe and fulfyll those thynges that were of charite and almesdede. And yn thys wyse he cumpasid his sermon that nowe he sterid his audience to gladnesse' (p. 13). The use of the word 'cumpasid' in this context is significant because in addition to meaning to 'devise' or 'plan', it also has spatial connotations, meaning to 'surround, enclose, go from place to place'.[80] The sermons that Rahere delivers alongside the neighbouring churches enable him to enclose the surrounding space within the sacred compass of his project, and not just secular, urban space, but the sacred spaces of 'dyuerse chirches' too. The verb is used again later in *The Book* in reference to Alfun, the church builder, who, having completed St Giles at Cripplegate, is then employed by Rahere to assist him in the building of St Bartholomew's:

> It was maner and custome to this Alfunine with mynystris of the Chirche to *cumpasse* and go abowte the nye placys of the chirche, besily to seke and prouyde necessaries to the nede of the poer men that lay in the hospitall and to them that were hyryd to the makynge vp of ther chirche. (p. 24, italics mine).

The Book then details two episodes in which Alfun is miraculously provided with supplies to sustain both the church builders and the poor and sick at the hospital, just as Rahere received the building supplies from St Bartholomew. A brewer, suggestively named Eden, whose malt is in short supply, nevertheless makes a donation and as a result, not only are her own supplies undiminished, like the feeding of the five thousand, they begin to multiply (p. 26). A stubborn butcher who 'nat oonly to the asker wolde nat yeue but was woonte with scornyng wordes to ynsawt [insult] them' is promised by Alfun that any piece of meat from which he donates a portion will sell more quickly (p. 25). When he grudgingly complies, offering a piece of the 'vilest' meat, Alfun's promise is fulfilled and he finds that his business is booming. Both of these miracles are relevant to the local economy because Smithfield was the site of an important livestock market in the Middle Ages, and by the late fourteenth century, there were ninety-five inns in the area.[81] 'From that tyme', *The Book* concludes with satisfaction, the local people are 'more prompte to yeue ther almes' (p. 25).

As Alfun 'cumpasses' the 'nye placys of the churche', he demonstrates how good works that aid the church are rewarded by miracles and his peregrination through urban space encloses the sites of mercantile miracles within the protective enclosure of St Bartholomew's. Such imagery naturally resonates with a church that is part of an Augustinian priory as tropes of containment evoke the imagery of monastic enclosure in the Middle Ages. The local shops and businesses become part of the priory's enclosure and serve the monastery like its own kitchens and stores, sanctifying the work of the victuallers in the process. The term 'cumpass' also recalls the city walls, the material enclosure of urban space, and while St Bartholomew's was built outside the walls of London, the sacred enclosure mapped by Alfun and the ministers of the church creates an alternate 'encompassed' space to rival that of the metropolis.

The founding of sacred space thus involves both material and symbolic construction. The provisions that Alfun and his ministers have secured are for the sick and needy and for those 'hyryd to the makynge vp of ther chirche'. Here the primary meaning of 'makynge vp' is of course the construction process but by the turn of the fifteenth century, the word 'makynge' had garnered literary significance.[82] In Middle English literature the word 'makynge' is commonly employed for writing poetry: poets are 'makers' and they 'make' their text.[83] The process of 'making' a church was not just material. As we have seen, the building process at St Bartholomew's is advanced and underpinned by Rahere's preaching of sermons, texts that edify a community and strengthen its spiritual foundations. *The Book* comments that in Rahere's teaching 'was fownde those thyngis techynge that the holy gost by the Apostles and Appostolyke expositoures, haue yeue to the chirche vnmoueably & stedfastly to beholde' (p. 13). Rahere's good words exemplify the teachings of the Holy Ghost as mediated through the apostles and given 'vnmoueably and stedfastly' to the church. Both adverbs call to mind the physical foundations of the church, similarly unmoveable and steadfast, especially when secured by the sacred word. *The Book of the Foundation* consecrates St Bartholomew the Great by building the word of God into the church and ensuring that its material and textual 'making' is virtuous and efficacious.

Two of the early miracles in *The Book* foreground the theme of language and the ability of the church to restore speech and the power of enunciation to parishioners, essential if the church is to maintain its identity as a house of prayer. One concerns a woman whose tongue was so swollen 'that she myght nat schete here moweth'; indeed she is so 'opynly grennyng' (gnashing her teeth, grinning, grimacing) that she is unable to 'hidde the swellynge' and her friends take her to St Bartholomew's church (p. 20). Rahere feels great compassion for her and draws the sign of the cross on her tongue in water that has been made holy by contact with the true cross: 'and yn the same howre all the swellynge went his way And the woman, gladde and hole, went home to here owne' (p. 20). In another miracle, a child who has been blind from birth is brought into the church and as soon as he enters the building, he falls to the ground. 'Vndir the hande of the heuenly leche that lightyth euery mane cummynge in-to this worlde', the child's 'Inward-borne blyndenesse fledde a-way':

> And than he knew his parentys with opyne yen that neuer he sawe before; And sundry thyngis by ther propyr namys distynctly he callide. (p. 23)

Both this miracle and the example of the woman with the swollen tongue present St Bartholomew's as a place in which language is gained and regenerated. The blind child who has never been able to see the world around him is suddenly able to declaim the 'propyr namys' of sundry things, a moment of creativity reminiscent of Adam naming the animals in Genesis (2.20). In healing the woman's tongue, a more complex miracle is taking place. The sins of the tongue were a major category in the literature of pastoral care and the swollen tongue not only means that the woman is unable to close her mouth, a bodily opening through which the devil might easily enter, but she resorts to 'grennyng' or gnashing her teeth, a trope frequently exhibited by biblical sinners who have been cast out of the kingdom of heaven (e.g. Matthew, 8.12, 13.42). Rahere's healing miracle not only restores the women's tongue to physical normality, it saves the woman from sin. She is no longer cast out of the kingdom of heaven but welcomed into the house of God on earth.

The 'makynge vp of ther chirche', then, involves Rahere, St Bartholomew, Alfun and their lay supporters in a material, symbolic, and linguistic construction process. As the master builder, St Bartholomew established the ideal, conceptual picture of the church that was then actualised by Rahere himself, who also laid the scriptural, pastoral and miraculous foundations of the new church and community. When Rahere received his vision of the church from on high, he was not just entrusted with a construction project, he was asked to edify a community and build a house for God on earth. In the consecration liturgy, we saw that a three-stage process of detachment, transformation and incorporation took place. The site was detached from the surrounding space and marked out as sacred, its material coordinates were sanctified, and both the congregation and the objects required for liturgical ritual were incorporated into the church. *The Book of the Foundation* makes manifest the sanctity of St Bartholomew's through the catalogue of miracles that took place there but rather than detaching the surrounding space from the church, the local neighbourhood and the wider Christian world are incorporated into the church's sacred purview. When Rahere revealed himself to the community as the founder of St Bartholomew's, he preached by diverse churches, bringing them into a mutually beneficial relationship with the new foundation through his pastoral peregrination. Like de Certeau's walker in the city, Rahere began to create a sacred map, at the centre of which, rather than Jerusalem, was the church of St Bartholomew the Great.

The 'excitament of holynes': The manifestation of sacred space

> Hedirto we haue writyn examplys of myracles the whiche were done In the dayes of goode remembrawnce of Rayer, Priore & foundatoure of this place to the laude of God and excitament of holynes. (p. 31)

The miracles that occurred during the days of Rahere were performed, *The Book* declares, 'to the laude of God and excitament of holynes'. The word 'excitament' (encouragement) is a unique term, according to the Middle English Dictionary, cognate with the verb 'exciten', which has a complex range of meanings.[84] It can mean 'to bring out' or 'produce', 'to encourage, exhort, or move' (often to virtuous action or devotion), to 'stir up or rouse' in the case of an emotion or 'to stimulate or quicken' a thought or perception.[85] As an 'excitament of holynes', then, the miracles that took place at St Bartholomew's not only produce the 'holynes' necessary for the existence of the church as a sacred space, they also inspire devotion on the part of both the participants and readers of *The Book of the Foundation*. Furthermore, the miracles act as a kind of stimulus for the sanctity that the church already possesses; the narration of the miracles stirs up or quickens that sanctity once more. And that sanctity is not static or inert, as the examples I will discuss below demonstrate, it is dynamic, mobile, contagious and fundamentally spacious.

Mary Carruthers describes the term 'translation', meaning 'to carry from one place to another', as a very active kind of word, and in Middle English 'exciten' and its derivative 'excitament' are similarly vigorous.[86] The 'excitament' of sacred space in *The Book of the Foundation* has much in common with the concept of translation. One of the primary characteristics of the sanctity that emerges is its ability not only to be carried from one place to another, but to transform that place into space as a result, to recall de Certeau's formulation with which I began this chapter. The geographical places in the narrative become sacred spaces because of their connection to the original sacred location, St Bartholomew's, as a result of prayers to the saint or the presence of a material object from the church. In the next section I will show how this translation of sanctity places St Bartholomew's at the centre of a sacred map, but here I will examine in closer detail the kind of sacred space that the miracles in *The Book* 'excite'. It is a sacred space that recalls the 'multimediality' of the consecration ceremony. The sight, sounds, objects and idea of the church come together to make manifest the sacred space that *The Book* commemorates and celebrates.

Mircea Eliade's concept of manifestation remains essential to the definition of sacred space. Eliade argues that the sacred 'transcends this world but manifests itself in this world, thereby sanctifying it and making it real' and this is a formulation to which *The Book* readily attests.[87] For Eliade, manifestation is crucial because it enables us to recognise the sacred:

> Man becomes aware of the sacred because it manifests itself, shows itself, as something wholly different from the profane. To designate the *act of manifestation* of the sacred, we have proposed the term *hierophany*.[88]

A 'hierophany', Eliade continues, is 'an irruption of the sacred that results in detaching the territory from the surrounding cosmic milieu and making it qualitatively different'.[89] The consecration ritual, as we have seen, aims to make the church 'qualitatively different' from the surrounding space but in order for its continued existence and potency to be visible and recognisable in the world, the sacred must be made manifest repeatedly. This repetition is a fundamental part of the hierophany, it 'does not merely sanctify a given segment of undifferentiated profane space; it goes so far as to ensure that sacredness will continue there. *There*, in *that place*, the hierophany repeats itself.'[90] When *The Book* reminds us that the miracles that 'we haue writyn' were performed in the days of Rahere, the text is quick to reaffirm Rahere as the 'Priore & foundatoure of *this* place' (p. 31, italics mine). The proximal deixis anchors the miracle stories to St Bartholomew's and to its founder, whose tomb is still visible in the church; indeed, the deixis even brings the reader into proximity with the foundation as they read about 'this place'. *The Book*'s role in recalling and re-enacting the miracles is essential because, as Eliade argues, when the sacred does not 'manifest itself, it must be provoked'.[91] Eliade explains this as the performance of a 'sort of *evocation*' which establishes the space as sacred once and for all:

> A *sign* is asked, to put an end to the tension and anxiety caused by relativity and disorientation – in short, to reveal an absolute point of support.[92]

The hierophany establishes stability as a result of its status as a 'fixed point, a centre' in the otherwise 'homogeneous and infinite expanse, in which no point of reference is possible and hence no *orientation* can be established'.[93] We might argue that medieval Smithfield is anything but a homogeneous and infinite expanse of space, but it is certainly the aim of *The Book of the Foundation* to present St Bartholomew's as the fixed, stable centre around which all other space orbits. I suggested earlier that *The Book* does not admit tension and anxiety, a factor that is all the more evident when the translated text is read in the context of the political upheaval at the end of the fourteenth century, and as Eliade points out, the manifestation and evocation of the sacred deliberately suppresses anxiety and establishes stability and strength in its place. The narration of miracle upon miracle could be read as an 'excess of signification', indicating the foundation's lack of confidence in its own sacred identity.[94] But when read in the light of Eliade's theory of manifestation, the miracle catalogue emerges as powerful proof of the foundation's sanctity, endlessly repeatable and therefore living and real. And while each miracle might have the same fundamental purpose – 'the laud of God and the excitament of holynes' – their strategies for constructing St Bartholomew's as a sacred space are by no means undifferentiated. Each miracle is a particular production of sacred space and it is to this varied catalogue that I will now turn.

The first characteristic that must be recognised is that the sacred space of St Bartholomew's is fundamentally spacious and remarkably non-specific in architectural terms. Most often *The Book of the Foundation* refers to miracles occurring within 'this church' (e.g. p. 20) and those who require healing are sent to 'the church' (e.g. p. 23). The church has monumental status, it is *the* church in the textual world, and the deictic 'this' ensures that *The Book*'s miracles are firmly anchored within the familiar and respected setting of St Bartholomew's. The specific places within the church that do feature are the holy altar (p. 36 and p. 52), the altar of the apostle (p. 22 and p. 38) and the Lady Chapel (p. 40), and within the priory close, the kitchen (p. 28) and the chapter house (p. 52) also appear. The latter contribute to the sense of a working priory which both spiritually and physically nourishes its people, the ideal space of 'recreacioun' that Rahere vowed to found. The rather vague spatial coordinates within the church are, in part, a result of the length of time it takes to build a medieval church; by the late twelfth century when *The Book* was originally written, for example, the presbytery of St Bartholomew's was complete but the nave was not constructed until the thirteenth century. Sacred space was always a work in progress and its material fabric could change significantly over time. The lack of spatial coordinates, therefore, works to the church's advantage: it enables the entire space to be sanctified and allows those who heard *The Book*'s narratives of individuals being healed within its confines to imagine for themselves the particular space in which it occurred. While the lack of detail might be frustrating to an architectural historian, it is a distinct advantage in a text that achieves new life in translation more than two hundred years after its original composition. The reader is free to map the events of the text on to the church as they know it and to produce a sacred space from the architectural place as it currently stands.

The Book's refusal to locate precisely the events that it narrates within a specific part of the church also contributes to the sense of a sacred space that is not confined to a single location within the building or priory complex. The depiction of the medieval church as the gate of heaven suggests that the physical boundaries of space can be traversed by sacred practice and the characterisation of sanctity as fluid and mobile is promoted throughout *The Book of the Foundation*. The centre of sanctity is the church building but that sanctity can move outwards into the surrounding environment to create sacred outposts, spaces which are sanctified by association and in which the miraculous occurs. Sacred space can thus be theorised in direct opposition to place which, in de Certeau's theory, is 'definable, limited, enclosed'.[95] Space, conversely, is 'constantly being produced by the practices of living', practices which in relation to sacred space originate in the liturgical ritual of the church, and consequently 'one's own spacing may, then, transgress the boundaries of maps and cities that define places'.[96] This can be seen most clearly in two miracles in which men who have been wrongfully imprisoned are released from their bonds. The sanctity of St Bartholomew's is shown to promote spatial freedom for those who call upon the church and its saint for aid.

In the first miracle, a poor man has been wrongfully accused by a wicked beadle and imprisoned in a cell. He is made to wear a 'coller of Iren of grete weighte' and he is fastened with a chain 'rennyng thorow the myddyl of the wallys, that they myghte kepe hym the more surly' (p. 37). The man is doubly imprisoned but his cell is near enough to St Bartholomew's that he is able to hear the performance of the liturgy and the church bells:

> Vpon a day whane of custome, the chanons of the chirche of seynt Bartholomewes a-fore the mornynge the matens endid and began to synge Te deum laudamus. And the peyll of bell was roonge the forsayed pore mane, the whiche was artid in bondys, herynge the sownde of the bellis and the melodye of ympnys – the howse sothly, that he was crucyat yn was nygh by to the chirche – And he began with deuoute soule and lamentable voice to crye and, as he cowde or myght, to calle vpone seynt Bartholomewe. (p. 37)

The man is stirred to pray to St Bartholomew and miraculously he finds himself 'I-losid' from his imprisonment and the door to his cell is suddenly 'opyne' (p. 37). Dragging his iron collar and fetters with him, he leaves the prison but the clanking of his chains wakes the wicked beadle who, when he sees 'his fugityue by the mone-light' (p. 38), attempts to follow him. But 'thorow the wylle of God nethir he myght meve his fote, nethir breke owt with his voyce' and so the poor man, 'skapyng by seynt Barthilmew help', enters the church to give thanks (p. 38). The man prostrates himself before the altar of the apostle and makes it known 'to them that stoid abowte the ordir of the benefeit I-ȝeuen to hym' (p. 38). The sanctity of St Bartholomew's frees the innocent but imprisons the guilty and, crucially, the miracle immediately enters into the communal memory of the space as the man recounts his experience to those within the church.

In this narrative, the bells and the canons' singing are crucial to the man's escape. Yi-Fu Tuan argues that 'sound itself can evoke spatial impressions'; the liturgical sounds of the church transfer the sanctity of St Bartholomew's to the prison cell and the man is able to transgress the boundaries of his prison and enter the space of the church, which his confinement had denied him.[97] Here the biblical dictum 'knock and it shall be opened to you' is found to be literally true as once the poor man has knocked spiritually at the saint's door by means of his prayer, his prison doors open. That the liturgical rituals of the church might instigate miracles also serves as a reminder of the importance of church services and the benefits of supporting the Augustinian canons and their ritual practice. A number of pre-Reformation bells survive from St Bartholomew's and one of them from c. 1510 is inscribed *sancta Bartholomeo ora pro nobis* ('Saint Bartholomew pray for us').[98] When the bell is rung the text inscribed upon it is activated and the sounds of the church's prayers ring out across the city, encircling the urban community in its protective space. Text, object and ritual practice coalesce in the working life of the church to the 'excitament of holynes'.

St Bartholomew's thus appears as the sacred nucleus of Smithfield, radiating outwards into the local area to gather in potentially profane spaces such as the prison. This is also evident in the second miracle concerning the release of prisoners. A man who is 'y-bownde' in a cart is suddenly freed when he calls upon St Bartholomew 'whan the passage was made by the same chirche' (p. 51). The man 'skippid owte of the Carte and enteryd the chirche' immediately (p. 52) and we are told that 'yn this wyse he skapid the handis of his ennemyes' (p. 52). As in the earlier miracle, the escape from enemies alludes to the church's legal position as a sanctuary set apart from secular space. In this episode, the church's sanctity emanates into the city streets as a result of the man's prayer to the saint. As the cart passes by and enters the church's sacred force field, the man is freed from the cart and embraced within the church's legal protection.

The protective quality of St Bartholomew's as a sacred space, as well as its mobility, can also be seen in one of the many miracles involving the rescue of sailors from storms in *The Book*. These episodes draw on Christ's calming of the storm in Matthew 8, a miracle that demonstrates Christ's power and reinforces the importance of faith on the part of the disciples. *The Book* makes the connection clear when the sailors call upon St Bartholomew with the words of the disciples: 'Lord, Lord, saue vs, we perysch' (p. 53, cf. Matthew, 8.25). In a similar episode in Book II, chapter 7, the rescue of a single surviving sailor involves more than just the power of St Bartholomew, however. When the apostle appears to the sailor and calms the storm, he declares that a ship from Dover will rescue him and he presents the man with a 'pece of breid' from the church (p. 44). The man is rescued as promised and he then displays the piece of bread 'to the confirmacion of the heuenly benefeit [...] magnifiynge God, whiche puttyth a terme to the see whiche all thynge whatsumeuer he will he doith' (p. 44). The piece of bread clearly invokes the Eucharist and functions both as a 'confirmacioun' of the miracle and as a representative of the church and its far-reaching powers. St Bartholomew performs the role of the priest when he administers the bread to the sailor as a sign of his salvation, both literally from the storm and spiritually as a result of his devotion to the foundation. The church is glorified by the presence of the saint who performs its ritual practice and by the presence of the sacramental bread in the storm. The hostile space of the sea is not only neutralised but sanctified through the miracle that takes place there. The piece of bread claims the miracle for St Bartholomew's church as well as for St Bartholomew himself.

The man's revelation of the miracle and the bread as its material proof ensures that the episode becomes part of the social memory at St Bartholomew's. Katajala-Peltomaa suggests that rescues at sea or escapes from captivity were frequently experienced by men and were 'closely linked to men's roles in late medieval society' as their activities frequently took them outside of the domestic sphere.[99] Miracles that occur to individuals in isolated or private spaces must be narrated in order to enter the public record, however, and another miracle in *The Book*, involving a man who cannot sleep, follows this pattern and involves the foundation's material culture once again. In this episode, the restorative powers of St Bartholomew's, amply demonstrated by the many healing miracles that take place at the church, are transferred to a parish church in Yarmouth through the presence of the relics of the saint:

> In VII. ȝeire of his vnfortune whan the relikys of the same chirche of seynt Batholomewe were browght and put yn to the oratorye of sente Nicholas at Ȝermoweth this man drewe to the same relykys deuoutly. And mekely prostratte himself, askyng and sekyng remedy. (p. 27)

Dawn Marie Hayes discusses the practice of taking relics on tour in order to boost the reputation, and financial status, of the home church.[100] That the man in Yarmouth is cured of his insomnia by the relics is indicated both by his devotion to them – the innocent man freed from prison also prayed 'with deuote soule' – and by the text's key phrase, 'askyng and sekyng':

> He fownde that he sowght he range at the doyr and oure porter opynde to hym and shewid to hym magnyfycently the bowellis of his mercy. And grovelynge to the grownde, he multiplied his prayers, and began to slepe. (p. 27)

Prayer in the church opens the door to sleep. When the man approaches the door, 'oure porter', who we assume is St Bartholomew, opens the 'bowellis of his mercy' and the man can finally sleep. The allusion to the commandment from Matthew (7.7) and the conception of mercy as a space that can be opened brings sleep within a Christian rhetoric.[101] This is a very personal sacred space but it is one that is only accessible through the presence of St Bartholomew's relics. That the miracle takes place in a rival sacred space, the church at Yarmouth, highlights a crucial element of competition between churches, to which I will return, but what is important to note here is that even miracles that occur in spaces outside of the church are, nevertheless, claimed in support for the sanctity of St Bartholomew's.

The relics are not the only objects from St Bartholomew's that are shown to have a significant role in the construction and maintenance of sacred space: liturgical books, *ex voto* offerings and measuring threads also play an important role in *The Book*. An early miracle in the text concerns an antiphonal which 'a certeyne man' took away from the church (p. 19). The antiphonal is crucial for the performance of the liturgical office. As *The Book* notes, it 'was necessarie to them that schulde synge ynne the chirche', especially because there 'was nat at that tyme grete plente of bokys yn the place' (p. 19). The book cannot be found and when St Bartholomew appears to Rahere in his chamber, Rahere explains that the 'profitable boke' which 'to the honoure of God' and 'in the holy temple of thy glorie they were wownte to synge' has been 'hidde yn ony place or stolyne a-way' (p. 19). St Bartholomew tells Rahere to enter the city early in the morning and to let loose his horse in the 'Iewes strete': 'And yn to what howse thy hors wilfully putte yne his fote knowe welle of me ther thy boke schall be fownde' (p. 19). Rahere does precisely as he is commanded 'and with the ennemyes of pees he spake pesibly And the boke that he sowghte he fownde' (p. 20). The narrative concludes with the peaceful recovery of the book and its return to St Bartholomew's.

The 'Iewes strete' probably refers to the street now known as Old Jewry, a fifteen-minute walk from St Bartholomew's.[102] The identity of the individual who removed the book is unspecified, although it's recovery is located in the Jewish street, and this leads Claire Hilton to conclude that 'it is more likely that a Christian took it and pawned it to the Jew', rather than the Jew committing the theft.[103] Hilton notes that it was 'common for Jews to take articles on pledge', including church items before this practice was banned in 1201, and certainly the miracle is more interested in the peaceful recovery of the book from the local area than in the opportunity it might provide to stage a narrative of conversion from Judaism to Christianity.[104] Although the Jews are described as 'the ennemyes of pees' in the passage, this may merely refer to their non-Christian status and it is certainly striking that despite this, Rahere is able to speak 'pesibly' with them and secure the book's return.[105] The narrative itself certainly does not assign any blame to them and it is plausible therefore that the Jewish street appears as part of the local geography, as a place of moneylending and, ultimately, of cooperation with St Bartholomew's. Rahere is not hindered by the Jews and with the recovery of the antiphonal, the canons are able to resume their liturgical practice, performing rituals which, as we saw in the example of the man freed from prison, are a potential source of sanctity. That this miracle occurs so early in *The Book* shows that Rahere is setting his house in order so that it can function efficaciously as the house of God on earth, in a supportive relationship with its neighbours. And a crucial element in the working life of the church is the provision, and protection, of its sacred texts.

Throughout *The Book*, individuals who are the recipients of St Bartholomew's miraculous powers enter the church to make offerings and give thanks. This is especially important in the case of the miracles that take place outside of the physical structure of the church as the association with St Bartholomew's must be clearly demonstrated. The entry of those who have been saved or healed into the church reaffirms the church and its patron saint as the source of the miracle, ensuring that our attention is continually fixed upon St Bartholomew's throughout the text. *Ex voto* offerings were a common way for those who had experienced the benevolence of the saint or the foundation not only to express their gratitude but also to place an object which stood in for themselves or their particular miracle at the heart of sacred space.[106] Basic offerings might include candles, such as those donated by the sailors who were saved in

Book I, chapter 17, but a more personal and symbolic offering might include an object which represents either the individual or the miracle in detail. The merchants who are delivered from a fierce storm in Book II, chapter 3 declare that they have 'herde of seynt Barthilmewe, that a-monge the knyghtis of the heuynly kynge ys worthy to be callid vppone, whiche plesawntly condescendith to the prayers of deuoute askers' and they declare:

> Lette vs, therfore, lyfte vp oure handis to heuyn and avowe with clere deuocioun that whane we cum whidir we purpose to Lundone we shall bere thedir in the honoure of seynt Barthilmewe, a Shippe of syluer aftir the fourme of oure Shippe made on oure costys and collecte or gaderyng made amongse vs offerynge yt to that chirche yn mynde of oure delyueraunce. (p. 39)

Having made their vow, the merchants call upon St Bartholomew who 'with his holy hande drewe forth the shippe' to the shore (p. 39), giving the merchants safe passage across the sea. When they come to London, the merchants fulfil their vow and forge a 'litill shippe [...] of siluyr' which they then take to the church:

> And to the prior I-callid, with summe of his Chanouns they tellid the processe of all this storie, yeldynge thankys to almyghty God And to the glorious Apostle And martir, seynt Barthilmewe. (p. 40)

The silver ship stands in for the merchants' ship and functions as a tangible and material sign of the miracle. The fact that the ship is made of silver rather than wax demonstrates the value that the merchants place upon the miracle and, furthermore, it contributes to the visual display within the church. But the donation of the silver ship is, crucially, accompanied by the merchants' narration of the episode to the prior and canons: 'they tellid the processe of all this storie, yeldynge thankys'. The ship's meaning is actualised by the merchants' story and the miracle is once again incorporated into the social and sacred memory of the community at St Bartholomew's.

Another common form of *ex voto* offerings were candles whose wicks were the length of the person, or animal, to be healed. *The Book* gives the example of a woman from Windsor whose livestock had all died from disease except for a single cow. She is advised by her friends to appeal to St Bartholomew:

> She, yeuynge grete credence to holsome cownsell Anoone began to mesure her cowe that she myght haue the mesure for a light to

> ben offeryd of that lengith, and so here vow to be parformyd. And a mervelous thynge! Annoon the cowe reuyuyd and began to ete. (p. 60)

The act of measuring the animal and producing the candle is enough for the woman's cow to be healed but, importantly, the woman then visits the church and lights the candle, giving thanks to God and to the apostle for the miracle. The practice of measuring for candles demonstrates the medieval belief that the measure of a man or creature could stand in for the physical body. Similar measures were taken of Christ's body – his height, for example, or the wound in his side – and devotion to those measurements was seen to be especially efficacious.[107] Measurements are particularly interesting when it comes to thinking about space as they represent the space that an individual takes up, and that individual can then be symbolically present in the church while the candle burns. Lighting candles was often seen as a way of praying to God and in the case of the measured candle, an individual or even an animal is able to pray and participate in the communal rituals of the church while being at a spatial remove. This is especially important for those who are too ill to attend church in person. The measured candle enables them to be present in sacred space and access its healing powers.

The final chapter of *The Book* also describes a miracle in which a measured thread plays an instrumental role but in this episode, the thread measures a house rather than an individual. A huge fire is threatening to engulf the town of Hastings 'by vengeawnce of God' (p. 62). A man who is just returning from 'be-ȝoonde the see with his shippe, chargid with wyne' decides to call into the church on his way home and 'for hym-self and for all that partenyd to hym, meke prayers he offerid vp to God And to the holy Apostle' (p. 62). Meanwhile, at home in Hastings, the man's wife can see the flames advancing down the street and she calls upon St Bartholomew 'bisily with ynwarde herte' and 'duplynge prayers', making a 'vowe of light to be browghte to his chirche yn-to his honoure' (pp. 62–3). In addition to making a vow to bring a candle to the church, the woman then begins to 'compasse the howse' with a long thread and 'leyfte hit ther fixed':

> And loo! A mervelous thynge to seye and beforne dayes vnherde the fyer ferid the feith of the womman And one euery parte bernyd And all thyng turnyd yn-to Asshis And nat presumyd to touche the threid but flow ouer to the next howsys, the howse that was mesurid with the threid, hit myght nat hurte. (p. 63)

The thread represents the woman's faith spatially as 'with the feith of the womman hit [the fire] was putte a-wey' and the incident could be read as an example of a particularly female spatial practice, given the traditional association of women with spinning and the contrast with her husband, whose mercantile activities take him away from the home. The practice of measuring for candles was also particularly associated with the tomb of Rachel in the Holy Land as women would often wrap a red string seven times around the tomb and make it into a candle or even a piece of jewellery to act as a fertility aid.[108] In the latter case, the spatial replication of the tomb enables the woman to carry the sacred space back with her, rather like a pilgrimage badge such as the images of Becket's shrine available from Canterbury Cathedral. In the example in *The Book*, however, the woman's measurement is directly related to her vow to St Bartholomew and as a result, she is able to perform a pseudo-consecration that protects her house from the fire. The house becomes a sacred space that is afforded the same physical protection as the church and *The Book* reinforces this in the conclusion to the narrative:

> Loo, howh by the merytis of the blessid Apostle Barthilmewe the fyer hadde forȝeit the myght of his vertu that the howse shulde nat feill his brennyng, that bar his tokyne. (p. 63)

The house will not burn down because it bears the apostle's 'tokyne', in this case the thread that the woman has associated with the saint through her vow. The Middle English Dictionary defines 'tokyne' as a physical object that is 'used to represent an action, a concept, state'.[109] It is fitting that 'token' should be the final word of *The Book* as a whole, for both the woman's thread and the manuscript of *The Book of the Foundation* are tokens of the sanctity of St Bartholomew's church. The narrator informs us that 'ȝeit abydyth that mervelous and glorious myracle of that howse to be seyn' (p. 63), implying that the house continues to be worthy of admiration and reverence. In its newly translated form, *The Book* also 'abydyth' to the 'excitament of holynes' of Rahere's foundation.

Just as we saw in the liturgical ritual for consecration, the miracles associated with St Bartholomew's exhibit what Manfred Pfister called 'multimediality'. They draw upon not only 'verbal but also acoustic and visual codes' in their performance of sanctity.[110] The sound of the canons' liturgical practice was a catalyst for the innocent man's miraculous escape from prison. The vows and prayers made to the saint, often materialised in candles or threads, ensured the safety of individuals, animals and houses. The material culture of the church also played an important role in the establishment of sacred outposts, from the presence of the Eucharistic bread in the storm to the relics of the saint that went on tour to Yarmouth. Each of the miracles discussed above caused a transformation in space and a translation of the sanctity of St Bartholomew's into a new, frequently hostile, space. The interaction with other spaces is important because it establishes the relationship between the foundation and its local and national environment. If we look more closely at the places with which St Bartholomew's is associated, it becomes clear that this is a deliberate strategy on the part of *The Book* not only to locate the church but to establish a competitive identity. St Bartholomew's is not merely a sacred space, it is the most sacred space on the medieval pilgrimage map.

Competition and rivalry: Mapping sacred space

Sacred spaces are intensely potent, magnetic and attractive, and as Mircea Eliade argues, they become a fixed point in the landscape around which other spaces and communities are oriented. The sacred, Eliade states, 'founds the world'.[111] St Bartholomew's church functions as the fixed point around which spiritual and urban life takes place in *The Book of the Foundation*. Sanctity flows outwards into the urban environment but the recipients of the miraculous always return to the church to give thanks, affirming the church as the source of sanctity. The construction of the church as a centre of sanctity encourages pilgrimage and donations to the church, a 'ritual journeying' that, as Alexandra Walsham notes, 'was a defining feature of contemporary religious experience'.[112] Pilgrimage boosts a church's profile both spiritually and financially, and this would have been especially welcome in the early fifteenth century when the 'Great Restoration' of the church was underway. All roads lead to St Bartholomew's.

The Book of the Foundation not only promotes the efficacy of St Bartholomew's in its own right, it also establishes a competitive relationship between the church and its neighbouring spaces, both sacred and secular, in order to establish its dominance. The amount of geographical specificity in *The Book* is in striking contrast to the lack of architectural detail that I mentioned earlier. The text catalogues in detail the locations from which individuals who are healed at the church originate, at the level of neighbouring parishes and churches such as St John's (p. 23) or St Martin-in-the-Fields (p. 47) and radiating outwards to include nearby towns such as Dunwich, Sandwich and Windsor (pp. 28, 43, 60). Links are even established with places as far afield as Greece and Rome, spaces of great cultural and religious significance. This contributes to the mapping of space with St Bartholomew's as the sacred centre around which local and international affairs orbit, analogous to, even replacing, the position of Jerusalem on medieval maps. Such references attribute an inclusivity to the sacred space of St Bartholomew's; anyone from anywhere can be healed there, but the 'excess of signification' could, as I suggested earlier, be read as a sign of anxiety.[113] The detailed origins of the pilgrims could be a sign of the church's lack of confidence in its own position and the perceived need to supersede, or at least establish an advantageous connection with, potential rivals. This would be crucial for the initial foundation of the church as a new sacred space in London, but it would also have been beneficial during the 'Great Restoration' when the church was in need of additional financial support for the rebuilding, at a time when there were many other sacred spaces competing for the laity's attention in medieval London. Rather than editing out the competition, *The Book of the Foundation* enables St Bartholomew's to garner more sanctity by association.

If we begin with Rome, Greece and Flanders, it is clear that the associations reflect in particular and strategic ways upon St Bartholomew's. In Book I, chapter 11, Rahere sends a representative to Rome after receiving the charter from Henry I (p. 16) and, once again, after Rahere's death, men are despatched to Rome to gain confirmation of the church's privileges from the bishops. After Jerusalem, Rome is the sacred and authoritative centre of Christianity and so the motivation for associating the church with the city is the logical step after the authorisation of the space by the king. In Book I, chapter 9, before the church has been built, three men from Greece arrive in England on pilgrimage and they prophesy the construction of St Bartholomew's and its subsequent fame:

> Wondir nat ȝe vs here to worschippe God where a fulle acceptable temple to hym shall be bylid. For the high maker of all thyng wyll that it be bylded; and the fame of this place schall attayne frome the spryng of the sunne to the goynge downe. (p. 12)

The prophecy adds to the mystique of the church's foundation but the association with Greece also establishes a link between

St Bartholomew's and antiquity. Paul Binski has explored the desirability of such an association in relation to Westminster Abbey's use of Cosmati pavements inspired by Roman mosaic work. Binski argues that the Cosmati pavement invoked a glorious imperial past and situated the royal patronage of the abbey within 'an older clerical and monastic tradition of esteem for the material culture of antiquity, as manifested by Rome and Byzantium'.[114] The reference to Flanders in the miracle of the rescued merchants who donate the silver ship to the church (pp. 38–40) is perhaps more pragmatic and historical than symbolic. In the eleventh century, Flanders had become a major economic power and indeed in the fourteenth and fifteenth centuries substantial trade links between London and Flanders were established and cultivated. The sailors from Flanders would therefore appeal to the 'local' audience of *The Book* as much as the references to English towns, especially since trade and travel are a central means through which known space is expanded and appropriated. Alfun the church builder encompassed local mercantile spaces within the church's sacred remit and the association with Flanders is a similarly effective means both of manifesting the sacred and garnering social power.

In addition to the evocation of the wider realm within which St Bartholomew's is situated, the text also confronts two symbolic spaces associated with wilderness, disorder and chaos: the sea and the forest. We have already seen St Bartholomew neutralising the threat of the sea by calming storms and saving sailors from drowning, and the church is also placed in a productive relationship with the forest in two miracles in which individuals have become mad as a result of demonic possession (pp. 45–6). In the first miracle, a young man called Robert, who was 'from his yonge age norysshid yn courte', is 'raueshid from his resonable wyttys' when 'it happid hym thorow a thyke woode to make his passage' (p. 45). Robert pauses in the wood to rest and his 'olde ennemy' in the 'form of a right fair womane' appears in his sleep and he is driven mad by the vision:

> And the same houre he lost his wytte and resoun of all myght was priuate and what was for to be done or lefte, he knew nat ledynge him woidenes nowe this way now that way he wanderid rennynge vnknowynge what he did. Hastyly he went whedyr the ympetuousnes of the malicious woodenes ympellid hym. (p. 46)

Robert is taken into St Bartholomew's and 'yn shorte space his witte was recoueryd' (p. 46). The motif of the courtly figure sleeping in the forest and losing his sanity is well known from medieval romance and the Arthurian tradition, but it is usually the court rather than the church that acts as the representative of the ordered, civilised universe.[115] The ease with which the church can be inserted into this romance trope is endorsed by the presence of the 'olde ennemy' and, in the second miracle, the 'feende'.

This miracle also features a courtly protagonist, a knight called Rayf from the household of William Demunfychet. Rayf is 'made woid' by a fiend:

> And he, so woid I-made, slyde downe from his hors ant rent his clothis, the money that be bar he skaterid a-brode and thrywh stonys to them that he mette with And now erryng yn wodis nowe yn hillys And now a-monge he medyllyd hym self. (p. 46)

The knight wandering wildly in the forest, having given up his horse and worldly goods, is the epitome of disorder in medieval romance but, as is evident from the Wife of Bath's 'wanderynge by the weye' in the *Canterbury Tales*, spatial disorder can also imply moral disorder.[116] Rayf is miraculously restored to sanity after being brought into the church and remaining there for two nights (p. 46). Initially he 'gretely […] withstode' being taken inside sacred space, however, and this indicates the strength of the opposition between the devil and the church. But the sanctity of St Bartholomew's wins out and the knight recovers his mental well-being.

The Book of the Foundation is keenly aware of the significance of symbolic and geographical locations and how to employ them to promote the sanctity of St Bartholomew's. The strategy of positive association and inclusiveness evident in the use of European locations such as Rome and Flanders is not universally applied to the other spaces in the text, however. This is most apparent when we examine the relationship between St Bartholomew's and its immediate neighbours: St Bartholomew's Hospital, St Paul's Cathedral and Westminster Abbey. St Bartholomew's Hospital became one of the largest and most important hospitals in the country and it was founded by Rahere at the same time as the church.[117] And yet, *The Book of the Foundation* reports the construction of the hospital with relatively little interest or emphasis:

> The Chirche he made of cumly stoonewerke tabylwyse. And an hospitall howse a litill lenger of from the chirche by hymself he began to edifie. (p. 10)

In fact, Rahere's initial vow during his illness in Rome was to 'make an hospitale yn recreacioun of poure mene' in return for his health (p. 4), rather than a church, and this intention is reported by *The Book* before the vision in which St Bartholomew commands him to found the church (p. 5). Indeed, as Nellie Kerling suggests, a hospital may even have been in existence prior to Rahere's foundation in 1123.[118] Despite the church and hospital being linked by a common founder and location, the relationship between the two, even in the twelfth century, was 'often strained'.[119] Moreover, the situation became increasingly vitriolic until, after numerous previous attempts, the hospital finally gained complete independence from the priory and church in 1420. The crux of the matter was the balance of power underlying the relationship and the progressive worsening of the dispute is clearly attested in the hospital's cartulary. The entry for 2 February 1413 records:

> King Henry IV to Thomas, archbishop of Canterbury, informing him that disputes between the priory and St Bartholomew's hospital must be brought before the King's courts and not before the ecclesiastical courts.[120]

The transfer of jurisdiction is all the more significant given that the site had been granted freedom from such restrictions in Henry I's royal charter, discussed above. The violently partisan nature of the church's protection of its own interests can be seen in a letter cited in the priory records from Pope Lucius to a number of ecclesiastical figures in 1185:

> You shall know that it has come to our hearing that after our beloved sons the brethren of the hospital of St Bartholomew had placed in their own chapel, according to custom, the body of one of their brethren who had departed this present life, the prior and canons of St Bartholomew's desiring violently to remove the body contrary to custom and justice, pronounced a sentence of excommunication of their own initiative against the same brethren, when they resisted them to the best of their own power [...] and furthermore falling upon them with a reckless daring, laid violent hands upon them, and stretching out hands of greed towards the candles which were carried with laudable devotion by the faithful at the burial, converted them to their own uses.[121]

The prior and canons of the church are presented here as attempting to forcefully dictate the use of the hospital's own sacred space, their own chapel. The subtext of this is their belief that the body should in fact reside within the priory church, rather than the hospital, with the ultimate result that the church would profit from offerings made there, again rather than the hospital. It is significant that the canons' failure to remove the body and empty the space results in excommunication: the exclusion of the brethren from the spiritual space of heaven and the community of believers. The wrangling between the church and the hospital, and the former's attempt to assert a monopoly over sacred space, offers a clear explanation for the majority of *The Book*'s miracles taking place in the church. Only four of the forty-two miracles occur in the hospital (Book I, chapter 28 and Book II, chapters 19–21), and even in those cases, the subordinate relationship of hospital to church is stressed.

In Book II, chapter 19, a woman who has fallen into prostitution goes mad and *The Book* explains that 'she was browght to the hospitale of the seyid chirche and yn short tyme folowid contraxioun of all membris that yn no wyse myght she vse them frely' (p. 57). The hospital is clearly identified as belonging to the church and the second phase of the woman's physical malady, the spasm or constriction of her limbs, occurs during her stay there.[122] She is healed by the mercy of the blessed apostle but this does not take place soon after she enters the space of the hospital, as is often the case with the healing miracles at the church.[123] In the next chapter, 'a litill tyme' also elapses before the woman afflicted with the palsy is healed (p. 58). And while the text describes the hospital as 'the same howse', that is, the hospital mentioned in the previous chapter, the term 'howse' is regularly associated with the church throughout *The Book*, so the reference to the hospital is not unambiguous (p. 58). In the following miracle of this cluster (Chapter 21), a woman is brought to 'the forsaid hospitalle' who has contracted hamstrings and 'hadde kepte her bedde longe' (p. 58). St Bartholomew appears to her in her sleep, commanding her to stretch out her feet, and by evensong the next day she is healed (p. 58). Here, although the hospital is mentioned at the beginning of the narrative, the reference to her former bedridden state creates ambiguity as to whether St Bartholomew's miraculous command takes place while she is in the hospital or bedridden at home. Once again, *The Book* exhibits little interest in promoting and capitalising on the role of the hospital in the narrative.

In Book I, chapter 28 the relationship between church and hospital is acknowledged more directly, but ultimately the church still remains centre stage. In this narrative, the carpenter Adwyne is unable to use his arms or legs and he is 'browght to the chirche and put yn the hospitall of pore men' (p. 29). As is typical of the medieval hospital, St Bartholomew's serves the poor but as Adwyne recovers 'by certeyn incrementys' the use of his hands and legs, it is the 'almes of the *same chirche*' which are said to sustain him (p. 29, italics mine).[124] This narrative is less clear-cut because unlike the majority of the other miracles in *The Book*, Adwyne does not experience a complete and miraculous healing. His arms still remain 'crokyd', even though his improvement is attributed to the 'vertu of the Apostle' (p. 29). Carole Rawcliffe points out that many hospitals performed charitable works such as caring for pilgrims, the disabled, widows and children, and even 'honest tradesmen who had fallen on hard times'.[125] Adwyne falls into the latter category and the narrative concludes by asserting that 'nat longe aftir' his health improves, 'the crafte of carpentry yn the same chirche, and yn the Cite of Londone he exercisid' (p. 29). Adwyne is able to repay St Bartholomew for his help by using his trade, now restored to him, but it is the church and the wider city that benefit; the hospital is conspicuously absent.

Given the continuing attempts to settle the ongoing disputes between Rahere's two foundations in favour of the hospital's independence, the church canons may have felt that their space was in danger of being marginalised and downgraded. They could then have made use of *The Book of the Foundation* to fight back and assert not only their illustrious origins but their ongoing sacred credentials. Furthermore, in the late fourteenth century the hospital had begun to assemble a collection of prestigious texts, beginning with the important medical treatise, the *Breviarum Bartholomei*, and culminating in the hospital cartulary in 1456. Such documents function, as Kerling suggests, as symbols of status and prestige and the church may have decided to produce the Middle English translation of its foundation legend in response to the hospital's textual ambitions.[126] The battle for supremacy between the church and hospital had begun to be fought with literary and historical documents.

Roger Walden was also no stranger to disputes over ecclesiastical space. During his time as bishop of London he was involved in the resolution of cases in which individuals' authority over a church was contested.[127] This sense of sacred space as contested, in competition with its neighbours and the outside world, can be seen mostly clearly in the relationship between St Bartholomew's and St Paul's Cathedral in *The Book of the Foundation*. The very first healing miracle in the text concerns a sick man called Wolmer who had been afflicted with various physical deformities for thirty years and had been taken to St Paul's where he waited, 'askynge almes of them that enterid yn' (p. 18). But when Rahere builds St Bartholomew's, the 'fame of the newe werke as it were a full swete odur dyffusyd by the mowthis of all the peple' reaches Wolmer and he 'conceyuyd a swete desire' to be taken to the new church (p. 18). The motif of the sweet smell is common in medieval hagiography and mystical texts and it often signifies the presence of the divine. Here it represents the sanctity of Rahere's enterprise emanating throughout the population. Wolmer is carried into St Bartholomew's and after his prayers to the apostle, 'with-owte tariynge' he is healed (p. 18). St Bartholomew's therefore clearly surpasses St Paul's in its miraculous abilities.[128] Not only is Wolmer healed, but he is healed immediately.

The use of the phrase 'newe werke' in the Middle English translation is especially resonant here and serves to emphasise the competitive relationship with St Paul's. This phrase was being used from the 1270s to describe the great rebuilding at St Paul's and its literary currency is attested by the late fourteenth-century alliterative poem *St Erkenwald*:

> Þen was hit [St Paul's] abatyd and beten doun and buggyd efte newe—
> A noble note for þe nones and New Werke hit hatte.[129]

Although the Latin original also uses the phrase, at the time of the translation of *The Book of the Foundation* the phrase 'newe werke' had gained particular connotations of which the translator and his readers may not have been oblivious. The phrase is also used in the passage discussed above in Book I, chapter 10 in which the people marvel at the building and the 'fownder of this newe werke' (p. 13) and when Wolmer is healed, he is described as a 'newe man' (p. 18). The new work of St Bartholomew's is more than just a new church, it is a sacred endeavour that rivals the great religious centres of London. That St Paul's should have been chosen as the representative location may have been due to its geographical proximity to St Bartholomew's (it is a five- to ten-minute walk) but the cathedral also had personal relevance to both Rahere and the likely sponsor of the Middle English translation, Roger Walden. Both Rahere and Walden held prebends at St Paul's and Rahere was a canon there before his foundation of St Bartholomew's, additional evidence for Walden's interest in the text and identification with the founder.[130] St Bartholomew's certainly gains in statue if it can surpass even the sanctity of London's cathedral church.

Another location with which St Bartholomew's is in implicit competition is Westminster Abbey. During the reign of Richard II, Plantagenet patronage of Westminster both as a sacred space and a site of government continued and Richard II showed a particular affection for and devotion to the cult of St Edward the Confessor, who re-founded Westminster Abbey in the eleventh century. He visited St Edward's shrine during the Peasants revolt, for example, and also included the saint on the famous Wilton Diptych.[131] At the time of the original Latin text of *The Book of the Foundation*, the canonisation of Edward had only recently taken place in 1161 and the translation of his relics in 1163. Also in the 1160s, Aelred of Rievaulx was commissioned to write his *Vita sancti Edwardi*, drawing on Osbert of Claire's 1138 *Vita beati Eadwardi regis*.[132] It is within both of these historical contexts, therefore, that Book I, Chapter 8 should be considered, in which the future existence of the church is revealed to Edward in a dream. The chapter begins by asserting:

> Heir we may nat silence kepe, but euydently expresse, that by relacioun of oure senyoures, we haue fownde, dyuynly schewid this to be a place of prayer longe beforne tyme to the glorious kynge Edwarde the confessoure. (p. 11)

Edward receives a vision in which he is 'warnyd of thys place with an heuynly dreme made to hym, that Gode this place hadde chosyne' for the building of a church (p. 11). Edward then visits the place that God had showed him and he prophesies that the place will be 'gret before God', which *The Book* then confirms by declaring that 'experience hath approuyd yt And euery feithfulmane may cleirly beholde the same' (p. 12). Given Edward's involvement at Westminster Abbey, his invocation as a supporter of St Bartholomew's is of considerable importance and represents the highest validation of both a royal and saintly kind.

Edward himself is described variously as 'blessid', 'glorious' and 'holy' in the chapter, locating his prophecy within a hagiographic discourse. But more significantly, his prophetic vision is located within sacred space itself:

> Whan he was in the Chirche of God replete with manyfolde bewte of vertu [...] as a religious and full of the spirite of prophicie, he schoone bright beholdyng thynges fer of as they were presente. And

> thynges to cumme, as they were nowe existente with the yis of his soule by the holy goste for he was Illumyned. (p. 11)

Readers of both the original Latin and the Middle English translation would most likely assume that the 'chirche of God' was Westminster. But even if this was not the precise location within which Edward had his vision, a new sacred space emerging from and being authorised within an established sacred space is a validation of the most powerful and unambiguous kind.

One final sacred space that was being re-established in the late twelfth century and that also forms part of the 'architexture' in which St Bartholomew's is constructed as a competitive site, is Canterbury Cathedral. While *The Book* itself contains no explicit references to Canterbury, its original composition during the period in which Canterbury occupied a central position in the public consciousness is striking. In 1170, archbishop Thomas Becket was murdered in the cathedral and by 1173, he had been canonised. A year later, Henry II, the king who appears in the second part of *The Book*, went on pilgrimage to Canterbury to visit the burial place of his archbishop, a ritual that was to last until the end of his life. In 1174, however, disaster struck and the cathedral was engulfed by fire. But rebuilding began shortly afterwards and the body of the saint was translated into a magnificent shrine upon the cathedral's completion in 1184.[133] These are precisely the dates within which *The Book of the Foundation* was originally composed, c. 1174–89, and indeed historically, St Bartholomew's was not without connection to Canterbury. E. A. Webb cites a charter from 1162 which details the church and canons being taken into the protection of none other than Thomas Becket and his confirmation of the Smithfield site to them.[134] The canons of St Bartholomew's cannot have been unaware of the impact of the cult of St Thomas that flourished during the last quarter of the twelfth century. Furthermore, in the eleventh century, Canterbury Cathedral acquired a relic of St Bartholomew himself, an arm that was gifted by Queen Emma.[135] The creation of the foundation legend by the canons of St Bartholomew's can, therefore, be read in two interrelated ways. Firstly, it reclaims St Bartholomew himself for the London church, despite Canterbury's ownership of the relic, and secondly, it establishes St Bartholomew's church in Smithfield as more than a match for the cathedral church of the murdered archbishop. Taken in concert with the text's treatment of Westminster Abbey and St Paul's, *The Book of the Foundation*'s presentation of St Bartholomew's as the most sacred space in medieval England is unmistakable.

Conclusion: Friends of the church

St Bartholomew the Great is still a thriving Christian community today and one that continually looks back to its sacred history for support and validation in its twenty-first-century life. The history of the foundation is a prominent component of the church's website and is also reflected in the name of the community choir, the 'Rahere Singers'.[136] Visitors to the church in Smithfield, and virtual visitors online, are encouraged to support St Bartholomew's church, just like the medieval audience of *The Book of the Foundation.* A range of projects and funds are promoted by the church; for example, a legacy bequest to the 'general Fabric Fund' could help to maintain the building. As the church's website declares, 'St Bartholomew the Great has survived centuries of upheaval; help ensure that it continues to survive for generations to come.'[137] Individuals can become Friends of the 'St Bartholomew the Great Heritage Trust', 'uniting those who have a particular interest in and affection for the Church' in order to preserve and maintain the 'fabric, ornaments, furniture and monuments of the Priory Church', the very material culture that is so important in *The Book of the Foundation.*[138] The church is currently planning a columbarium, a set of memorial niches for the internment of ashes, so that modern day worshippers can become a part of the fabric of the building after death, like their medieval forebears.[139] A major restoration project is also part of the 'Mission Action Plan' of the Parish of Great St Bartholomew's for 2016–21.[140] Appropriately named the 'Great Project', perhaps recalling E. A. Webb's designation of the fifteenth-century building works as the 'Great Restoration', this initiative not only intends to improve the facilities for all of the groups who work in and use the church but also aims to communicate the church's history and heritage to a wider audience (pp. 9–10). The parish's 'Mission Action Plan', in draft form at the time of writing, sets out an ambitious vision of the church's future but it is a future that has its roots in the medieval past and in *The Book of the Foundation* itself. The 'Plan' confidently asserts:

> We affirm the Priory Church of Saint Bartholomew the Great as a sacred place. 'This Spiritual House', Bartholomew told Rahere, according to *The Book of the Foundation*, 'Almighty God shall

> inhabit, hallow and preserve unspotted for ever and ever and His eyes shall be open and His ears intending on this House night and day, that he who asks may have, he who seeks shall find and he who knocks may enter. For one who, being converted and penitent of his sin, in this place praying shall be heard in Heaven, or seeking, with a perfect heart, help from whatever tribulation, without doubt shall find it. To those who knock with pious longing at the door of the Spouse attending angels shall open the gates of Heaven taking up and offering to God the prayers and vows of a faithful people.' It is therefore our duty and responsibility and our joy, as those to whom this building and its heritage are entrusted: to maintain, enhance, and improve the fabric of the building; to keep it as a dedicated place of prayer; to offer within it worship that is acceptable to God; to welcome visitors and to share with them our history and heritage; to use such means as enable 'the very stones' to witness to the Christian faith; and to increase participation in the life of the Church both within the congregation and in local outreach. (p. 4)

The Book of the Foundation has once more been translated, this time into Modern English, in order to affirm that St Bartholomew the Great truly is a 'sacred place'. The 'very stones' of the building are a witness to the Christian faith and to the continued vitality of the foundation and its congregation in the city of London. St Bartholomew's church is, and always has been, more than just a medieval religious building. It is a space of miracles, an architectural marvel and a sacred centre that more than rivals the great churches of medieval Christendom and modern London. In my previous chapter I quoted Henri Lefebvre's definition of the 'spatial code' as 'not simply a means of reading or interpreting a space, rather it is a means of living in that space, of understanding it, of producing it'.[141] *The Book of the Foundation* is still able to help the community of St Bartholomew's to live in their church, to understand it and to continue to produce the sacred space at its heart.

But the parish community is not always the idealised, supportive group that *The Book of the Foundation* imagines and aims to produce. Sadly, the twenty-first century 'Mission Action Plan' admits that there have been incidents of theft from the church and inappropriate behaviour in the churchyard, such as fighting and drinking (p. 12). Behaviour in the medieval church, too, often left a lot to be desired and as a result the sanctity of the church was threatened. Rahere understood the importance of sermons in the construction of his new foundation and the community he had gathered within it. In late medieval England, the literature of pastoral care, from sermons to penitential handbooks, was more important than ever as churches sought to educate the laity in order to protect, sustain, and enliven their sacred spaces.

Notes

1 This chapter builds upon material from Laura Varnam, '*The Book of the Foundation of St Bartholomew's Church*: consecration, restoration, and translation', in Joseph Sterrett and Peter W. Thomas (eds), *Sacred Text, Sacred Space: Architectural, Spiritual, and Literary Convergences in England and Wales* (Brill: Leiden, 2011), pp. 57–75, used with permission. *The Book of the Foundation of St Bartholomew's Church*, ed. Norman Moore, EETS OS 163 (Oxford: Oxford University Press, 1923), p. 32. All subsequent quotations refer to this edition by page number. I have silently removed the oblique strokes that Moore includes throughout his edition, inserting full stops and commas where necessary. I have, however, followed his capitalisation throughout.

2 Moore, *The Book of the Foundation*, p. xi and Laura Varnam, 'The Howse of God on Erthe: Constructions of Sacred Space in Late Middle English Religious Literature' (DPhil thesis, Oxford University, 2007), pp. 36–40.

3 See E. A. Webb, *The Records of St Bartholomew's Priory and of the Church and Parish of St Bartholomew the Great, West Smithfield* (Oxford: Oxford University Press, 1921), vol. II, especially pp. 11–12. Webb christens the building work the 'great restoration' in vol. I of the *Records*, p. xxiv.

4 Henri Lefebvre, *The Production of Space*, trans. Donald Nicholson Smith (Oxford: Blackwell, 1991), p. 118.

5 Etienne Balibar and Pierre Macherey, 'On literature as an ideological form', in Robert Young (ed.), *Untying the Text* (London: Routledge, 1990), pp. 79–99, p. 83.

6 Michel de Certeau, *The Practice of Everyday Life*, trans. Steven F. Rendall (Berkeley: University of California Press, 1984; paperback 1988), p. 117.

7 De Certeau, *Everyday Life*, p. 117.

8 *Ibid.*.

9 *Ibid.*, p. 115.

10 *Ibid.*, p. 118.

11 *Ibid.*, pp. 123–4. Italics original.

12 *Ibid.*, pp. 98–9.

13 Keith D. Lilley, *City and Cosmos: The Medieval World in Urban Form* (London: Reaktion, 2009), p. 15. Lilley explores the circular depiction of Jerusalem on medieval maps as a model both for the medieval city and for the wider cosmos.

14 Lefebvre, *The Production of Space*, p. 118.

15 Balibar and Macherey, 'On literature as an ideological form', p. 83.
16 I consulted the manuscript in the British Library on 23 June 2006.
17 British Library, MS Cotton Vespasian B IX, folio 83r (labelled in pencil f. 81).
18 See Norman Moore's introduction to his edition of the text, pp. ix–xii, and Norman Moore, *The History of St Bartholomew's Hospital* (London: C. Arthur Pearson, 1918), vol. I, pp. 1–10. Moore's is the only published edition of the Middle English text; the Latin is, as yet, unpublished in full. A section of the Latin can be found in John Caley and Henry Ellis's edition of Dugdale's *Monasticon Anglicanum* (London: James Bohn, 1846), vol. VI, pp. 294–95. E. A. Webb has translated the Latin; see *The Book of the Foundation of the Church of St Bartholomew London, Rendered into Modern English from the Original Latin Version Preserved in the British Museum, Numbered Vespasian B IX* (London: Oxford University Press, 1923).
19 Webb, *Records of St Bartholomew's*, vol. I, p. xxiv.
20 Sari Katajala-Peltomaa, *Gender, Miracles, and Daily Life: The Evidence of Fourteenth Century Canonization Processes* (Turnhout: Brepols, 2009), p. 247 and p. 287.
21 Katajala-Peltomaa, *Gender, Miracles, and Daily Life*, p. 104.
22 *MED* 'devocioun' (n.) 1 and 3.
23 Christopher Brooke, *London 800–1216: The Shaping of a City* (London: Secker and Warburg, 1975), pp. 327–8.
24 Dawn Marie Hayes, *Body and Sacred Place in Medieval Europe 1100–1389* (Routledge: London, 2003), pp. 25–32.
25 Webb, *Records of St Bartholomew's*, vol. II, p. 3.
26 Paul Connerton, *How Societies Remember* (Cambridge: Cambridge University Press, 1989), p. 3.
27 Webb, *Records of St Bartholomew's*, vol. I, p. xxiv. *MED* 'restoracioun' (n.) '1d) restoration to a former state; e) restoration or renewing of something that is lost'. The word also has associations with healing, '1a) restoration to health, a cure'.
28 Eric Hobsbawm, 'Introduction: inventing tradition', in Eric Hobsbawm and Terence Ranger (eds), *The Invention of Tradition* (Cambridge: Cambridge University Press, 1983), pp. 1–14, p. 4.
29 Paul Strohm, *England's Empty Throne: Usurpation and the Language of Legitimation 1399–1422* (London: Yale University Press, 1998), especially Chapter 1, 'Prophecy and Kingship', pp. 1–31.
30 For a discussion of the monument, see Julian Luxford, 'The idol of origins: retrospection in Augustinian art during the later middle ages', in Janet E. Burton and Karen Stöber (eds), *The Regular Canons in the Medieval British Isles* (Turnhout: Brepols, 2011), pp. 417–42, pp. 434–8.
31 See Webb, *Records of St Bartholomew's*, vol. I, pp. 52–3 and 70–5. Webb points out the resemblance between Rahere's monument and

that of the favourite of Richard II, Sir Bernard Brocas, located in Westminster Abbey, p. 75.

32 May McKisack, *The Oxford History of England: The Fourteenth Century, 1307–1399* (Oxford: Clarendon, 1959), p. 297. Both K. B. McFarlane and the chronicler of the *Historia Vitae et Regni Ricardi Secundi* get Walden's name wrong, calling him Robert and John respectively. See K. B. McFarlane, *England in the Fifteenth Century* (London: Hambledon, 1981), p. 106, and *Historia Vitae et Regni Ricardi Secundi*, ed. George B. Stow (Philadelphia: University of Pennsylvania Press, 1977), p. 148. Only Gervase Mathew remarks in passing that he was part of 'an able group of ministers and secretaries'; see *The Court of Richard II* (London: John Murray, 1968), p. 152.

33 It is therefore somewhat surprising that Walden does not get a single mention in Margaret Aston's *Thomas Arundel* (Oxford: Clarendon, 1967).

34 U. C. Hannam, 'The episcopal registers of Roger Walden and Nicholas Bubwith', *Transactions of the London and Middlesex Archaeological Society*, n. s. 11 (1954), 123–136, p. 123. For a fuller description of Walden's various positions, see Webb, *Records of St Bartholomew's*, vol. I, pp. 185–8, and R. G. Davies, 'Roger Walden', *Oxford Dictionary of National Biography* www.oxforddnb.com/view/article/28445 [accessed 27 September 2016].

35 Nigel Saul, *Richard II* (London: Yale University Press, 1997; paperback 1999) pp. 127 and 339n. Saul notes that outside Westminster, the Porchester rebuilding was the 'most ambitious programme that Richard undertook', p. 339, n. 39. Antony Steel concurs with Saul that Walden is 'worth remembering for his reorganisation of the signet office in what proved to be a lasting form', *Richard II* (Cambridge: Cambridge University Press, 1962), p. 218.

36 Davies, 'Roger Walden', p. 1.

37 Webb, *Records of St Bartholomew's*, vol. I, p. 192. Italics mine.

38 'varia fortuna vectus', 'inconstans, incerta [...], instabilis', *Thomæ Walsingham, Quoandam Monarchi S. Albani, Historia Anglicana*, ed. Henry Thomas Riley (London: Longman, Green, Longman, Roberts and Green, 1864), vol. I, p. 224.

39 J. H. Wylie, *The History of England under Henry IV: Volume III, 1407–1410* (London: Longmans, Green, and co, 1896), p. 128.

40 See *Chronique de la Traison et Mort de Richard Deux Roy Dengleterre*, ed. and trans. Benjamin Williams (London: Aux dépens de la Société, 1846), p. 227. John Walden died in 1417 and both he and his wife Idonia were buried in Walden's Chapel at St Bartholomew's. Idonia even left a bequest in her will for a chantry to be established for her brother-in-law, Roger; see Webb, *Records of St Bartholomew's*, vol. I, p. 194.

41 See the *Traison et Mort*, p. 259 and Wylie, *The History of England under Henry IV*, p. 126. Significantly, Walden was the only figure who was spared execution for his involvement in the plot.

42 'magis militaribus et mundialibus negociis quam clericalibus aut liberalibus imbutus', see *The Chronicle of Adam Usk*, trans. C. Given-Wilson (Oxford: Clarendon, 1997), pp. 81–3.

43 'laicum literatum'; see *Eulogium*, ed. Frank Scott Haydon (London: Longman, Green, Longman, Roberts and Green, 1863), vol. III, p. 377. 'insufficienti et illiterate'; see 'Annales Ricardi Secundi et Henrici Quarti, Regum Angliae', in *Johannis de Trokelowe et Henrici de Blaneforde, Monachorum S Albani, necnon quorundam anonymorum, Chronica et Annales, Regimantibus Henrico Tertio, Edwardo Primo, Edwardo Secundo, Ricardo Secundo, et Henrico Quarto*, ed. Henry Thomas Riley (London: Longmans, Green, Reader and Dyer, 1866), p. 213. Translations graciously provided by Ralph Hanna.

44 Opinion is divided as to whether Walden was buried in St Bartholomew's or St Paul's. One eyewitness account claims that Walden was buried at St Paul's; John Stow, on the other hand, suggests that he was buried in a tomb next to Rahere's monument at St Bartholomew's; see Webb, *Records of St Bartholomew's*, vol. I, pp. 188–91.

45 Moore, *The Book of the Foundation*, p. xii.

46 Paul Strohm notes the proliferation of and support for such rumours in 'The trouble with Richard: the reburial of Richard II and the Lancastrian symbolic strategy', *Speculum*, 71 (1996), 87–111, pp. 93–6.

47 British Library, MS Cotton Vespasian B IX, folio 75v.

48 An omission in the translation in Book II, Chapter 18 is also intriguing in this regard. The Latin reads *Henricus secundus rex anglie* but *The Book* omits the name Henry and merely states 'in that tyme that the second, kynge of Englond besegid Walys' (*The Book of the Foundation*, p. 53). The omission of Henry leaves the identity of the 'second' king open to interpretation.

49 Emma Cownie, 'The cult of St Edmund in the eleventh and twelfth centuries: the language and communication of a medieval saint's cult', *Neuphilologische Mitteilungen*, 99 (1998), 177–97, p. 182.

50 Webb, *Records of St Bartholomew's,* vol. I, p. 61, paragraphs 5 and 6. Italics mine.

51 Lefebvre, *The Production of Space,* p. 142. See Paul Binski, *Westminster Abbey and the Plantagenets: Kingship and the Representation of Power 1200–1400* (London: Yale University Press, 1995) and Nigel Saul, 'Richard II and the city of York', in Sarah Rees Jones (ed.), *The Government of Medieval York: Essays in Commemoration of the 1396 Royal Charter* (York: University of York, 1997), pp. 1–13.

52 Saul, *Richard II*, p. 12.

53 Binski, *Westminster Abbey*, p. vii.

54 *Ibid.*, p. 4.

55 See *Ibid.*, pp. 175–206.

56 Strohm, 'The trouble with Richard', p. 90.

57 Strohm, *England's Empty Throne*, p. 1.

58 *The Chronicle of Adam Usk*, p. 81.
59 See Webb, *Records of St Bartholomew's*, vol. I, pp. 74–5.
60 *MED* 'recreacioun' (n.) 1.
61 Mary Carruthers, 'The poet as master builder: composition and locational memory in the Middle Ages', *New Literary History*, 24 (1993), 881–904, p. 900. Italics original.
62 Carruthers, 'The poet as master builder', pp. 897–8 and 900. Italics original.
63 *MED* 'halwen' (v.).
64 Webb, *Records of St Bartholomew's*, vol. I, p. 50.
65 *MED* 'table-wise' (adv.). The Latin reads *decenti lapideo tabulatu* which Webb translates as 'suitable stone blocks in courses', Webb, *Records of St Bartholomew's*, vol. I, p. 391.
66 *MED* 'comli' (adj.) 1a) and 2b).
67 I will discuss this allegorical reading of church architecture in more detail in Chapter 4.
68 Jill A. Franklin, 'The eastern arm of Norwich Cathedral and the Augustinian priory of St Bartholomew's, Smithfield, in London', *The Antiquaries Journal*, 86 (2006), 110–30, p. 110.
69 Franklin, 'The eastern arm of Norwich cathedral', p. 116.
70 *Ibid.*
71 *Ibid.*, p. 123.
72 Webb, *Records of St Bartholomew's*, vol. II, p. 110.
73 Franklin, 'The eastern arm of Norwich cathedral', p. 124.
74 *The Rationale Divinorum Officiorum of William Durand of Mende: A New Translation of the Prologue and Book One*, trans. Timothy M. Thibodeau (New York, 2007), pp. 73–4.
75 Bede, *The Ecclesiastical History of the English People; The Greater Chronicle; Bede's Letter to Egbert*, ed. and trans. Judith McClure and Roger Collins (Oxford: Oxford University Press, 1969), pp. 56–7. On the Christianization of pagan sacred space, see Alexandra Walsham, *The Reformation of the Landscape: Religion, Identity, and Memory in Early Modern Britain and Ireland* (Oxford: Oxford University Press, 2011), pp. 28–48.
76 Mircea Eliade, *The Sacred and Profane: The Nature of Religion*, trans. Willard R. Trask (Orlando: Harcourt, 1987), p. 69.
77 See Colin Morris, *The Sepulchre of Christ and the Medieval West: From the Beginning to 1600* (Oxford: Oxford University Press, 2005).
78 See Nick Nichols, 'The Augustinian canons and their parish churches: a key to their identity', in Burton and Stöber (eds), *The Regular Canons*, pp. 313–37, and James G. Clark, 'The Augustinians, history, and literature in late medieval England', in Burton and Stöber (eds), *The Regular Canons*, pp. 403–16.
79 Webb, *The Records of St Bartholomew's*, vol. II, p. 248.
80 *MED* 'compassen' (v.) 1a), 4a) and b).

81 Alec Forshaw and Theo Bergström, *Smithfield Past and Present* (London: Robert Hale, 1980), pp. 20–1.
82 *MED* 'makinge' (ger.) 3b).
83 *MED* 'makinge' (ger.) 5. The verb 'maken' means 1a) to create, 2a) to construct or produce, 3a) to found (a city, church, monastery) and 5a) to write or compose; see *MED* 'maken' (v.1).
84 *MED* 'excitement' (n.).
85 *MED* 'exciten' (v.) 2, 3, 4 and 6.
86 Mary Carruthers, *The Craft of Thought: Meditation, Rhetoric, and the Making of Images 400–1200* (Cambridge: Cambridge University Press, 1998; paperback 2000), p. 119.
87 Eliade, *The Sacred and Profane*, p. 202.
88 *Ibid.*, p .11. Italics original.
89 *Ibid.*, p. 26.
90 Mircea Eliade, *Patterns in Comparative Religion*, trans. Rosemary Sheed (London: Sheed and Ward, 1958), p. 368. Italics original.
91 Eliade, *The Sacred and Profane,* p. 27.
92 *Ibid.*, pp. 27–8. Italics original.
93 *Ibid.*, p. 21. Italics original.
94 Helen Barr argues that Richard II's excessive use of visual display and symbolism could be attributed to such an anxiety, *Socioliterary Practice in Late Medieval England* (Oxford: Oxford University Press, 2001), p. 87.
95 Graham Ward, 'Introduction', in Graham Ward (ed.), *The Certeau Reader* (Oxford: Blackwell, 2000), pp. 1–14, p. 13, n. 3.
96 Ward, 'Introduction', p. 13, n. 3.
97 Yi-Fu Tuan, *Space and Place: The Perspective of Experience* (Minneapolis: University of Minnesota Press, 1977), p. 15.
98 Webb, *Records of St Bartholomew's*, vol. II, p. 113.
99 Katajala-Peltomaa, *Gender, Miracles, and Daily Life*, p. 104.
100 Hayes, *Body and Sacred Place*, pp. 31–2.
101 Curing insomnia through entry into an otherworldly space guarded by a porter is reminiscent of classical conceptions of the god of sleep and his realm, part of the popular vogue for dream theory in the late fourteenth century. See Chaucer's *Book of the Duchess*, in *The Riverside Chaucer*, ed. Larry D. Benson et al. (Oxford: Oxford University Press, 1987; paperback 1988), p. 332, lines 153–77.
102 Thanks to Anthony Bale and Dean Irwin for this identification. See Joe Hillaby, 'The London Jewry: William I to John', *Jewish Historical Studies*, 33 (1992–4), 1–44, especially pp. 4–8 on the Latin term *vicus judeorum*. Thank you to Dean Irwin for sending me this article.
103 Claire Hilton, 'St Bartholomew's hospital, London, and its Jewish connections', *Jewish Historical Studies*, 30 (1987–8), 21–50, p. 22.
104 Hilton, 'St Bartholomew's hospital, London, and its Jewish connections', p. 22.

105 *MED* 'enemi' (n.) 1b) an adversary of God, an unbeliever or heathen; one who is opposed to (or fails to observe) a Christian doctrine or virtue.
106 See Ronald C. Finucane, *Miracles and Pilgrims: Popular Beliefs in Medieval England* (London: Macmillan, 1977), pp. 97–9.
107 On devotion to the measurement of the side wound, and the related indulgence, see Douglas Gray, 'The five wounds of Our Lord II', *Notes and Queries*, 208 (1963), 82–9, p. 88.
108 Susan Signe Morrison, *Women Pilgrims in Late Medieval England: Private Piety as Public Performance* (London: Routledge, 2000), p. 20.
109 *MED* 'token' (n.) 1.
110 Manfred Pfister, *The Theory and Analysis of Drama*, trans. John Halliday (Cambridge: Cambridge University Press, 1988), p. 7.
111 Eliade, *The Sacred and Profane*, p. 30.
112 Walsham, *The Reformation of the Landscape*, p. 49.
113 The phrase is Helen Barr's, *Socioliterary Practice*, p. 87.
114 Binski, *Westminster Abbey*, pp. 105–6
115 Corinne J. Saunders, *The Forest in Medieval Romance* (Cambridge: Brewer, 1993), pp. 44–94, espccially pp. 64–5.
116 *MED* 'wandren' (v.) 2c) to be unstable in one's mode of living, be idle; 3a) wander as an exile, b) fig. to endure spiritual exile, be spiritually homeless or lost. *The General Prologue* in *The Riverside Chaucer*, p. 31, line 467.
117 Euan C. Roger suggests that St Bartholomew's is only surpassed by St Leonard's, York; see 'Blakberd's treasure: a study in fifteenth-century administration at St Bartholomew's hospital, London', in Linda Clark (ed.), *The Fifteenth Century, XIII: Exploring the Evidence. Commemoration, Administration, and the Economy* (Woodbridge: Boydell, 2014), pp. 81–107, p. 81.
118 Nellie J. M. Kerling, *The Cartulary of St Bartholomew's Hospital* (London: Lund Humphries, 1973), p. 1.
119 Kerling, *Cartulary*, p. 2.
120 *Ibid*., entry 49, p. 19.
121 Webb, *Records of St Bartholomew's*, vol. I, p. 81.
122 *MED* 'contraccioun' (n.) a) and b).
123 For example, Wolmer regains the use of his limbs 'with-owte tariynge' when he enters the church and prays at the altar of the apostle (p. 18); Robert recovers from his madness 'yn shorte space' after entering the church (p. 46); and a blind man regains his sight 'when he come, trewly, to the chirche of seynt Barthylmewe' (p. 51).
124 Carole Rawcliffe, *Medicine and Society in Later Medieval England* (Stroud: Alan Sutton, 1995), p. 205.
125 Rawcliffe, *Medicine and Society*, p. 205.
126 Kerling, *Cartulary*, p. 2. The growing association of St Bartholomew's with book production in the fifteenth century is discussed by Margaret Connolly in relation to the scribe John Shirley who was living in the close

in the 1450s; see *John Shirley: Book Production and the Noble Household in Fifteenth Century England* (Aldershot: Ashgate, 1998), p. 57.

127 See Hannam, 'Episcopal registers', pp. 131–2. A man named Walter Clyde attempted to become rector of the church at Caldwell even though the situation was already taken by John Rider, and Nicholas Overton appealed to the bishop as he feared that he was going to be dispossessed of his position as rector at the church of St Mary Magdalen, Milkstreet, by a John Shadworth who had forced him to flee from the church (folios 6v–7v in the register for 1405).

128 This hierarchy of sacred space with St Bartholomew's at the pinnacle recurs in Book II, Chapter 25 in which a young boy whose mother has taken him to 'many placys of seyntis' to cure him of his madness 'opteyned no remedy' until they visited St Bartholomew's (p. 25).

129 Clifford Peterson (ed.), *Saint Erkenwald* (Philadelphia: University of Pennsylvania Press, 1977), p. 73, lines 37–8.

130 Rahere held the prebend of Chamberlain's Wood and Roger Walden the prebend of Willesden. See Norman Moore, *The Church of St Bartholomew the Great, West Smithfield: Its Foundation, Present Condition and Funeral Monuments* (London: Adlard and Son, 1908), p. 8, and Webb, *Records of St Bartholomew's*, vol. I, p. 186.

131 Binski, *Westminster Abbey*, p. 187, and Saul, *Richard II*, figure 13 and 14.

132 Emma Cownie comments upon the large number of saints' lives being produced in the last quarter of the twelfth century during which *The Book of the Foundation* was originally composed; see Cownie, 'The cult of St Edmund', pp. 182–5.

133 Austin Lane Poole, *From Domesday Book to Magna Carta, 1087–1216* (Oxford: Clarendon, 1955), vol. II, pp. 197–216.

134 Webb, *Records of St Bartholomew's*, vol. I, pp. 97–8.

135 Nicholas Brooks, 'The Anglo-Saxon cathedral and its community, 597–1070', in Patrick Collinson, Nigel Ramsay and Margaret Sparks (eds), *A History of Canterbury Cathedral* (Oxford: Oxford University Press, 1995), pp. 1–37, p. 30.

136 http://greatstbarts.com/index.html [accessed 27 September 2016].

137 http://greatstbarts.com/Pages/Support_Us/wills.html [accessed 27 September 2016].

138 http://greatstbarts.com/Pages/Support_Us/friend.html and http://greatstbarts.com/Pages/Support_Us/charities.html [accessed 27 September 2016].

139 http://greatstbarts.com/Pages/Information/columbarium.html [accessed 27 September 2016].

140 http://greatstbarts.com/Documents/Other_Documents/Church-MAP%202016–2021%20v.1.pdf [accessed 27 September 2016]. All subsequent quotations refer to this document by page number.

141 Lefebvre, *The Production of Space*, p. 47.

3
Sacred and profane: Pastoral care in the parish church

The fourteenth-century conduct poem *How the Goode Wife Taught Hyr Doughter* begins by establishing the centrality of the church in the life of the medieval laywoman. Good conduct on the part of the daughter is founded upon supporting the parish church: spiritually, financially, and through good behaviour.

> Doughter, and thou wylle be a wyfe,
> Wysely to wyrche in all thi lyfe
> Serve God, and kepe thy chyrche,
> And myche the better thou shal wyrche.
> To go to chyrch, lette for no reyne,
> And that schall helpe thee in thy peyne.[1]

The verb 'kepen' here has multiple meanings that encapsulate the attitude to the parish church that the pastoral care material under discussion in this chapter aimed to cultivate. To 'kepe' the church means to support it in both an abstract and concrete sense: to guard and defend the place and structure; to protect and preserve it from harm and damage, sin and the devil; and to take care of it, in material and affective terms.[2] To 'kepe' also means to hold or to take into one's possession, and this is performed linguistically in the *Goode Wife* by the possessive pronoun 'thy'.[3] The text goes on to substantiate how the daughter should keep her church. She must pay her tithes 'gladly' (11), make offerings (12), help the poor (13–16), and maintain a high standard of behaviour in the church itself:

> When thou arte in the chyrch, my chyld,
> Loke that thou be bothe meke and myld,
> And bydde thy bedes aboven alle thinge,
> With sybbe ne fremde make no jangelynge.
> Laughe thou to scorne nother olde ne yonge,
> Be of gode berynge and of gode tonge;
> Yn thi gode berynge begynnes thi worschype,
> My dere doughter, of this take kepe. (19–26)

When she is in church, the daughter must prioritise prayer over 'jangelynge', the sin of gossip and idle speech that is a constant concern in pastoral care material. The Good Wife instructs her daughter to 'take kepe' of her advice because 'worschype' begins with 'gode berynge', but it is not merely the worship of the individual that is at stake here. It is the worship of the church itself.

The pastoral care material that I will examine here arose in the wake of the Fourth Lateran Council's decrees on educational reform and yearly confession in 1215. The flourishing tradition of vernacular literature that resulted ranges from sermons and collections of narrative exempla to penitential handbooks and catechetical material, the aim of which was to remedy the ignorance of the clergy and to educate the laity in the basic tenets of the faith. As John Mirk puts it in his *Instructions for Parish Priests*, 'whenne þe blynde ledeth þe blynde, / In to þe dyche þey fallen boo.'[4] But more than just providing basic knowledge, such texts, in conjunction with the visual and material decorations of the parish church, taught the laity how to conduct themselves as good Christians, in particular with respect to the space of the church itself. The requirement for yearly confession meant that the laity needed to be able to identify their sins, and a major area of concern was the sins that took place in and around the parish church. This is crucial because it is specifically the sanctity of the church that is threatened by lay misbehaviour. It is the duty of the parish priest to teach his congregation how to behave in order to avoid committing the sin of sacrilege but the narrative exempla that he draws upon risk depicting the church as a magnetic space that attracts sin rather than sanctity. Before I examine the narratives of desecration in more detail, I want to show how the Good Wife's advice to 'kepe thy chyrche' is deliberately and systematically promoted by pastoral care material in order to inculcate in the congregation a loyalty to their parish church that would ultimately result in a desire to maintain and increase its sanctity. If the laity care about their parish church, they are far less likely to endanger its sacred status.

In John Mirk's *Instructions*, he explains that the parish priest must teach the laity how to behave 'whenne þey doth to chyrche fare':

Þenne bydde hem leue here mony words,
Here ydel speche, and nyce bordes,
And put a-way alle vanyte,
And say here pater noster & here aue.

No non in chyrche stonde schal,
Ny lene to pyler ny to wal,
But fayre on kneus þey schule hem sette,
Knelynge doun vp on the flette,
And pray to god wyth herte meke
To ȝeue hem grace and mercy eke. (265–75)

As in the *Good Wife*, idle speech must be abandoned in favour of prayer and the congregation must conduct themselves appropriately by kneeling in devotion rather than 'lolling about', as the modern editor of Mirk's *Instructions* puts it.[5] Mirk goes on to explain why games are forbidden in the church and churchyard, alluding both to Genesis, 28.17 and to Christ expelling the moneylenders from the temple (Matthew, 21.12–13):

For cryst hem self techeth vs
Þat holy chyrche ys hys hows,
Þat ys made for no þynge elles
But for to praye In, as þe boke tells. (340–3)

God's house is a house of prayer and Mirk returns to the appropriate reverence due to the church in his list of questions for the parish priest when examining his congregation on the Ten Commandments. Under sloth, the priest is to ask if the individual has 'come to chyrche late / And spoken of synne by þe gate' (1165–6). The use of 'gate' here could refer to a gateway: a dangerous, liminal space that marks the transition between the profane space outside and the consecrated space of the church and churchyard.[6] But the Middle English Dictionary defines its use with the preposition 'bi' as 'on the way, during the trip', which presents the journey to the church through the streets as fraught with the potential for gossip and sin.[7] The penitent is asked if they has been 'slowe to goddes seruyse / Or storbet [disturbed] hyt by any wyse' (1167–8). The priest continues:

Hast þou letted [prevented] any mon
Þat to chyrche wolde haue gon?
Hast þow spoken harlatry
Wythynne chyrche or seyntwary?
[…] Hast þow wyþowte deuocyone
I-herde any predycacyone? (1169–78)

These questions ask the individual not only to identify inappropriate conduct – gossiping, hindering a neighbour from attending church – but also to confess a lack of spiritual commitment, for example, hearing a sermon 'wyþowte deuocyone'. This is important because where sinful behaviour threatens the church, good behaviour performed with genuine devotional intent strengthens the sanctity of the space and can even be a cause of miracles.

Mirk's instructions on appropriate devotional behaviour also apply to church attendance on holy days. In the examination for the third commandment, he asks:

Hast þow holden þyn halyday,
And spend hyt wel to goddes pay?
Hast þow I-gon to chyrche fayn
To serue god wyþ alle þy mayn?
Hast þou any werke þat day I-wroȝt,
Or synned sore in dede or þoȝt? (989–94)

The prohibition of working on the Sabbath gave rise to group of medieval wall paintings known as the 'Sunday Christ' or 'Sabbath-breakers' in which Christ's body is shown to be wounded by the tools used by those who work on holy days.[8] The importance of attending church on such days is powerfully reinforced by John Audelay's *Our Lord's Epistle on Sunday*, a poem which records Christ's letter to St Peter in which Christ warns that his wrath shall come upon those who do not keep the Sabbath. Christ declares that if anyone runs an errand on the Sabbath rather than going to church, 'al evylis Y wil send him':

Herefore fro you I wil turne my face,
And betake you into your enemyse hond,
And withdraw fro you mercé and grace,
And blynd you both with schame and schond,
And drown you within a lytyl stownd—
As I did Sodom and Comor,
That the erthe swolewd to hel ground
Sodenly or thai were ware!
Have mend, seris, here apon,
Beware betyme, or ye be schend!
And your mysdedis, loke ye amend,
And serve your God. Foresake the Fynd![9]

These threats of violence act as a negative counterpoint to the pastoral care material that promoted the very real benefits of presence in the church, especially at mass. Mirk explains, for example, that on the day 'þat þow syst goddes body, / Þese benefyces schalt þou haue sycurly':

Mete & drynke at thy nede,
Non schal þe þat day be gnede;
Idele othes and words also
God for-ȝeueþ the bo;
Soden deth that ylke day,
The dar not drede wyþowte nay;
Also þat day I the plyȝte
Þow schalt not lese þyn ye syȝte. (318–25)

In Audelay's 'Epistle', quoted above, Christ declares that he will 'blynd you both with schame and schond [shame and disgrace]' but this can easily be avoided, as Mirk suggests. Seeing the host at mass protected the individual from sudden death and losing their sight, as well as providing forgiveness for idle words and oaths. Physical protection was also believed to be offered by the sight of St Christopher, a popular saint in medieval wall paintings, frequently depicted 'opposite a door where they could be easily seen' (Figure 3).[10] Roger Rosewell records a now-lost Norman-French inscription from Woodeaton, Oxfordshire, which read 'ki cest image berra ce jur de male mort ne murra [who sees this image shall not die an ill-death this day]'.[11] Presence in God's house afforded the individual the protection of its sanctity. Failure to attend risked sudden death and damnation.

Presence in the church at particular times could also garner considerable benefits. In his sermon for the feast of Corpus Christi in the *Festial*, John Mirk discusses the establishment of the ritual by Pope Urban IV and his attempt to increase his congregation through the promise of pardons:

> Þan for þis holy pope þoght to draw Goddys pepul wyth þe bettyr wylle to come to chyrch þis day, he graunteth alle þat ben worthy, þat is, very contrite and schryuen of hure synnes and ben in chyrch at boþe evensonges of þis fest and at masse and at matynys, for vche of þeise a hundred dayes of pardon, and for vche oþer oure of þis day fourety dayes of pardon, and for vche day of þe vtas a hundred dayes of pardon, to dyron for here mede for euremore.[12]

Pardon is promised for those who are 'worthy' and worthiness is defined here not only as individual virtue but as presence in the church 'at boþe evensonges of þis fest and at lasse and at matynys'.

3 St Christopher. Medieval wall painting, St Botolph's, Slapton, Northamptonshire.

The repeated reference to 'þis fest' and 'þis day' makes the pope's pardons available to the contemporary congregation listening to the sermon, reinforcing the advantages of church attendance. In his sermon for the feast of St Margaret, Mirk even goes so far as to suggest that church attendance is preferable to fasting and personal devotions to the saint:

> Gode men, suche a day ȝe schal haue þe fest of Seynt Margrete. And þagh it be a lyght haly-day save þeras þe schyrch is edyfyed in hur name, ȝitte I warne ȝow, for, as I suppose, þer ben somme þat haue suche love to hure þat he wyl faston hur evon: bot þan ȝe þat faste hur evyn ȝe quyte ȝow not to hyr os ȝe schulde bot if ȝe comon to chyrch on morowun and heren a masse of hure. For scheo wyl cun ȝow more þank to makyn a masse isayde in worchep of hur þan to faston many evenes brede and watur wythoute masse. For þe masse ioyeth alle þe angellys of heven, it fedeth and comfordeth þe soules in purcatorie and sokoreth alle þat leveth in

> erthe in scharite. And he þat fasteth þe evyn he helpyth hymselfe and no forthur. (p. 181)

Fasting 'helpyth hymselfe and no forthur' whereas the communal celebration of mass benefits the entire community of the faithful, both on earth and in purgatory, and even the angels in heaven. Prayer for the dead was a crucial part of the living community's work in the church, and in his sermon for All Souls Day, Mirk tells a story that shows how the dead can return the favour and help the living. It concerns a man whose house is next to the churchyard 'so þat þe dore oponyd towarde þe chyrch' (p. 242). Whenever the man passes the churchyard he 'wolde seyn *De profundis* for alle criston soules', and one day when he is pursued by his enemies on the way back to his house, he prays again and 'anone þerwyth alle þis chyrch-ȝorde rose ful of bodyes, vchone wyth an instrument in hys hond of hys crafte, and dryuon aȝeyne hys enmyes' (p. 242). The man's prayers are repaid as the dead arise from the churchyard and drive away his enemies. In Mirk's sermons, communal church attendance is rewarded by pardon from sin and protection from enemies.

It was not just presence in any church that was encouraged in pastoral care material, however. Presence in the local parish church was essential; 'kepe *thy* church' as the Good Wife reminds us. The fifteenth-century sermon collection *Jacob's Well* declares:

> Þou shuldst on þe halyday kepyn þin owyn parysch cherche and heryn þe full dyvyne seruyse, and nowȝt styrten owt to oþere cherchys fro þe techyng of þi curate, þat þou schuldyst noȝt here Goddys woord [...] ffor grettere sygne of hate to God mayȝt þou noȝt schewe þan to fle þat place þere þou schuldyst here his woord.[13]

There is a clear drive here to encourage parishioners to remain loyal to their own parish churches and their clergy, a cause also supported by Mirk's *Instructions* in the directives on confession. Priests are told that when a man comes for confession:

> Fyrst þow moste ask hym þen,
> Wheþer he be þy paresschen,
> And ȝef he vnswere and say nay,
> Theche hym home fayre hys way,
> But he schowe þe I-wryten,
> Where by þou myȝt wel I-wyten,
> Þat he hath leue of hys prest
> To be I-schryue where hym lust. (813–20)

Without written permission, the laity should not seek absolution from another priest. The fifteenth-century *Speculum Sacerdotale* concurs, emphasising the legal position:

> Sires it is to wite that it is noȝt *laweful* to no preste for to receyue þe suget of a-nother preste vnto penaunce but ȝif it be þrouȝ ignorance or with the leve of that preste that he was schryven to a-fore. And therfore ȝif the parischen of thi neyghboure come to the, þou owest noȝt for to receyve hym to penaunce or confession but ȝif it be done hym to vnderstonde that he haue *licence* of his curette or ellis that his curet is noȝt sufficient to heere his counsel ne able to counsel him.[14]

Such strictures do not, of course, mean that parishioners refrained entirely from seeking absolution from another priest. Margery Kempe, for example, had a number of confessors in additional to her own parish priest, Robert Spryngolde, at St Margaret's in Lynn.[15] Katherine French has discussed the popularity of the mendicant orders and the potential threat to the livelihood of parish priests who feared both 'the loss of revenue and influence when their parishioners sought out confession with a mendicant or requested burial in mendicant or monastic churchyards'.[16] There was considerable competition for lay attention in this period, from the mendicant orders but also from local and international pilgrimage sites, as I discussed in Chapter 2, and this might explain why writers like Mirk and the anonymous sermon-authors were keen to refocus attention on both the parish church and its ministers as the primary source of spiritual sustenance and sanctity. Seeking out an alternative sacred space or an alternative priest may, of course, have appealed for different reasons. Confession to a minister outside of the parish may have been motivated by embarrassment on the part of the penitent and a desire for 'privacy', as French points out, or by recognition of the minister's spiritual status.[17] A penitent's own parish priest may not have been 'sufficient' to offer counsel, as the *Speculum Sacerdotale* suggests, or alternatively a parishioner might seek out a priest with a holy reputation, if we consider Margery Kempe and Richard Caister, the vicar at St Stephen's, Norwich. Pilgrimage to a holy site confers clear spiritual benefits and burial in an alternative churchyard may have reflected a desire to be laid to rest alongside relatives outside of the parish or, in the case of monastic churchyards, to signal devotional allegiances and social status.[18] While the impulses behind church-hopping and confessor-hopping may have been different, the concerns raised in pastoral literature highlight how essential the laity were for the livelihood of the parish as a whole. It was crucial that parish priests did not allow the laity's spiritual and financial capital to be dispersed elsewhere, no matter how tempting it might be.

A major strategy that priests could employ in their sermons to establish a relationship of proximity, familiarity, and affection between the laity and their local place of worship was the 'þis cherche' formula. The dedication sermon in the *Speculum Sacerdotale* begins by declaring his subject to be 'þe feste of the dedicacion of *this chirche*' (p. 163, italics mine). John Mirk also employs the formula in his sermon for the feast of St Alkmund in the *Festial*, stating:

> Goode men and woymen, such a day N ȝe schull haue Seynt Alkmundys day. Therefore comyth to þe chirche, forto worschip God and Saynt Alkamunde, þe whech is patron of þys chyrche.[19]

The church referred to here is Shrewsbury St Alkmund with which Mirk himself, and the abbey of Lilleshall of which he was later a canon, was associated, making the formula especially resonant. Dedication feast days and feast days for the patron saint of the church were times at which the parish priest would especially encourage attendance in, and loyalty towards, the specific church in question but we also find the formula used in sermon exempla to impress upon the congregation the need for good behaviour within the church in which the sermon is delivered. In *Jacob's Well*, the narrator tells the story of the demon, commonly known as Tutivillus, who records the idle speech of the congregation on his scroll, and comments:

> I trowe þe feend hath nede to drawe lengere & braddere his rolle *here*; for it is ellys to lytel to wryten on alle þe talys tolde in þis cherch.[20]

The addition of 'here' makes the mapping of the exemplum on to 'þis cherche' even more emphatic; *here* in *this* church, Tutivillus would need a large scroll indeed to record all the idle speech of the parishioners. The formula was also used in a now-lost fourteenth-century stained glass window given by Sir Hugh Hastings and his wife Margery to Elsing church, Norfolk. Hugh and Margery were represented in the window kneeling and holding a miniature church, with the following inscription: 'pray to thi son made Marye in whose worchipe yis chirche hā wrowt huwe ye hastyng Margorie mi wyf Ledi forgit us nowt'.[21] In this inscription, Hugh asks Mary to intercede with Christ, as it is in her worship that 'yis chirche' has been made. Russell West-Pavlov argues that deictic language is 'the linguistic means by which a speaker anchors utterances in the concrete place of enunciation ("here", "there", "this table")'.[22] The anchoring of Hugh's prayer in his church is doubly secure here as the utterance is inscribed in the window and also features a miniature representation of the church, held in Hugh's own hands.

Deictic language establishes a reciprocal relationship between language and space. The proximal deixis of 'þis cherche' brings the listener into close proximity with the space as it gives a specificity to the church being invoked, 'þis' church in which the sermon is performed. West-Pavlov argues therefore that deictic language 'does not merely gain purchase upon the space', the space itself 'can be said to ground, indeed more actively, to inform or infiltrate the language'.[23] The relationship is reciprocal. The sermon need not necessarily be performed in church space for this connection to be established, however; the deictic operations of the text can be just as successful in a reading context. Anna Fuchs argues that 'here' can be the 'shared knowledge contexts (or frames, scenes, background etc.) activated in communication'.[24] An individual will have a mental image of their own parish church which functions as a 'shared knowledge context' that can be applied to sermon texts and penitential material. The individual's idea of 'a church' is fundamentally informed by their experiences in their own parish church and the sermon's 'here' calls that physical and architectural context to mind. There is a symbiotic exchange between the church building and the sermons preached within it, and that exchange generates a sanctity that is animate and dynamic. Moreover, it is a sanctity that inspires personal commitment. West-Pavlov argues that spatial language, such as the 'þis cherche' formula, 'never ceases to remind one of one's debts to the place in which one stands', or indeed the place which one mentally imagines.[25] This indebtedness is a crucial resource for the parish priest to draw upon as he encourages his congregation to remain loyal to their parish church, a building which offers them protection and salvation as their communal and spiritual home.

Animating the church: The relationship between text and image

In his sermon for Corpus Christi, John Mirk delivers the commonplace of church art that has been subject to considerable revision by art historians: 'ymages and peyntoures ben lewed mennus bokys' (p. 157).[26] The role of church art in the education of the laity is more complex than the concept of *libri laicorum* would suggest. Church art is not an alternative form of teaching provided due to the laity's inability to access textual material. Visual and textual representation work in a symbiotic relationship in order to edify the congregation. As Herbert Kessler argues, by the late Middle Ages pictures were 'no longer simply "books of the illiterate," but, rather, multivalent devices used by various groups in diverse ways and deeply implicated in oral as well as written culture'.[27] As I discussed in my introduction, the interpretation of images involved communal dialogue; 'perception was a performance', as Michael Camille argued.[28] Here I will examine the pastoral care material that was shared between the textual and visual fields in order to offer a performative reading of the relationship between narrative exempla and religious art that directly contributes to the sanctity of the church. A priest could use images such as the Seven Deadly Sins or the recording demon Tutivillus as a visual aid in his sermons but even where no direct connection was made, the saints, angels, and demons that populated the medieval church informed the laity's understanding of narrative exempla. Mirk explains that 'þer ben many thowsand of þe pepul þat cowde not ymagyn in here herte how Criste was don on þe rode bot os þei lernyn it in sytght of yamges and poyntowres' (p. 157). Church art provides an image for the laity to embody and enhance their understanding of the crucifixion. The laity's idea of the crucified Christ, or of an angel or devil, is shaped by the iconography of the church – their local church in particular. But as we shall see, the relationship is reciprocal. Text and image supplement and enrich one another and the creative synergy between church decorations and pastoral texts works to animate the church and present it as a living actor in the drama of salvation.

John Mirk's sermon for the feast of St Margaret is frequently cited as evidence for the pedagogical value of images in the church. Having described Margaret's victory over the devil, he explains:

> Herefore, where þat Margrete is peyntyd oythur corvon, scheo hath a dragon vndyr hur fette and a cros in hur hande, schewing how be þe vertu of þe cros scheo gate þe victory of þe fende. (p. 182)

Mirk uses the sermon to enlighten his audience as to the meaning of St Margaret's iconography where it is 'peyntyd oythur corvon' and, at the same time, to reinforce the authority of his own narrative with reference to external imagery in the church. The fifteenth-century treatise on the Decalogue, *Dives and Pauper*, concurs with Mirk's reading. When Dives repeats the axiom that imagery is 'a tokene and a book to þe lewyd peple' and asks Pauper to 'teche me ȝet a lytyl betere to knowe þis tokene and to redeyn þis book', Pauper explains the significance of the individual 'tokens' that identify the saints in visual imagery in similar terms.[29] St Peter is 'peyntyd wyt keyis in his hond in tokene þat Crist betoke Seynt Petyr þe keyis of holy cherch and of þe kyngdam of heuene' (pp. 91–2); St Katherine is painted with her wheel 'in tokene of þe horrible qheelys qheche þe tyraunt Maxence ordeynyd to rendyn here lyth fro lyth' (p. 92); and St Margaret is painted 'wyt a dragoun vnder here feet and wyt a cros in here hond in tokene þat qhanne þe dragoun deuowryd here she blissyd here & be vertue of þe cros þe foul dragoun brast and she cam out of hym heyl and hool' (p. 93). The attributes of St Paul, St John the Baptist and St John the Evangelist are also rehearsed, saints who, like St Margaret, were a ubiquitous presence in both the parish church and in sermon material. The visual and textual representations of the saints are mutually reinforcing.

In the fourteenth and fifteenth centuries, Middle English texts even began to find their way into wall paintings and stained glass windows. In addition to Hugh Hastings' stained glass window, there are also a small number of examples of dialogues taking place which, as Madeleine Gray has recently argued, 'seems geared to constructing a dynamic and active space with speech scrolls reminiscent of late medieval drama'.[30] Gray includes the example of St Christopher conversing with the Christ-child at Horley (Oxon). Christopher asks, 'what art you and art so yonge, bar I never so hevy a thynge' and the Christ-child answers, 'Yey, I be hevy no wonder ys, for I am yey kynge of blys'.[31] The narrative situation of the wall painting is brought to life by the dialogue. Christopher Woodforde also records Middle English speech in two lost stained glass windows. In the Heydon blasphemy window, the Virgin Mary addressed the swearers, lamenting that Christ's 'lemys be rent asundyr ryth' by their speech.[32] In the Works of Mercy window at Lammas, the needy addressed the Virgin and she replied; the homeless man, for example, declared 'hostel I crave' and the Virgin answered, 'Come wery in and you shall have.'[33] This creates an 'active and dynamic' space, as Gray suggests, founded on the interplay between vernacular text and image, which actualises the possibility that images in the church have the capacity for speech, whether directly in the form of speech scrolls, in the examples mentioned, or indirectly when their characters are given a voice in medieval sermons. I will explore the notion that devotional images speak to the viewer in more detail below, focusing in particular on speaking crucifixes in sermon exempla and, at the end of the chapter, on lyric poetry that dramatises Christ's speech from the cross on Good Friday. Medieval Christians were encouraged to view the painted church as a performative space for narrative encounters with Christ and the saints.

Narrative and image can also be mutually supportive even without the presence of vernacular text in a wall painting or stained glass window. Miriam Gill has charted the relationship between medieval wall paintings and sermons, detailing what she classifies as 'direct connections, common material, and general associations'.[34] Direct connections are references in sermons such as those made by John Mirk and the appearance of tropes such as the Warning to Swearers or the Warning to Gossips in both visual art and texts. I want to extend this analysis here to consider the connections made as a result of the performance of sermons within the church itself and the effect that this has on the lay audience. Sermon exempla give visual decorations a voice and a narrative, and produce a sanctity that is performative, animate, and full of potential. In his work on images, David Freedberg argues for a symbiotic relationship between image and beholder that creates just such a 'potentiality', predicated on sight as the primary sensory engagement.[35] He suggests that we should consider 'not only what beholders do, but also what images appear to do; not only what people do as a result of their relationship with imaged form, but also what they expected imaged form to achieve, and why they have such expectations at all'.[36] The exempla that were the staple of medieval sermons encouraged the expectation that the images and carvings in the church could come alive at any moment; they were just waiting to be activated by the preacher's performance and the laity's response.

Popular subject matter in medieval church art included the lives of saints, the life of Christ (especially the Passion), the life of the Virgin, the Last Judgement or Doom, morality images, and numerous depictions of angels and devils. The appearance of such subjects in sermon exempla creates an exchange between the events of the narrative and the particular visual representations in the church in which the tale is delivered. If we take the example of angels, the fifteenth-century preaching compendium *The Alphabet of Tales* includes an exemplum in which St Gregory is performing the mass and the 'Aungels of our Lorde ansswerd hym and sayd "et cum spiritu tuo"'.[37] The majority of churches in the period had carvings, windows, or wall paintings depicting angels, many of which were shown taking an active part in church rituals, from censing to singing. At Hailes, Gloucestershire, a wall painting depicts two angels censing the east window and at Brent Eleigh, Suffolk, angels cense a space which almost certainly held a pedestal and statue of the Virgin and child before the Reformation.[38] Censing angels also appear in stained glass at Ludlow, Shropshire and Field Dalling, Norfolk. Norfolk is justly famous for its churches that feature hammerbeam roofs decorated with angels who hold instruments of the passion, liturgical objects, or musical instruments.[39] There is also a lively tradition of angels singing and playing a variety of musical instruments in stained glass windows such as the harping angels at Tattershall, Lincolnshire; the angel playing the hurdy-gurdy at York St Denys; and the angelic orchestras at Fairford in Gloucestershire, Orchardleigh in Somerset, and, most famously, in the Beauchamp Chapel at Warwick, St Mary's, which even includes a portable organ and a glockenspiel.[40] The Beauchamp Chapel also features a choir of angels in the tracery lights singing *Gaudeamus omnes in domino* for the Assumption of the Virgin Mary.[41] In this window the angels present the words and music to the viewer as they sing, not only offering a script for liturgical imitation but performing an eternal hymn of praise to God and Virgin within the church itself. The medieval lay person listening to narratives such as the one in the *Alphabet* could not fail to make the connection between the visual imagery around them in the church and the textual angel of the exempla. Their idea of an angel will be directly informed by their church's iconography. If the angel in the church has a feathered body, like those at Yarnton in Oxfordshire, for example, the angel of their imagination would be similarly garbed. When they listen to a narrative in which an angel assists the priests in his ministrations, it is the angel that they see before them that becomes the active participant in the scene.

An even stronger case can be made that images of devils in the church are animated and enlivened by the popular tales of demonic interference in parish life. In the *Alphabet*, a devil appears to an abbot and asks him to accompany him 'vnto a gaderyng samen of our brethir' (p. 392). The abbot is astonished when the devil leads him to the church but the devil replies provocatively, 'knowis þou not at withouten vs þer is no gaderyng?', parodying the idea of the church as the gathering place of the Christian community. In the narrative, the devils busy themselves in the church, preventing the monks from performing their offices until the abbot prays and they 'vanyshid away' (p. 393). In a church in which devils appear, whether in carvings, stained glass, or wall paintings, no 'gaderyng' of the community takes place without them. Unlike the *Alphabet*'s exemplum, in which they are dismissed at the end of the tale, in their visual form in church decoration devils do not vanish away when the priest prays – they remain powerfully visible and active in church space. Images of devils carrying off sinners in wheelbarrows (e.g. the Last Judgement window at Fairford, Gloucestershire) or weighing down the scales against a sinner (e.g. Martham, Norfolk) act as a warning of the judgement that is to come and, as we shall see, a number of exempla show that even burial in the sacred space of the church will not protect a sinner as devils enter the church and violently exhume the bodies of those who do not belong.[42]

One devil in particular appears in both church decoration and exemplary narratives, the demon who records and incites idle gossip, known as Tutivillus.[43] He features in didactic material on the subject of jangling and he is associated with gossiping women in particular.[44] In the wall painting at Slapton, Northamptonshire, for example, a huge demon sits behind two gossiping women, perhaps encouraging them in their sin by pushing their heads together (Figure 4). In the tracery lights at Stanford-on-Avon, demons creep towards two women who face each other, the blue demon encouraging the woman on the right by prodding her. Demons also appear to encourage the gossiping women in wall paintings at Peakirk, Northamptonshire, and Seething, Norfolk; in both cases, pushing the women's heads together.[45] In three-dimensional art, Tutivillus appears in the form in which we tend to find him in the narrative exempla, recording parishioners' idle gossip on a scroll or, more rarely, collecting monks' skipped syllables in a sack. An unusual bench end in the parish church of Charlton Mackrell, Somerset, conflates both traditions as Tutivillus is carrying a sack and writing on a scroll.[46] On a misericord in Ely cathedral, the central demon has his arms around the two women who neglect their rosary and prayer book, and in the supporters on either side, another demon writes on a scroll and attempts to pull out the scroll with his teeth.[47] Tutivillus also came to have a role in medieval drama, as Margaret Jennings has explored.[48] He is the principal devil in the morality play *Mankind* and he also appears in the Towneley 'Last Judgement' play, in which he claims

4 Tutivillus and the gossiping women. Medieval wall painting, St Botolph's, Slapton, Northamptonshire.

jurisdiction over a much greater range of sinners than merely 'thise kyrkchaterars':

> Yit of thise kyrkchaterars
> Here ar a menee,
> Of barganars and okerars
> And lufars of symonee,
> Of runkers and rowners.
> God castys thaym out, trulee,
> From his temple, all sich mysdoers;
> I cach thaym then to me.[49]

Tutivillus is a demon who catches the laity in the act of sin, and I will explore his specific role in pastoral care exempla below, but what this range of visual and theatrical depictions makes clear is the interplay between narrative, imagery, and performance in the edification of medieval Christians. The pastoral aims of the parish priest are supported by a multimedia approach to salvation.

The potential for visual imagery to be dramatically animated was explicitly shown in miracle stories in which material objects come to life and interact with the laity as a direct result of virtuous or sinful behaviour. I have argued elsewhere that such narratives portray devotional objects such as the crucifix or pietà as performative, agential, and interactive, drawing on Dan Hicks' argument that we should view objects not as static, unresponsive matter, but as 'events'.[50] I want to extend that argument here to show how the miraculous animation that takes place significantly increases the sanctity of the church and demonstrates how profoundly that sanctity relies upon lay practice. The expectations that the medieval laity had of the visual imagery that surrounded them in the church, to return to Freedberg's argument, are in part established by the miracle narratives that I will now discuss, and these narratives play a decisive role in making the sanctity of the church manifest for all to see.

A number of narratives depict religious images that come to life and interact with an individual to their spiritual benefit. In *The Alphabet of Tales*, for example, a priest who has been vexed by the temptations of the flesh is told by the pope to present a ring to an image of St Agnes 'þat was paynttid in his kirk' and 'on his behalfe charge hur þat sho sulde suffre hym wed hur' (p. 33). The priest does as he is commanded and the painted image of St Agnes 'putt furth hur ryng-fynger & profird it to hym, & he putt on þe ryng' (p. 33). The image of the saint 'drew in hur fynger agayn' and all the priest's temptations pass away (p. 33). Devotion to the saint, materialised in the miracle of the ring, saves the priest and the tale concludes by informing us that the evidence of the miracle is still visible: 'in Rome in hur kurk, at þis day, þe same ryng shewis yitt on hur fynger' (p. 33). In another exemplum from the *Alphabet*, a young boy is playing handball outside the church and he wishes to safeguard a ring that 'a maydyn þat luffid hym be flesshly luff had gyffen hym' (p. 438). He takes the ring into the church and sees the image of the Virgin:

> And when he come befor þe ymage of our Lady, he stude mervelland and beheld hur fayrnes, & he set hym down on his kne and deuotelie sayd afor hur his Ave Maria. And when he had done he said vnto hur; 'Forsuth, Ladie, þou erte fayrer þan any oþer & mor fayr þan sho þat gaff me þis ryng, and þerfor I forsake hur. I, fro hens furth, I will luff the, so at þou wyll luff me agayn.' And he profurd þe ryng vnto þe ymage fynger, and þe ymage put furth hur fynger streght & he putt it on. And þan þe fynger closyd agayn vnto þe ymage as it was are. (p. 438)

The boy is so impressed by the fair statue of the Virgin that he forsakes the maiden but he later marries, breaking his promise to the Virgin, and on his wedding day he has a dream that the Virgin appears in his bed between him and his wife, presenting her ring finger. The man wakes up and thinks that the vision is a mere 'fantasye' but when the Virgin reappears and threatens him, 'he was ferd for hur' and he forsakes his wife for the wilderness where 'devotelie he servid our Ladie vnto his lyfis ende' (p. 439). This example suggests that devotion to the material culture of the church is a lifelong commitment, a commitment that extends even after death, as evidence from wills demonstrates. Richard Marks includes the example of a man called John James who asked that he be buried 'right under the foote of the ymage of our lady' where he sat during services, enabling him to continue his devotions to her image through his burial within the church.[51]

In another tale concerning the Virgin, a knight who has lost all his goods goes to the woods to make a pact with the devil. He is promised full restoration to his former state if he renounces God and Mary. The man renounces God but he refuses to renounce Mary and he travels back into the town and comes upon a church in which he kneels before an image of the Virgin, weeping and making such great sorrow that 'all þe kurk rang' (*Alphabet*, p. 371). The image of the Virgin and child then comes to life and the Virgin begs Christ's forgiveness for the knight:

> Our Ladie spak vnto hur Son & said; 'O, þou swete Son! Hafe mercie of þis man!' And þe childe at satt on hur kne wolde not speke again vnto his moder, bod turnyd his head awayward fro hur. And sho prayed hym agayn, & sayd þat þe man was dessayvid, and with þat he turnyd his bak opon hur and said; 'This man hase denyd me, what shulde I do vnto hym?' And þan þe ymage of owr Lade rase vp & sett hur Son apon þe altar, and fell down on hur kneis at His fete and said; 'I pray þe, swete Son, þat for my sake þou forgyff hym his syn.' And onone þe child liftyd vp His moder and said vnto hur; 'Moder, yit I neuer denyed þe thyng att þou axkid me. And now, beholde, for þi sake I forgyff hym.' (p. 371)

In this endearing narrative, when the Christ-child refuses to acknowledge the knight, the Virgin places him on the altar and prays for forgiveness, which is finally granted 'for þi sake'. The exemplum demonstrates the efficacy of the Virgin's intercession and the power of lay practice to generate miracles. It is as a direct result of the knight's devotion to the Virgin that the image comes to life and the Virgin saves the knight from damnation.

The miraculous animation of the church's imagery acts as a moral barometer for the laity's virtue and vice. This can be seen even more clearly in exempla concerning the crucifix. In the *Gesta Romanorum*, when a woman goes to kiss the feet of the crucifix, 'the crucifix drewe a-wey his fete' and berates the woman: 'Go from me, for thou arte not worthy to kysse my fete, for the synne thou beres in thyn herte, for shame, and longe haste done.'[52] The gesture of drawing away the feet embodies the woman's sinful distance from Christ and the crucifix then speaks to make the significance of this action clear. *Jacob's Well* tells the tale of a man who was 'so slawe & sluggy in goddys seruyse' that 'slawly he com to þe cherche, & selde, & late, & whenne he com þedyr, he in slepyng or in iangelyng, ocupyed hym, þat he herde neythir goddys seruyse ne goddys woord, &, wyth his ianglyng, lettyd manye oþere fro þe heryng of dyvin seruyse' (p. 110), thus breaking all of the instructions for church attendance and good behaviour outlined by John Mirk. When the man dies and his funeral service is conducted, the crucifix 'on þe bere [bier] loosyd his handys fro þe crosse, & stoppyd his eerys wyth his handys' (p. 110). The meaning of this miracle is then explained by God himself who declares:

> Þis cursyd man wolde neuere for slauthe heryn my woord, ne don þer-after, ne heryn my seruyse in holy cherch deuoutly; þerfore, his soule is in powere of feendys dampnyd. Þerfore, myn ymage on þe cros stoppyth his erys, to schewe ȝou þat I, god, stoppe myn erys in heuen, þat I here no prayere, prayed for hym in holy cherche. Þerfore prayeth no more for hym, for he is dampnyd. (p. 110).

God's eyes and ears are trained upon the church, as the Bible states (2 Chronicles, 6.40). But when an individual refuses to 'heryn my seruyse in holy cherch *deuoutly*', then God stops his ears, as the miraculous animation of the crucifix demonstrates. In the version in the *Alphabet*, the crucifix is located not on the bier of the deceased but 'in þe rude-lofte' (p. 67), a gallery above the rood screen and the choir. This foregrounds the consequences of the man's devotional failings even more publicly. The sermon in *Jacob's Well* reinforces the exemplum's purpose in promoting church attendance by concluding: 'þerfore, leuyth ȝoure slouthe & ianglyng in tyme of goddys seruyse, & heryth it deuoutly, & goddys woord also; and ellys god wyll noȝt here prayerys in holy cherch, prayed for ȝow' (pp. 110–11). Lack of devotion has a clear impact on an individual's salvation and the material culture of the church miraculously confirms this.

The most popular story of the miraculous animation of the crucifix is known as the Merciful Knight and it appears in *Jacob's Well*, the *Alphabet*, Robert Mannyng's *Handlyng Synne*, Mirk's *Festial*, and as a stand-alone narrative in Oxford, Bodleian Library MS Ashmole 61.[53] In this exemplum, a knight forgives his father's murderer when he begs for mercy in the name of Christ. The pair then go to the church to creep to the cross on Good Friday and 'whanne þe kny3t kyssed þe crosse, þat for3af his faderis deth to þe oþer kny3t, þe crucyfixe halsyd hym abowtyn his necke, & seyde, "þou for3yue þis kny3t þi faderis deth for my loue, & kyssed hym; þer-fore I for3eue þe alle þi synnes & kysse þe"' (*Jacob's Well*, p. 253). As a direct result of the virtuous behaviour of the knight, the crucifix is miraculously animated. The figure of Christ embraces the knight and explains that his action is an imitation of the knight's own embrace of the murderer. When the murderer begged for mercy from the knight, he appealed directly to Christ's example: 'I pray þe for loue of him þat deyid on cross to 3yue mercy to mankynde, haue þou mercy on me' (p. 252). This establishes a chain of imitation. The knight imitates Christ and the crucifix then imitates the knight by embracing him.

This imitation is even more important in the version in Mirk's *Festial* as it is used to encourage participation in church ritual and the protection of sacred space. The narrative appears in Mirk's sermon for Good Friday, and the knight has lost his son, making his forgiveness of the murderer on this day even more significant. Mirk prefaces the exemplum by explaining the Good Friday ritual of creeping to the cross:

> Þan aftur þe orisones þe crosse is browte forth, þe wyche yche criston man and womman schal worchep þis day in worchep of hym þat as þis day dyed on þe crosse. And pray to God to for3euen alle þat has trespased a3eynus 3ow, as Cryste prayed hys Fadur to for3euen þilke þat dedon hym to þe deth, þis day hongynge on þe crosse. (p. 108)

The repeated deixis, 'þis day', anchors both the crucifixion itself and the exemplum that is to follow in the present moment of church ritual. Christ is made present, '*hongynge* on þe crosse', and the cross of Calvary and the crucifix in the narrative are aligned with their material representation in the parish church, on the rood screen and on the altar. Replication and imitation are central to this narrative and Mirk linguistically re-enacts the *imitatio Christi* at the heart of the Good Friday ritual when he declares that men and women 'schal worchep on þis day' the cross as they 'worchep' Christ. As Holly Johnson points out, although 'we cannot be sure exactly when, amidst the Good Friday rituals, the congregation heard a sermon', Mirk's use of the future tense here suggests that the sermon was preached before the ritual of creeping to the cross.[54] This would mean that the exemplum had even greater resonance with the audience because they would go on to perform precisely the ritual whose importance and miraculous potential the preacher has just described.

In Mirk's version, the church setting is given increased importance as the murderer, pursued by the knight and a great company, sees the people entering the church to participate in the Good Friday rituals and follows suit. The murderer enters the church, not only to 'heron and sene Goddus seruice', but also to seek sanctuary and 'put hym holy in Godys mercy' (p. 109). Once inside the church, the murderer realises that he has 'trespased to heygly aȝeynus hym', echoing the Pater Noster, and he begs for forgiveness and performs an *imitatio Christi*:

> He felle downe flatte to þe grounde wyth his armes spradde abrode, as Cryste sprade his armes on þe crosse, and sayde to hym: 'For hys lofe þat þis day sprade his armes on þe crosse and dyed for þe and me and alle mankynde, and forȝaue alle þat dydun hym to þe deth, haue mercy on me and forȝef me þat I haue trespased aȝeynus þe.' (p. 109)

The murderer's linguistic and embodied imitation inspires the knight's forgiveness but a major component in his decision is the fact that he meets the murderer within the church itself. Immediately after the murderer's speech, Mirk tells us that 'þis oþur knythe þoȝte welle hit hade bene a *to horybul synne* for to haue done oȝte amysse to hym *þare in þe chirche* whille þat he mekud hym so and so lowly prayed hym of mercy for Cristes sake' (p. 109, italics mine). The knight not only respects the status of the church as a sanctuary, he is fully aware that he would be committing sacrilege if he were to shed blood in sacred space. When the knight then approaches the crucifix and is embraced, the Christ figure declares 'I forȝeff þe, os þow hast forȝeuen *for me*' (p. 109, italics mine). The knight forgives the murderer 'for Cristes sake' but also so as to refrain from shedding blood in the church. For Mirk, then, the exemplum demonstrates the miraculous potential of the church's material culture when inspired by virtuous behaviour that not only imitates Christ but also safeguards sacred space. The crucifix approves of the knight's mercy and of his decision not to desecrate the church. Mirk concludes the exemplum by encouraging his audience to participate in the network of imitation by worshipping the crucifix on Good Friday and embracing each other as a community in their own church, just as Christ and the knight did:

> Þus schulde ȝe vchone forȝeue oþur for Cristus luff, and klyppon and kysson and ben frendus, and þan wil Cryste klyppon and kysson ȝow and ȝeffon ȝow þe ioy þat euer sal laston, to þe wyche ioy God bryng vs alle. Amen. (p. 109)

The laity listening to the exemplum could not help but see the promise that Christ will 'klyppon and kysson ȝow' as both figurative and literal when they gazed upon the crucifix in their own parish church on Good Friday and proceeded to creep to the cross.

The response of the parish congregation is also foregrounded in the version in *Handlyng Synne*. Mannyng concludes by explaining that 'al þe parshe boþe old and ȝyng, / Parseyuede & sagh þat clyppyng', and as a result:

> Þe myracle sone oueral was kyd,
> And eury man þer of gan telle,
> Prestes yn prechyng þer of gun spelle,
> So þat eury man yn þe cuntre
> Leuede weyl þe more yn charyte.[55]

The story of the crucifix's miraculous embrace of the knight is well known throughout the parish and as a result, every man in the country 'leuede weyl þe more yn charyte'.

The miraculous animation of the church's images in the exempla above, from crucifixes to statues, reinforces the sanctity of the space in three ways: firstly, by the very fact of the miracles themselves; secondly, through the promotion of devotion to church ritual and the avoidance of sacrilege; and finally, by the encouragement of virtuous behaviour on the part of the congregation. But as the narratives to which I will now turn demonstrate, sacrilege was an ever-present threat in the parish church and, paradoxically, it provided an opportunity for the powerful reassertion of sanctity. The irruption of the profane in the parish church was necessary to the continued performance of the sacred, and the devils and demons who police the profane ironically safeguard the sanctity of

God's house. Their determination to claim sinners for themselves maintains the opposition between sacred and profane and purges God's house of pollution and contamination.

'Sin is behovabil': The sacred and profane

The feast day of the dedication of a church was an opportunity for the parish priest to remind his congregation of the sanctity of the space and their duty to maintain and safeguard that sanctity through virtuous behaviour. Both John Mirk's *Festial* and the fifteenth-century *Speculum Sacerdotale* sermon collection include a dedication sermon but their approaches to the celebration are rather different. Edward Weatherly argues that while 'most of the stories in the *Festial* teach a moral, those in the *Speculum Sacerdotale* attempt to arouse devotion through wonder at the miraculous'.[56] This is precisely the strategy that the *Speculum* author employs in the dedication sermon. He emphasises the great sanctity of the church and presents an idealised space in which everything is as it should be:

> In siche a day ȝe shul haue þe feste of the dedicacion of this chirche, in the whiche place we come and worschepeþ God in, of the whiche þer ben gret sacramentes, for this place is hous of praying, hous of sanctificacion. In it are prayers made, in it are askers of grace herd and sped, in it are heuenly þyngis wonne, in it ben þe sacramentis. Deuelis ben out dryven, gilty are delyuered, seke men made hole. (p. 163)

There is no doubt here about the status of the church as a sacred space. Devils are expelled, the guilty are saved, and the sick are healed. It is a house of prayer and a house of 'sanctificacion'. An unusual word in Middle English, 'sanctificacion' means hallowing and honouring but it also signifies the action of 'God's grace making a believer or baptismal water holy or free of from sin', and indeed the word is used in this way in the *Speculum*'s sermon for Pentecost that celebrates the birth of the church.[57] The author commands: 'Let vs clense vs a-ȝeyns the tyme of syche a solempnyte fro alle spottes of flesche and of spirit þat we may be worþi in þat day to take þe Holy Gost to oure sanctificacion and be his temple' (p. 159). The dedication sermon performs this act of sanctification linguistically by declaring in the present tense all of the practices and characteristics that constitute sacred space:

> Riȝtwis men are commendid to God, ordynaunces and institucions of holy chirche ben rehersid, wickyd men are acursid. In it is the

habitacion of God, concourse of angels, reconsiliacion of man, and the lowenes of erþe is in it fellaschiped to the hyenes of heuene. And this place is holy hous of God and ȝate of heuene. (p. 163)

The repeated deixis, 'this chirche', 'this place', anchors the idealised church of the sermon to the material building in which it is preached. The sermon invokes the Genesis, 28.17 description of the house of God and the gate of heaven but it takes this a stage further by suggesting that earth is 'fellaschiped' to heaven in the church, that is, joined or united in community. The church is also the site of the 'reconsiliacion' of man, and this is significant because of the responsibility that the sermon then places on the individual to protect the sanctity of the church. 'Reconsiliacion' here applies to the re-establishment of harmony between God and man and the verb 'reconcilen' is used to refer to the readmittance of sinners to the church after excommunication.[58] 'Reconcilen' also refers to the re-consecration of a church after desecration has taken place; in *Jacob's Well*, the author asserts that if 'þou diffoulyst þe place' then it 'nedyth to be reconsyled aȝen' (p. 130).[59] The connection which this establishes between the individual and the church is fundamental to the sermon's argument. The author continues:

O Lord, what this place is gretely to be a-dredde! For the place is holy, þe sacramentis that in it be made are holy, and seruyce þat in it is seide and songyn is holy, and God to whome al that parteyneþ is holy. And so, sires, owith ye to be holy in herte and in body þat ye may be the temples of God. (p. 164)

The holiness of the church inspires the same feeling of dread that Jacob expressed (Genesis, 28.17) and this is performed in the sermon by the retreat from the deictic 'this' to the definite article, 'the place'. The sanctity of the church requires a reciprocal holiness from the congregation who 'owith', with a sense of moral and legal obligation, to be 'holy in herte and in body' in order to become the temple of God.[60] The preposition 'in' is transferred from the church ('in' it prayers are made, 'in' it askers of grace are heard) to the body of the individual Christian, drawing on the imagery of the temple of God from 1 Corinthians, 3.16–17:

For it is writen þus: '*Templum Dei sanctum est quod estis vos. Et quicumque violauerit templum Dei, disperdet eum dominus Deus.*' He seiþ: 'þe temple of God is holy and that be ȝe, scilicet, men. And therfore who-so-euer fowleþ þat temple of God, the lord God schall

> destroye hem.' And therfore let vs kepe vs clene fro alle fowlynge of flesche and of body that we may worþily worschepe this solempnyte. And þerfore comeþ to your chirche and prayeþ God that he prayed in that temple, come and here the prayers and yeue large blessynge and graunte syche werkys for to worche þat ye may come to euerlastynge blisse. Amen. (p. 164)

The church and the body of the individual believer are interchangeable, and any act that 'fowleþ' (pollutes or defiles) either body is an act of sacrilege for which God will take vengeance.[61] The body of the individual must be kept clean in order to protect the purity of the church but as many of the narrative exempla that I will examine here demonstrate, not only was that obligation rarely kept, its violation provided a powerful opportunity for the sanctity of the church to be reaffirmed.

In her work on concepts of pollution and taboo, Mary Douglas defines dirt as disorder and argues that although 'disorder spoils pattern, it also provides the material of pattern'.[62] Moreover, eliminating dirt is 'not a negative movement but a positive effort to organise the environment'; 'far from being an aberration from the central project of religion', rituals of purification 'are positive contributions to atonement'.[63] While the sinful behaviour of the laity does pollute the sanctity of the church, I argue that the cleansing that takes place as a result makes more than a 'positive contribution to atonement'; it is, paradoxically, a necessity for the sanctity of the church to remain a visible, tangible presence. To return again to Mircea Eliade's argument, sanctity must be made manifest and that manifestation is effected here by narratives of pollution and disorder.[64] Such narratives demonstrate that sin is, to borrow Julian of Norwich's term, 'behovabil' (beneficial or necessary) because it provides the opportunity for the sacred order to be powerfully re-established and the profane to be expelled.[65]

John Mirk's dedication sermon supports this argument. Rather than emphasising the sanctity of the church, as the *Speculum Sacerdotale* does, Mirk's sermon underscores its dependence upon the congregation's good behaviour. He begins by establishing three primary reasons for church consecration: 'for þe chyrch clensyng, for devoute preying, and for þe dede byriing' (p. 249). The church is 'ordeynot þat criston pepull schulde come togydyr in charite to worcheppon hure God in rest and pes' and God 'ȝeveth hem hys blessyng and walkyth amongus hem' (p. 249). But this arouses the jealousy of the fiend and he 'secheth alle hys malys to sayon if he mowe be any way dryvon God away from hem, for wel he wotte þat God abyduth not þereas debate is and descencion' (p. 249). As a result, the consecration ceremony was established and Mirk declares, crucially, that:

> be holy preyer and halowinge scheo [the church] is clansed of þe fende and of hys malys, and hath no power aftur to comyn in chyrch but hit so be þat sum wykkyd lyuer þat is belafte wyth þe fende bryng hym ynto chyrch wyth hym. For also long os a man is owte of charite, þe fende is in hym and hath power oure hym. (p. 249)

The consecration ceremony is entirely efficacious in expunging the presence of the fiend, although as Mirk's exemplum goes on to demonstrate, he refuses to go quietly. At the consecration of a church, Mirk narrates, 'a swyn ran among þe pepules feet hyder and þidur, and so ȝode oute at þe chyrch dore', through which 'God schewuth opynly how þe fende be halowing of þe chirch was dryven oute of þe chyrch' (p. 249). But to show his displeasure, the fiend returned the following night and 'ran on þe chyrch wyth such a noyse þat he ferut alle þat herdon it' (pp. 249–50). Returning again the subsequent night, the fiend makes a 'more hydous noyse, as þagh alle þe chyrch hadde fallon down at onus' but then he finally leaves (p. 250). The devil's noise represents an attempt to establish an alternative, profane order, parodying the liturgical performance of the consecration ceremony itself. It sounds as though the church is on the point of collapse, but in fact the fiend's performance serves as a palpable, physical sign of the efficacy of the consecration ceremony. The foundations of the building tremble but ultimately the church is proven to be unshakeable, both physically and symbolically.

The same is not the case, however, in an exemplum known as the 'Usurer's Church' in *The Alphabet of Tales*. This exemplum shows that the consecration ceremony relies on the church-building process being virtuous in and of itself, otherwise the liturgical ritual is powerless to expel the fiend – or indeed to be performed at all. In the narrative, a usurer 'of his ravyn & his vsurye had byggid a kurk' (p. 198), and when the bishop and clergy arrive to consecrate the building, they sec a devil sitting upon the high altar:

> 'Why halows þou my kurk? Sese! for þe iuridiccion þeroff longis vnto me; ffor it is byggid all of ravyn and vsurie.' And with þis, þe bisshopp and his clerkis wer ferd and went þer ways. And onone as þai wer getten oute þer-of, þer was a grete noyce þer-in, and þe devull sett fire þerin & burnyd it vp & destroyed itt euere dele, att all folke mott se. (p. 199)

Here, because the church is built from ill-gotten gains, the devil is able to destroy it and assert legal 'iuridiccion' over 'my kurk'. In the version in *Jacob's Well*, the devil tells the bishop to 'cese of þin halwyng, for þis cherche longyth to me' (p. 203), which implies that the devil has his own profane consecration in mind. Both of these buildings are churches in appearance only. Their material coordinates have been constructed in order to frame a sacred space but because they have been built with the wages of sin, the sacred potential of the building cannot be activated. Without virtuous foundations, material architecture cannot become sacred space and the devil has every right to demolish it. The implication of this narrative, however, is that the innumerable churches that do remain standing across medieval England must have been constructed by virtuous builders and, therefore, their very existence testifies to the efficacious expulsion of the devil. As Mirk declares in his consecration sermon, the devil has no power to re-enter the church, unless a 'wykkyd lyuer [...] bryng hym into chyrch wyth hym' (p. 249).

This is shown to literally be the case in an exemplum in *The Alphabet of Tales* when a proud woman with an elaborate headdress enters the church:

> Sho was gaylie atyrid in cowrchevis, and sho had a passand lang tayle folowand hur, and þer was þer-vppon dawnsand a huge multitude of fendis, as it had bene blak men of Ynde, skornand with þer mowthes and clappand with þer handis. And they war als thykk as it had bene fyssh in a nett. (p. 395)

The simile 'as it had bene fyssh in a nett' parodies the parable of the fishing net (Matthew, 13.47–50), as the woman's train catches devils and brings them into the church. But the priest responds not by immediately banishing the fiends but by making them visible to the woman and the rest of the congregation for their edification:

> He commaundyd all þe peple to stand styll, and he coniurid þies fendis at þai sulde nott go away, & he made his prayer & besoght God att þe peple myght se þaim; & so þai did. And when þis womman saw at þe fendis had so mekull power on hur for þe pryde of hur clothyng, & at þe peple yrkid for to luke on hur, sho went home and skyftid hur clothing & wold neuer were tayle after. (p. 595)

The priest's strategy of making the consequences of the woman's pride visible to the congregation shames her into repentance. She removes the excess material from her clothing both because she recognises the power that the fiends have over her and because the people ‘yrkid for to luke on hur’. The meanings of the verb ‘irken’ range from reluctance to disgust.[66] In a wall painting depicting gossiping women at Eaton, Norfolk, the fiends present appear to be defecating and farting, and Miriam Gill has argued that the painting’s didacticism works by a strategy of ‘revulsion and aversion’.[67] The same applies here as the people are reluctant, or indeed too disgusted, to look upon the woman’s ‘tayle’, with a possible pun here on ‘tayle’ as genitalia.[68] Fashionable dress as a conduit for sin is also depicted in two wall paintings of the Seven Deadly Sins at Alveley, Shropshire, and Raunds, Northamptonshire.[69] At Raunds, the sins are vomited out of the mouths of dragons that issue from the clothing of a fashionably dressed woman who represents Pride. The figure of Death pierces the woman’s right side with a long spear, and in a parody of Christ’s side wound giving birth to the church, the woman’s body engenders the deadly sins. At Alveley, the sins emerge from her lower body and, as in the *Alphabet* exemplum, she is wearing a long train. Both paintings offer a stark warning of the hidden cost of proud clothing, but whereas the woman in the *Alphabet* repents and shortens her garments, the women in the paintings eternally issue forth the deadly sins, ready to be caught up by the clothing of another unwary parishioner.

The threat that the laity pose when they bring the devil into the church with them is foregrounded in the *Alphabet* exemplum because the episode takes place at the ‘kurk-dure’ (p. 595), a dangerously open space that must be carefully policed by the clergy. Boundaries are a particular area of concern in the protection of sacred space because where they are not maintained, pollution may more easily occur. Mary Douglas argues that ‘uncleanness is matter out of place’ and this idea is fundamental to the medieval definition of sacrilege.[70] In *Handlyng Synne*, Mannyng explains that sacrilege includes instances in which ‘þyng vnhalewed were forgete, / Þat in holy cherche were lete’ or conversely if ‘halewed þyng yn ouþer stede lay’ (8613–15). Objects must be kept in their rightful place, consecrated or otherwise. Sacrilege also covers ‘vyleyny’ in the churchyard (8652), and here Mannyng focuses in particular on the pollution that comes from the defecation of animals. He singles out priests that ‘late here bestes fyle þer ynne’ (8662), and the verb ‘filen’ here has a double meaning, both to pollute through the voiding of excrement and to desecrate or profane by rendering morally corrupt through sinful acts.[71] Mannyng then tells an exemplum concerning a knight whose manor is near the church and 'as often falles, / Broke were þe cherche ȝerd walles' (8677–8), resulting in the knight's beasts having 'fyled oueral' the churchyard (8682). A bondman confronts the knight, declaring that it is wrong to 'late ȝoure bestes fyle þus þese graues' because 'þere mennes bones shuld lye: / Bestes shulde do no vyleynye' (8689–90). The knight's 'vyleynye' is all the more apparent because it is exposed by a lower-class bondsman or 'vilein'.[72] When the knight protests that he will not 'wrschepe swyche cherles bones' (8694), the bondsman educates him that 'erles' and 'cherles' are made from the same earth and will be buried in the same churchyard (8699–8704), and it is only after this lesson has been delivered that he 'closed þe cherche ȝerd' so that no beasts may 'fyle þer ynne' (8711–13). The pollution of the churchyard enables Mannyng both to emphasise the importance of maintaining the boundaries of sacred space and to make a broader point about social hierarchy being dissolved in death. The churchyard is 'oure long hous [...] to reste yn tyl þe day of dome' and therefore we must 'ȝyf we were kynde, / Kepe hyt clene with gode mynde' (8657–60). Keeping the churchyard clean constitutes 'kynde' or natural behaviour; it is villainous to do otherwise.

While the churchyard is in danger of pollution from animal defecation, the interior of the church is threatened by the congregation's misbehaviour. As we have already seen, visual representations of Tutivillus appear to show him encouraging the laity to gossip, and in a lively exemplum in *Jacob's Well*, a fiend gleefully requests that an abbot accompany him to the church to 'se what we do' there (p. 237). Once inside the church, the abbot discovers 'dyuerse feendys [...] rennynge al abowte in þe cherche', tempting the congregation into sin in a variety of ways, from 'puttynge here fyngerys to þe eyȝen of summe' so that they fall asleep to 'skyppedyn a-forn hem in lyknes of wommen' so that they are 'temptyd to leccherye' (p. 237). The fiends also 'grecyd here lyppes wyth here oynementys in here box' so that the laity 'iangelyd, & telde talys' (p. 237). In an appearance with his fellow devil, Ruffin, in the alliterative stanza in John Audelay's *Book* known as *Over-Hippers and Skippers*, Tutivillus's role is to record rather than to tempt:

> Over-hippers and skippers, moterers and mumlers,
> Tytyvyllis tytild here wordus and takes ham to hys pray;
> Japers and janglers, haukeers and hunters –
> The holé servys of God thai schend when they say.

> Rofyn wyl rede hom ful redely in his rolle anoder day,
> When thay ben called to here cowntis and to here rekenyng –
> How thay han sayde here servys, the Prince of Heven to pay.[73]

Tutivillus 'tytild', that is chronicled or inscribed, their words and 'takes ham to hys pray', punning on 'prey' and the prayers that the laity should be offering, rather than disturbing 'the holé [holy] servys of God'.[74] Ruffin assists Tutivillus by reading the account of the laity's sins when they are called 'to here cowntis and to here rekenyng' (Matthew, 12.36–7) and he appears again in Audelay's *Virtues of the Mass*, sitting by a window 'with pen and enke and parchemen' to write down the gossip of the women in the church.[75] In this poem, there is so much jangling to record that Ruffin fills his scroll, and when he pulls it with his teeth to make more space, he falls backwards and 'smot with his choule [jowel] / Agayns the marbys [marble] stone', making St Augustine burst out laughing.[76] When Augustine reports to Pope Gregory what has happened, he takes him to the window where 'blak blood he se espred / Apon the aschelere [masonry] even.'[77] The fiend's injury leaves a profane mark upon the masonry, and this story could be employed to explain and make didactic use of an imperfection in the church.

Audelay reminds the reader to 'kepe you out of Godis wreke, / Fore ther is no word that ye speke, / Bot ye don syn!'[78] But in this version of the narrative, the focus is displaced from the sin on to the misfortunes of the demon. In his zealous pursuit of recording the laity's gossip, Ruffin hurts himself and the exemplum concludes with Augustine and Gregory gazing at the spectacle of the demon's black blood upon the church pavement, rather than holding the gossips to account. In John Mirk's version of the Tutivillus story, however, the attention is firmly upon the sin itself and how the demon can help to rectify it. Mirk includes the narrative under his second reason for church consecration in the dedication sermon, 'devoute preying' (p. 249). He laments the state of the church, observing that while God himself declares that 'my hous is an hous of prayeres', 'more is þe harme now, it is makut an hous of dadul, of wyspering and rownyng and of spekyng of vanite and of othur fulthe' (p. 250). The church has become a house of 'dadul' or gossip, as Mirk's exemplum explains:

> Wherefore I rede how, as an holy byschop was at hys masse, hys dekon turnot to byddon þe pepul bowen hem downe to þe blessyng. Þan seygh he too wommen rowne togedyr, and þe fende satte in

> here nekkys wrytyng on a long rolle as faste os he mythe. Þan aftur masse be bydyng of þe dekon þe byschop sende aftur þese wommen and askud hem how þei haddon ben occupyod in þe masse-tyme. Þan saydon þei how þey haddon sayde hure Paternoster. Þan þe bischoppe commaundud þe fend to redon þat he hadde wryton. And whan he had red all þat þei hadde talkud of, þei fellon doun to þe grounde and askud for mercy mekly, and so weron browth oute of þat cursyd boke. (pp. 250–1)

In *Jacob's Well*, Tutivillus declares that he writes down 'þise talys of þe peple in þis cherche, to recordyn hem a-fore god at þe doom for here dampnacyon' (p. 115) but in Mirk's narrative, the fiend presents his evidence to the ecclesiastical hierarchy within the church itself. The deacon tells the bishop what he has seen during the mass and when the women deny gossiping, compounding their sin, the bishop 'commaundud þe fend to redon þat he hadde wryton'. The documentary evidence provided by Tutivillus is the direct cause of the women's repentence and, consequently, the cleansing of the church from idle gossip. Once the women repent, their gossip is expunged from the fiend's 'cursyd boke' and order is restored in the church. The fiend and the bishop collaborate in protecting the church's status as a house of prayer and although the bishop appears to be unable to command the women to tell the truth, he does command the fiend to present his evidence. In Mannyng's version of the exemplum, the fiend hides 'pryuyly byhynde here bak', hoping to hide his activities from the unsuspecting congregation and priest in order to use the information he has collected to further his own fiendish agenda (9287). Mirk's fiend, however, not only sits openly in the church scribbling down the gossip, but actively assists the bishop in rooting out sin, performing a collaborative role by keeping a close watch on the congregation while the bishop performs the mass and publicly declaring their sins once it has ended. Moreover, by the end of the narrative, the fiend has become an instrument of reconciliation because by revealing the sacrilegious behaviour of the gossips, he causes them to repent, the implication being that if he had not recorded his evidence, they would have continued in their sin and the church would still have been polluted by their jangling.

In the treatise on the divine service for the Bridgettines at Syon Abbey called *The Myroure of Oure Ladye*, Tutivillus declares, 'I do myne offyce that is commytted vnto me', and in this way he imitates the clergy's performance of their ritual offices.[79] His office in Mirk's exemplum is to detect and provide evidence for the successful prosecution of sin in the church – he is both a witness and a legal scribe, and Michael Camille relates this to the increase in the role of scriptoria in the law and production of legal documents in the Middle Ages.[80] Churches were closely involved in legal business in this period as they were often venues for ecclesiastical courts, and so the activities of Tutivillus in Mirk's narrative would not only have been familiar to a lay audience, but additionally unnerving because they would have been aware of the power wielded by legal scribes and the earthly punishments that could await them as a result of a court's decisions.

The concept of the devil's own ritual practice can also be found in the pastoral care topos of the devil's church or tavern. At the beginning of Chaucer's *Pardoner's Tale*, the company of young folk that 'haunteden folye' can be found performing 'the devel sacrifise / Withinne that develes temple in cursed wise.'[81] The dancing girls, singers, and fruit-sellers in the tavern are described as 'the verray develes officeres' that 'kyndle and blowe the fyr of lecherye', establishing a profane order in an alternative profane space.[82] *The Book of Vices and Virtues* similarly locates the devil's space in the tavern and, moreover, constructs it in deliberate opposition to sacred space:

> Þe tauerne is þe deueles scole hous, for þere studieþ his disciples, and þere lerneþ his scolers, and þere is his owne chapel, þere men and wommen redeþ and syngeþ and serueþ hym, and þere he doþ his myracles as longeþ þe deuel to do. In holy chirche is God ywoned to do myracles and schewe his vertues: þe blynde to seen, þe croked to gon riȝt, brynge wode men in-to hire riȝt wytte, doumbe men to speke, deue men here herynge. But þe deuel doþ þe contrarie of al þis in þe tauerne.[83]

The devil's tavern has its 'owne chapel' and the miracles of God have their counterpart in the devil's miracles which include gluttony, lechery, swearing, lying, and 'many oþere manere synnes' (p. 54). The tavern is described as a 'stronge castel or hous for to werre wiþ God and alle þe halewen' (p. 54) but what is evident from the texts and visual images that I have been discussing in this chapter is that to think of the house of God and the devil's house as oppositional spaces is a simplification. There is a devil's chapel ready to emerge from within the parish church itself as a direct result of lay misbehaviour. Furthermore, the devil's officers do not always wage war upon God and the saints. In relation to the burial of the dead, they often intervene to purify the church from profane contamination.

In Mirk's dedication sermon, he explains that the third reason for church consecration is 'for þe dede byriing' (p. 249). Burial in the church or churchyard ensures that the dead are prayed for by the living community and, moreover, it guarantees that 'þe bodyes of þe dede schul lyg þer in reste wythowte travayle or vexing of þe fende' (p. 251). Mirk elaborates with particular reference to burial within the church building:

> Wherefore þe fende hath no power to do nowte to none þat is byryed in criston byrines, bot hyt so be þat he haue so trespased þat he be not worthy to lygge þere. For Iohn Belut telluth how none schulde ben beryed in chyrch but þe patrones of þe chyrch, and prestes and clerkys þat defenduth þe chyrch from gostely enmyes wyth hure preyeres, and othur patrones þat defenduth hem from bodyly enemyes. For such haue ben byried þat in þe morow þe cors hath ben caste oute of þe chyrch and alle þe cloþus lafte in þe byrynes. (p. 251)

In this case, the corpse will be 'caste oute of þe chyrch' in order to cleanse the building of the profane matter that is 'out of place' in its sacred confines, to return to Mary Douglas's theory of pollution.

In Mirk's sermon the impetus for church cleansing comes from angels who appear to the ecclesiastical hierarchy in order to encourage them to keep their own houses in order. In the first exemplum, an angel tells the churchwarden to remove the sinful individuals that he has buried or he will be dead within thirty days, 'and so was, for he wolde notte don os he was bydon' (p. 251). In the second, longer exemplum, the king of France is damned because rather than defending the church, 'he berafte Holy Chyrch hure ryghtes' (p. 251). An angel informs the bishop and orders him to open the king's tomb and 'see þe sothe' (p. 251). When this is done, a great dragon flies out, leaving the tomb 'brennyng wythine os it hadde ben a knylle-mowth' and Mirk concludes, wryly, that therefore 'byriing in holy place helputh not ham þat ben dampned' (p. 251). In this narrative, the king's body appears to have been metamorphosed into a dragon, a creature commonly associated with the devil, and he casts himself out of the holy place, leaving the tomb burning like the mouth of a kiln, an image that we might associate with hell. The burning fissure in the church building is palpable evidence of the violence that the king did to the church by attacking its holy rights and the fiendish creature that flees from the tomb demonstrates not only that the church will not tolerate the presence of an unrepentant sinner, but that the profane dead are themselves all too eager to escape sacred space.

The sanctity and integrity of the church cannot be maintained if it is polluted by a sinner and so the body, the sign of the sin, must be expelled from its physical confines. Sacred space cannot help the sinner but the sinner can, paradoxically, help a sacred space by creating the opportunity for performative purification. Sanctity must be made manifest in order to be visible and the expulsion of sinful bodies is a clear example of the inability of sacred space to tolerate profane contamination. This purification process is often aided by devils that enter the church to claim jurisdiction over the sinful dead. In *Handlyng Synne*, for example, Mannyng tells the story of a man called Valentine who was 'playtour' (lawyer or advocate) at a church, 'more for mede þan goddes onour' (8748–50). Valentine is buried inside the church and the same evening the churchwardens are awoken by a 'ruly and shryl' cry, as though someone 'were put out aȝens hys wyl' (8757–8). When they go to investigate, they see many fiends around the man's body:

And of hys graue þey vp hym pulde;
Out of þe cherche drawe hym þey wlde;
Þe deueles drowe hym by þe fete
As hyt were kareyne þat dogges ete. (8763–66)

The wardens run away in fear and when they return the following morning, they search for the body, opening the doors of the church and looking about. They find the body lying outside the church, 'þe fete ybound to gedyr ful fast, / And as a foule kareyne kast' (8777–78). Mannyng's twofold use of the image of carrion emphasises the degradation of Valentine's body and the repeated use of the preposition 'out' – 'pute oute', 'oute of þe cherche', 'lyggyng þere wyþ owte' (8776) – reinforces the importance of expelling profane matter from the church building. Mannyng justifies Valentine's removal by the fiends and their attack on his body by arguing that Valentine's tomb, as well as his lack of virtue, is to blame:

Þer he lay fyrst, he was nat wrþy,
But hys soule had pyne þe more
For þe pompe & pryde þat he was leyd þore.
Lordes are bysy aboute to haue
Proud stones lyggyng an hygh on here graue.
Þurgh þat pryde þey mowe be lore,
Þogh þey had do no synne byfore.
Hyt helpeþ ryght noght þe tumbe of pryde,
Whan þe soule fro pyne may hyt nat hyde. (8780–88)

The usurer's church could not be consecrated because it was funded by ill-gotten gains but a proud tomb endangers salvation, even if the individual 'had do no synne byfore'. And yet despite this warning, fine tombs not only continued to be built but to be valued as ornaments of the churches in which they were erected.[84]

Sinners are frequently subjected to violent post-mortem punishment in addition to being forcibly removed from the church by fiends. In his sermon for the third Sunday of Lent, in which Mirk preaches against 'foly speche and rybaudy and harlotry' (p. 84), he includes an exemplum about an abbess who was a 'clene womman of hur body os for dede of lechery, but scheo hadde grete lust and gamon to talk þerof' (p. 85). When the abbess is dead, 'scheo was byried in þe schyrch':

> On þe nyghte aftur, fendus commyn and tokon vp þe body and beton it wyth brennyng schoureges fro þe navel vpwarde, þat it was also blake as pyche; bot from þe nauel dounwarde þei myght do noght þerto, for þat parte schone as þe sonne. (p. 85)

The abbess cries out, rousing two of her sisters, and her reanimated body explains to them that while she was 'clene maydon as for any dede of flesche', she had 'grete luste to spekon of fylthe of þe flesshe and oþur rybaudy, þerfore þat parte of my body þat is gylty it hath þe penaunce as ȝe sene' (p. 85). Like Tutivillus with his scroll of jangling, the fiends act as instruments of justice here, marking the abbess's body with the sign of her sin. The 'fylthe' that she speaks pollutes the church but her punishment provides an opportunity for her to repent in the presence of other members of the community. She concludes her speech by begging that her sisters 'preyen for me, for þorgh ȝoure preyeres I may ben holpyn. And beth ware be me in tyme comyng' (p. 85). The abbess's wicked living has allowed the fiends to enter the church and they have asserted their rights to punish the part of her body that has committed the sin, beating it with burning scourges until it is 'blake as pyche'. The tortures meted out to sinners by demons would be familiar from all visual depictions of the Last Judgement, and here the abbess's body, black as pitch above and shining like the sun below, encapsulates the doom of both the saved and the damned, and the choice that faces all medieval Christians in their conduct.[85]

In the version of the tale in *Jacob's Well*, the nun's body is literally divided in two by the fiends. We are told that the 'kepere of þe cherch', who guards and protects the material building and its contents, witnesses the fiends punishing the nun before the altar:

> Þe feendys, wyth a brennyng sawe, kuttyn here in þe myddys, & þe ouer part of here þei brentyn fro þe wast vpward for here ydell woordys. Þe nethir parte fro þe wast dounward was hole, for sche was chast in body. And on the morwe, on þe paument it was verryly sen where sche was brent. (p. 232)

The nun is cut in half with a burning saw and the sinful part of her body is burned. The association of the punishment with hell could not be clearer as the preacher concludes the sermon with direct reference to the afterlife:

> I drede me, þanne, ȝe þat arn ydell in word, thouȝt, & dede, schal be brent & sawyd wel werse þan sche was, but ȝe leuyn it. Þerfore, caste oute þe grauel & sand of ydelnes wyth good occupacyon, þat ȝe be sauyd fro sawyng & brennyng of feendys to ioye and blysse euerelastynge! (p. 233)

The nun's punishment acts as a violent and performative *memento mori*, reminding the audience of what will await those who are idle in 'word, thouȝt, & dede' in the afterlife, the tricolon a common warning to the laity of the vast array of opportunities for sin. The consequences for sacred space of the fiend's violence are considerable. The dismembering of her body before the altar acts as a ritual of purification in which the fiends are integral to the cleansing of sacred space. The violence of the bodily punishment is presented as necessary to purge the space of sin but for the duration of the act, the space transforms into a fiery hell, ruled by devils. It is only in the version in the *Alphabet* that the chaste half of the woman's body is 'putt in þe grafe agayn' (p. 305), restoring the sacred order. Both versions highlight the physical evidence left in the church as a result of the punishment. The pavement has been physically marked by sin and although this acts as a warning to the congregation, it is also a constant reminder that the church's imperfections are a result of the congregation's sin.

Fiends do not always enter the church and claim what is theirs without a fight, however. The *Alphabet* tells of a witch who instructs her children, a monk and a nun, to bury her in a tomb in the church covered 'stronglie both with lead & strong yrn' and bound with 'iij strang chynys' (p. 487). They are told to perform the mass and pray for her, and if she lies in the church 'sekurlie iij dayes', they should bury her in the earth (p. 487). The first two nights of her funeral vigil, 'feendys brak þe yatis of þe kurk' and break two of the chains upon her tomb but the middle chain remains intact. On the third night, 'aboute cokkraw', an appropriate time for a woman who has denied God, 'suche a throng of fendis' enter the church that 'þai at saw it semyd at þe temple turnyd vpsadown' (p. 487). The 'maste vgsom' fiend enters the church and calls the woman by name, commanding her to rise up from her tomb:

> And sho answerd again & sayde sho mot not for þe bondis at was bon aboute þe tombe. And he bad lowse þaim, and onone at his commandment þe chyne braste as it had bene hardis, & þe coueryng of þe tombe flow off. And þer he tuke hur oppynlie befor all men & bare her oute of þe kurk. And þer befor þe yatis þer was ordand a blak hors, & þat ane vglie, & here-vppon was sho sett. & þan onone sho & all þis felowshup vanysshid away. (p. 488)

Despite her elaborate security system, the fiend's commands break the witch's chains and she is released from burial in the sacred space of the church, proving Mirk's dictum that 'byriing in holy place helputh not ham þat ben dampned' (p. 251). The church is transformed into hell as the fiend performs a parody of Christ's harrowing, breaking down the church gates and unbinding the witch's chains (cf. Matthew, 16.19). In the version in *Jacob's Well*, the fiend declares that 'for þi synne þe cheyne schal breke' and the witch leaves the church 'roryng' before being set upon by a 'blak brennyng deuyl' who bears her to the 'pytt of helle' (p. 187). The *Jacob's Well* sermon concludes by making clear the relationship between the pit of hell and the sinner's own body, invoking the metaphor of the well of the soul that is the overarching allegory of the sermon cycle: 'Why? For þe scauel [spade] of schryfte had noȝt cast out þe wose [mud/slime] of here synne. Þerfore, beeth ware, & wyth þis scauel ferme [cleanse] ȝoure pytt!' (p. 187). The pit of hell and the pit of the sinner's body are equated. The word 'ferme', to cleanse, is often used to refer to the cleaning out of privies and here, rather than the temple of God, the body of the Christian is a polluted pit of sin.[86] In the prologue to *Jacob's Well*, the author explains that his purpose is to make a deep well out of a shallow pit (p. 1). The pit is the body and it is filled with cursed water, beneath which is the 'deep wose', the slime and mud, of the Seven Deadly Sins (p. 2). This slime will infect sacred space unless it is cleansed by the fiends who remove the offending material – in this case the body of the witch – and take it to where it truly belongs, the pit of hell.

What all of the narratives discussed here demonstrate is that sacred space thrives on the challenge provided by profane desecration. Gossiping in church and the burial of the unrepentant dead are an opportunity for the church to be cleansed and for the purification effected by the consecration ceremony to be reasserted and made manifest in present time. The agents of this cleansing are, paradoxically, fiends and demons such as Tutivillus who have been granted power over sacred space by the sinner's actions; wicked living, as Mirk recognised in his dedication sermon, empowers the fiend to re-enter the church and act accordingly. Mary Douglas argues that eliminating dirt and pollution represents a 'positive contribution to atonement' as through rituals of purification, 'symbolic patterns are worked out and publically displayed'.[87] The irruption of the profane in the sacred space of the church requires atonement but that atonement, as we have seen in the burial narratives, is not performed without a considerable display of violence and hostility. Mircea Eliade argues that the fundamental 'ambivalence' of the sacred is that it is at once 'sacred and defiled', and that defilement is shown in the physical traces left behind by the punishment of sinful bodies, such as scorched pavements or the devil's blood on the walls.[88] In the final section of this chapter, I will turn to the relationship between violence and sanctity in the parish church with reference to René Girard's argument that 'violence is the heart and secret soul of the sacred'.[89] Drawing together my primary arguments in this chapter – that the animation of religious objects contributes to sacred space and that the profane is necessary for the manifestation of sanctity – I will focus on the depiction of the crucified Christ in wall paintings and medieval lyrics to argue that violence is indeed at the heart of the sacred, but far from being secret, that violence is openly and repeatedly exposed to public scrutiny.

'Looke on my woundis, thynk on my passioun': Violence and the sacred

In the verses spoken by Christ on the cross in John Lydgate's *Testament*, the refrain centres on the idea of sacrifice. Christ is 'like a lambe offred in sacryfice'; 'for mannes offence', he is 'offered in sacryfice'; and Christ tells the reader that 'whan thou were lost, thy sowle ageyn to fynde / My blod I offred for the in sacryfice.'[90] Verses from the *Testament* are famously painted on the walls of Holy Trinity church, Long Melford, Suffolk, and I will return to the importance of this emplacement later, but here I want to focus on Christ as a sacrificial victim who sheds his blood for mankind's sin with reference to René Girard's theory of violence and the sacred. Girard argues that 'the operations of violence and the sacred are ultimately the same process', citing the root of 'sacred' in the Latin *sacer* which means both sacred and accursed.[91] For Girard, the sacred 'encompasses the maleficent as well as the beneficent', and I have already shown how the sanctity of the parish church is sustained by the violent punishment of transgressors.[92] Girard sees violence and sanctity as 'inseparable' and this is nowhere more evident in medieval Christianity than in Christ's sacrifice for the salvation of mankind. Christ offered himself up as a 'substitute for all the members of the community', thus acting in accordance with Girard's theory of the sacrificial victim.[93] Girard theorises that the 'more critical the situation, the more "precious" the victim must be' and there is no victim more precious in the Christian church than the Son of God.[94]

Christ's sacrifice was made present in the church on a daily basis through the ritual performance of the mass and through the visual imagery of Christ's bleeding and crucified body in crucifixes and in wall paintings such as the Last Judgement. In *Dives and Pauper*, an explicit link is made between ritual and crucifix when Pauper explains why priests have an image of the cross before them during mass:

> For euery messe synggyng is a special mende makyng of Cristys passioun, and þerfore he hatȝ aforn hym a crucifix to doon hym han þe more fresh mende as he owyȝt to han of Cristys passioun [...] Afforn þis ymage þe preist seyȝt his messe and makȝt þe heyest preyerys þat holy cherche kan deuyse for sauacioun of þe queke and of þe dede. He halt vp hese hondys, he lowtyȝt, he knelyȝt in caas, and al þe wurshepe he can doon he doth. Ouyrmore, he offryȝt vp þe heyest sacrifyce and þe best offryng þat ony herte can deuyse, þat is Crist, Godys sone of heuene vnder forme of bred and of wyn. (pp. 86–7).

The performance of the mass is a 'mende makyng', that is, an atonement that re-enacts Christ's passion, offering up God's son in the form of bread and wine, 'þe heyest sacrifyce and þe best offryng þat ony herte can deuyse'.[95] The role of the crucifix is to help the priest to have 'þe more fresh mende' of the passion, introducing a pun on 'mende' as penance and 'mende' as mind.[96] The mass is an atonement but it is also a 'mende makyng' in the sense that it brings Christ's passion to mind. Indeed, the ritual aims to make Christ's passion 'fresh' in the mind of the priest, 'fresh' here meaning 'of recent making or occurrence, new'.[97] This term is used by Margery Kempe in her *Book* when she weeps at the sight of the pietà in a Norwich church, declaring that Christ's death is as 'fresch to me as he had deyd this same day, and so me thynkyth it awt to be to you and to alle Cristen pepil. We awt evyr to han mende of hys kendnes and evyr thynkyn of the dolful deth that he deyd for us.'[98] The pietà, like the crucifix in *Dives and Pauper*, helps Margery to keep Christ's death in 'mende' as freshly as if it had taken place that day.[99] The word 'freshe' in Middle English is also used of Christ's wounds to indicate that they are newly inflicted. The *Prick of Conscience*, for example, declares that on Judgement Day, 'Crist sal shew þan his woundes wyde [...] þat fressche sal sem and alle bledand'.[100]

Christ's blood was a ubiquitous presence in the medieval church. As Caroline Walker Bynum reminds us, crucifixion was not a bloody death, but by the end of the Middle Ages, depictions of Christ in the textual and visual record were awash with blood as a result of the violence perpetrated on his body.[101] This is clear from Mirk's description of Christ's suffering in his Good Friday sermon: 'þei buffettud hym and hubud hym and bobud hym, and aftur strypud hym nakud and bete hym so dispytowslyche wyth scowreges alle hys body, so þat from hys toppe to his to was noþing lafte holle on hym, bot alle ranne on blode' (p. 107). Medieval wall paintings of the Doom frequently emphasise the presence of Christ's blood. At Rotherfield, East Sussex, for example, the figure of Christ is depicted raising his hands to display his wounds and blood runs copiously down his arms and from the wound in his side.[102] Christ's blood had multiple, often contradictory, significances in the period. It was a sign of the violence perpetrated on Christ by mankind, and therefore the fresh streams pouring out of the wounds in a Doom painting such as Rotherfield were accusatory, demanding repentance from the viewer. In a memorable story in Mirk's *Festial*, when Christ appears at the deathbed of an unrepentant man, he thrusts his hand into his side wound and flings a handful of blood in the man's face, declaring: 'þis schal be redy tokun betwyx þe and me in day off dome þat I wolde haue ȝeuen þe mercy and þou woldust notte' (p. 136). In the Eucharistic cup, Christ's blood was the embodiment of salvation. In the church, to shed blood was a heinous act of sacrilege but the presence of Christ's blood, conversely, was a 'sign of desecration that makes holy; hence it sets apart, consecrates'.[103] Christ's blood is both sacred and profane, both maleficent and beneficent, to return to Girard, and this can also be seen in narrative exempla concerning the desecration of the crucifix by the Jews.

In Mirk's sermon for the Exaltation of the Holy Cross, he tells the story of a Jew who came into a church and, 'for he segh no man þerine, he ȝode to a rode and, for grete envye þat he hadde to Criste, wyth his swerde he cutte þe rode þrote' (p. 227). The crucifix immediately starts to bleed and the Jew is covered in blood:

> Þe blode sprente on hys cloþes so þat hit be-spredde alle hys cloþes wyth blode. And whan he segh hymself so be-bledde, he was adredde. Wherefore he toke þis rode and hydde it in a priuey place. (pp. 227–8)

The attack upon the crucifix is both an act of desecration and a consecration. The Jew violently slits Christ's throat and then attempts to cover up what he has done by hiding the crucifix in a 'pruiey place', 'pruiey' here meaning secret but also punning on the noun 'privy' and its associations with pollution.[104] But the Jew's act results in a miracle that confirms the sanctity of the crucifix and the real presence of Christ. Bettina Bildhauer argues that 'what counts as Christ's body was often proven through blood, as when a desecrated host begins to bleed'.[105] If a material object such as the crucifix bleeds, it must count as the body of Christ. Like the Merciful Knight whose virtuous conduct caused the crucifix to embrace him, the sacrilegious behaviour of the Jew also generates a miraculous response. And as a direct result, the Jew converts to Christianity. He is accosted by a Christian man in the street who demands to know of the 'man-queller' where he has been and what he has done with the man he has slain. The Jew tries to deny the charge but Christ's blood on his clothing accuses him and he falls to his knees, acknowledging the 'grete myght' of the Christian God. He cries 'Cryste, mercy' with all his heart and converts. Mirk then commands the listener to follow his example: 'Now ȝe schul knelon adoun and pray to hym þat schedde hys blode on þe cros for ȝow and alle mankynde' (p. 228). When hearing this sermon delivered in the church, the cross upon which Christ died is visually and materially present, on the rood screen, in stained glass, and in wall paintings. The crucifix in the story and the crucifix in the church are aligned and the listener is reminded of their duty to venerate Christ and the cross.

The integral relationship between Christ's bleeding body and the church building is evident from a number of Middle English texts. In Lydgate's poem *Cristes Passioun*, Christ states:

> Whan Longious spere thorugh myn herte Ran,
> And blood & water went be my sides doun,
> Tyme of my passioun, þe byldyng fyrst began.[106]

Lydgate draws on the symbolism of blood and water representing the sacraments of baptism and Eucharist, and the birth of the church. But he materialises the image of Ecclesia being born from the side of Christ.[107] 'Þe byldyng' of the church as a sacred architecture and a community began at the very moment when Christ's body was wounded by Longinus's spear. The Middle English Dictionary suggests that in rare cases 'byldyng' can be used to gloss the Latin *aedificatio* and in Lydgate's lyric, Christ's words 'edify' the congregation about the history of the church.[108] In *Dives and Pauper*, the church building is related to the wounds in Christ's feet. When Dives asks how he should read the crucifix, Pauper explains that he must 'take heid' of all of Christ's wounds individually. For example:

> Take heid also be þe ymage how hese feet weryn naylid to þe tree and stremedyn on blode for to destroyin þe synne of slaugthe in Godys seruyse, and make an ende of slaugthe in Godys seruyse and hyȝe þin foot to Godys hous and to Godys seruyse. (p. 84)

Christ's bleeding feet testify to the importance of presence in the church. The reader must use their own feet to carry them to the church and perform the devotions that Christ's sacrifice demands.

This passage on Christ's wounds in *Dives and Pauper* concludes by interpreting Christ's position on the crucifix as a symbol of his readiness to embrace and welcome the viewer:

> And, as Seynt Bernard byddyȝt, take heid be þe ymage how his heid is bowyd doun to the, redy to kyssyn the and comyn at on wyt the. See how hese armys and hese hondys been spred abrod on þe tree in tokene þat he is redy to fangyn the and halsyn the and kyssyn the and takyn the to his mercy. See how his syde was openyd and his herte clouyn on too in tokene þat his herte is alwey opyn to the, redy to louyn the and to forȝeuyn the alle trespas ȝyf þu wylt amende the and askyn mercy. Take heid also how hese feet weryn naylyd wol harde to þe tree in tokene þat he wyl nought flein awey from the but abydyn wyt the and duellyn wyt the wytouten ende. (pp. 84–5)

Christ's feet are nailed to the cross to signify that he will 'abydyn wyt the' and his arms are spread abroad to show that he is ready to embrace the viewer and take them to his mercy. The interpretation of his arms recalls the embrace of the Merciful Knight discussed above, presenting the crucifix as a devotional object with the potential for miraculous animation. This potentiality is important for my final selection of material for this chapter, Middle English lyrics spoken by Christ from the cross. These lyrics give Christ a voice and, more specifically, they give the Christ of devotional images in the church a voice in the vernacular. The transference of this voice by the viewer on to the image in their parish church animates the Christ figure, investing him with the potentiality that Pauper identifies, and reinforces the sanctity of the church that is tied to the display of Christ's bleeding wounds.

A number of lyrics survive in which Christ speaks to the viewer from the cross, commanding that they stop and take heed of his wounded body, based on the 'Reproaches' or *Improperia* from the Good Friday liturgy. Holly Johnson notes that the *Improperia* were chanted during the ritual of creeping to the cross and argues that 'such rituals were intended to re-enact the events of Good Friday, making them present again and drawing the participants into these events as if they were there'.[109] The Middle English lyrics operate in precisely the same way, making Christ present in the vernacular for the lay audience. In the fourteenth-century lyric known as *Abide, Ye Who Pass By*, the reader is addressed as follows:

> Abyde, gud men, & hald yhour pays,
> And here what god him-seluen says,
> Hyngand on þe rode.
> Man & woman þat bi me gase,
> Luke vp to me & stynt þi pase,
> For þe I sched my blode.[110]

The viewer on the point of passing by the cross is accosted and obliged to 'abyde' and look up at Christ hanging on the cross.

> Be-hald my body or þou gang,
> And think opon my payns strang,
> And styll als stane þou stand.
> Bihald þi self þe soth, & se
> How I am hynged here on þis tre
> And nayled fute & hand.[111]

The viewer is commanded to behold for themselves Christ's crucified body, how he is hanging on 'þis tre'. The deixis brings the viewer into close proximity with the cross.

Behald my heued, bi-hald my fete,
And of ma mysdedes luke þou lete;
Behald my grysely face
And of þi syns ask aleggance
And in my mercy haue affyance
And þou sall gett my grace.[112]

The beholding of Christ's head, feet, and grisly face demands that the viewer refrain from committing more sins, but they are offered a promise of grace in return for their 'affyaunce' in Christ's mercy, 'affiaunce' meaning confidence and faith but also a pledge of loyalty or solemn promise.[113] Another lyric called *Thou Sinful Man that By Me Goes* works in a similar way. Christ addresses a reluctant viewer whom he must convince to 'turn þi face' towards him, reprimanding him, 'Man, fra me þou ga not ȝit!'[114] Both lyrics construct a viewer who is passing by the cross and employ proximal deixis to encourage the viewer to remain 'here' by the tree. In *Abide, Ye Who Pass By*, the viewer is compelled to stand 'styll als stane', fixated and unable to move away from the sight of Christ's body. Such lyrics operate as passion meditations, enabling the reader to imagine themselves at the foot of the cross in Calvary, as Nicholas Love advocates in *The Mirror of the Blessed Life of Jesus Christ*, but here the cross itself is transported to where the viewer stands in the present day. In the meditation for Good Friday, Love urges the reader to 'take hede now diligently with alle þi herte' and 'make þe þere present in þi mynde, beholdyng alle þat shale be done aȝeynus þi lorde Jesu'.[115] The Middle English lyrics function as a direct call for the layperson to behold the crucifix and to respond to the gift of salvation it represents by bearing witness to Christ's wounded body and refusing to walk away from their devotions. And given the prominence of the crucifixion group in parish church art, for example atop the rood screen, the laity are most frequently placed at the foot of the cross in the parish church, their own Calvary. The reader of the lyrics then transfers the voice of Christ to the crucifix in the parish church and as a result animates the material culture of the church by making Christ dramatically present in the space.[116]

Such lyrics are also important because they provide the devotee with what Sarah McNamer has described as 'scripts for the performance of feeling' that 'explicitly aspire to performative efficacy'.[117] This performativity is made possible, McNamer contends, by the first person, present tense speeches that are voiced by the reader; the address to the reader as 'you'; the encouragement of an affective response, including stipulating the required gestures (such as to behold or to remain standing); and the use of deixis.[118] I have already argued that deixis is an important strategy in the establishment of the relationship between the laity and the parish church and its use here functions similarly. That the 'here' of these lyrics and the location of 'þis cros' could be linked to the church is further evidenced in the instructions in the manuscript of a lyric called *Ihesus That Hast Me Dere I-boght*, from Longleat MS 29. A direct relationship is constructed between the devotional supplication in the poem and the material culture of the church in the instructions that preface the poem:

> In seiynge of þis orisoun stynteth & bydeth at euery cros & þynkyth whate ye haue seide. For a more deuout prayere fond I neuer of þe passioun who-so wolde deuoutly say hitte.[119]

Just as the lyrics demand that the reader 'abyde', the Longleat instructions require that the individual 'stynteth & bydeth' at 'euery cros' and think about what they have said in reciting the lyric, which is specifically called a 'prayere'. This encourages the reader to enact a repeat performance of the lyric when they see any cross, for example a wayside cross or a crucifix in the church, and it promotes the eager devotion that I argue is crucial for the status of the parish church in particular. The instructions declare that 'a more *deuout* prayere fond I neuer of þe passioun who-so *deuotly* say hitte' (italics mine), and as we saw earlier, the devotion of the congregation contributes materially to the sanctity of the church.

The Longleat instructions aim to inculcate in the reader an automatic response to the crucifix through repetition: if they think about Christ's words 'at euery cros', eventually the sight of any crucifix will bring his speech to mind. The association of Christ's words with church crosses is deliberately invoked in the Good Friday sermon in the *Speculum Sacerdotale* which includes an inset lyric narrated immediately after the preacher has directed the listener to look upon the crucifix in the church:

> Sires, beholdeþ before you the fygure of oure redemptour Ihesu Crist, as he hongeþ in þe crosse in þe same fourme þat he suffred deþ in and brouȝt mankynde for the peynes of helle. Where he cryeþ and seiþ to vs yche day in syche words (p. 112).

The preacher explains that Christ is depicted 'in þe same fourme þat he suffred deþ in', making an explicit link between his sermon and the visual culture of the parish church, and Christ's words from the cross are then delivered as follows:

Lystne, man, lystne to me,
Byholde what I thole for the.
To the, man, well lowde I crye;
For thy loue þou seest I dye.
Byholde my body how I am swongyn;
Se þe nayles howe I am þrouȝ stongyn.
My body withoute is betyn sore,
My peynes with-in ben wel more.
All this I haue tholyd for the,
As þou schalt at Domysday se. (p. 112)

The lyric repeatedly asks the listener to 'byhold' Christ's body and the violence that has been inflicted upon it. The preacher then develops the final line of the lyric's reference to Doomsday by resuming the sermon and stating that 'for in the ende of the world, he schal come and schewe hym and his woundes þat he suffred for vs, and there he schall shewe al the tokenes of his passion' (p. 112). The sermon therefore also relates to the depiction of Christ in paintings of the Last Judgement on the chancel arch in which he displays his wounds as he sits in judgement over the saved and the damned.[120] This collapses sacred time as the wounded Christ, present in the church, speaks to the viewer about his past wounds at the crucifixion that will still be visible in the future at Doomsday.

The advantage of giving Christ a voice in the parish church was recognised by John Clopton, the patron of Holy Trinity church, Long Melford in Suffolk. In the second half of the fifteenth century, the Clopton chapel was painted with verses from John Lydgate's Marian lament *Quis Dabit Meo Capiti Fontem Lacrimarum* and from the verses in the *Testament* in which Christ speaks from the cross. Both Gail Gibson and Shannon Gayk have discussed the presence of the *Testament* quotations in the church. Gayk notes that the passages chosen represent a 'selective excerpting of the most affective moments' of the poem and that the inscription of the lyric in the church is 'a pointer to a real devotional object and urges an emotional response to that image'.[121] The following passage from the *Testament* is inscribed in the church directly above the altar:

Behold o man lefte up thyn eye & see
what mortall peyne I suffred for your trespace

with pitous voys I creye and seye to the
behold my wounds behold myn blody face
behold the rebukis þ^{t} doth me to manace
and [...] reforme the to grace
was like [...] offerid in sacrifice.[122]

Gail Gibson argues that there 'must have once been a crucifix or a devotional image of Christ as Man of Sorrows, displaying his wounds' on the altar below and thus the injunction to 'behold' directs the viewer to the specific object before them, the crucifix that represents Christ's sacrifice.[123] The words of Lydgate's poem make Christ's voice present in the church and when those words are read by the viewer, the crucifix before them is animated as the voice of the inscription is actively associated with the figure of Christ. The presence of the viewer who looks upon the crucifix devoutly, as the Longleat instructions recommended, makes Christ's sacrifice freshly present in the church, and the inscription from Lydgate's poem encourages the viewer to take this sacrifice into their own body: 'Emprynte theese thyng in your inward thought / And grave hem depe ī your remembraunce.'[124] Here Lydgate uses the language of material representation, 'emprynte' and 'grave', to describe the transference of Christ's words into the viewer's thought and remembrance. Both verbs mean to inscribe or imprint, to make a mark, and, figuratively, to impress upon the mind.[125] The viewer is encouraged to subject their thought and memory to the same material process undergone by the crucifix, imprinting their thought and remembrance as the sculptural material has been imprinted with the image of Christ. I have argued throughout this chapter for the symbiotic relationship between the church and the individual Christian, often materialised in the animation of devotional objects. Good behaviour maintains and boosts the sanctity of the space; bad behaviour causes desecration and, paradoxically, the opportunity for sanctity to be re-established. There is a reciprocity between the church and the individual – both are the temple of God and, as the *Speculum Sacerdotale* dedication sermon argued, the individual owes it to the parish church as the house of God on earth to behave themselves. But there is also an exchange that takes place as a result of Christ's injunctions to 'behold' his body, as Sarah McNamer has persuasively argued.

In her analysis of the *Mirror of the Blessed Life of Christ*, McNamer identifies the verb 'behold' as a keyword in Love's vocabulary. But whereas the Middle English Dictionary defines 'biholden' as to look upon, scrutinise, pay attention to, and contemplate, McNamer argues that the definition needs considerable extension to take into account its use as 'a mechanism for generating sensory perception itself: for generating a specific way of seeing, in other words, that had the potential for producing – in the body, as well as in the mind – an impulse toward a particular form of compassion: the protective and ameliorative action of holding'.[126] To 'behold' Christ's wounded body is, according to McNamer, to 'see empathetically because it is also "to hold": to hold with the eyes'.[127] Citing the etymology of the verb in the Anglo-Saxon 'be-healden', McNamer suggests that to behold includes a 'sense of possession' that in Middle English 'implies a movement outward: it appears to function as a prompt to reach out and hold'.[128] This argument can be further substantiated with reference to medieval theories of optics which suggest that the function of the eye was 'simultaneously receptive, passive, vulnerable to sensations' and 'active: roaming, grasping or piercing its objects'.[129] As Suzannah Biernoff has demonstrated, 'sight was at once an extension of the sensitive soul towards an object, and the passage of sensible forms through the eye and into the brain'.[130] Looking involved an exchange between the viewer and the object that was conceived in part as physical.[131] Biernoff applies this theory to 'ocular communion' with Christ, commenting that 'vision, in the medieval world, did not leave the viewer untouched or unchanged':

> Given that perception was defined as assimilation, the objects of one's attention were of critical importance. To see was to become similar to ones object.[132]

To behold Christ's wounded body in the church was to become that body; to touch, to take possession, to *embody* the crucified saviour. The sermon exempla that I have examined in this chapter make explicit the embodied imitation that takes place when the individual Christian enters the parish church and beholds its visual decorations. The relationship between church and congregation which is at the heart of this material could not be more important for the continued manifestation of sacred space in the parish church. The building's sanctity stands and falls by its congregation's behaviour but as the next chapter will demonstrate, this relationship was no longer taken for granted at the turn of the fifteenth century. Indeed, it was under threat. The critique of the material church by the Lollards was a systematic attempt to divide the community from their material home. The church became a battleground, not between angels and demons as we have seen here, but between competing ideas of the meaning of the word 'church'. If the synergy between building and community constitutes not only the meaning of 'church' but the reality of its sanctity, what happens when that relationship comes under attack? Henri Lefebvre asks, 'what would remain of the Church if there were no churches?' and in what follows, I will explore what is at stake for the sanctity of the church when the relationship between the material building and its congregation, the 'living stones' (1 Peter, 2.5) of the church, is challenged and reimagined.[133]

Notes

1 All stained glass windows discussed in this chapter can be found in *Corpus Vitrearum Medii Aevi* unless otherwise specified: www.cvma.ac.uk/index.html [accessed 17 March 2017]. *How the Goode Wife Taught Hyr Doughter* in *The Trials and Joys of Marriage*, ed. Eve Salisbury (Kalamazoo: Medieval Institute Publications, 2002), pp. 219–24, lines 5–10. All subsequent quotations refer to this edition by line number.

2 *MED* 'kepen' (v.) 10a), 11a), 15b).

3 *MED* 'kepen' (v.) 3a) and 4a).

4 *Instructions for Parish Priests by John Myrc*, ed. Edward Peacock, EETS OS 31 (London: Trübner, 1868), p. 1, lines 2–3. All subsequent quotations refer to this edition by line number.

5 *Instructions for Parish Priests*, p. 9.

6 *MED* 'gate' (n.1) 1a).

7 *MED* 'gate' (n.2) 2a).

8 See Roger Rosewell, *Medieval Wall Paintings in English and Welsh Churches* (Woodbridge: Boydell, 2008), pp. 87–9 and figure 207, 'The Sunday Christ' at Breage, St Breaca.

9 *Oure Lord's Epistle on Sunday* in *John the Blind Audelay: Poems and Carols (Oxford, Bodleian Library MS Douce 302)*, ed. Susanna Fein (Kalamazoo, Medieval Institute Publications, 2009), pp. 112–17, lines 59 and 27–39. Fein notes that the 'archetype of this poem had a widespread distribution in the Middle Ages', although it only appears once in Middle English verse in Audelay's poem, p. 268.

10 Rosewell, *Medieval Wall Paintings*, p. 70.

11 *Ibid.*, p. 72.

12 *John Mirk's Festial*, ed. Susan Powell, EETS OS 334 (Oxford: Oxford University Press, 2009), vol. I, p. 155. The second volume of *John Mirk's Festial* was edited by Powell as EETS OS 335 (Oxford: Oxford University Press, 2011). The pagination in volume 2 continues consecutively from volume 1. All subsequent quotations refer to this two-volume edition by page number.

13 Folios 188v–189r, quoted in Leo Carruthers, '"Know thyself: criticism, reform, and the audience in *Jacob's Well*', in Jacqueline Hamesse (ed.), *Medieval Sermons and Society: Cloister, City, and University* (Louvain-le-Neuve: Fédération Internationale des Instituts d'Études Médiévales, 1998), pp. 219–40, pp. 229–30, italics mine.

14 *Speculum Sacerdotale*, ed. Edward H. Weatherly, EETS OS 200 (London: Oxford University Press, 1936), p. 67. Italics mine. All subsequent quotations refer to this edition by page number.

15 For example, the saintly vicar of St Stephen's, Norwich, Richard Caister (chapter 17) and William Sleightholme, who was also the confessor to St John of Bridlington (chapter 53), see *The Book of Margery Kempe*, ed. Barry Windeatt (Cambridge: D. S. Brewer, 2000). I discuss Margery's relationship with her parish priest in more detail in my forthcoming article, 'The importance of St Margaret's church in *The Book of Margery Kempe:* a sacred place and an exemplary parishioner', to be published in *Nottingham Medieval Studies*, 2017.

16 Katherine French, *The People of the Parish: Community Life in a Late Medieval English Diocese* (Philadelphia, PA: University of Pennsylvania Press, 2001), p. 178.

17 French, *People of the Parish*, p. 178.

18 See, for example, Robert Dinn, '"Monuments answerable to mens worth": burial patterns, social status and gender in late medieval Bury St Edmunds', *Journal of Ecclesiastical History*, 46 (1995), 237–55.

19 *Mirk's Festial*, ed. Theodor Erbe, EETS OS 96 (London: Kegan Paul, Trench, and Trübner, 1905), pp. 240–41. Italics mine. I quote Erbe here rather than the more recent edition by Powell because Powell's edition uses British Library, MS Cotton Claudius A II as a base text, which has modified Mirk's original sermon to apply to any church, stating that St Alkmund is patron of 'a chyrche'. See Powell's note on this, *John Mirk's Festial*, vol. II, p. 414.

20 *Jacob's Well*, ed. Arthur Brandeis, EETS OS 115 (London: Kegan Paul, Trench, and Trübner, 1900), p. 232. Italics mine. All subsequent quotations refer to this edition by page number.

21 Christopher Woodforde, *Norwich School of Glass-Painting in the Fifteenth Century* (London: Oxford University Press, 1950), p. 6.

22 Russell West-Pavlov, *Spaces of Fiction / Fictions of Space: Postcolonial Place and Literary DeiXis* (Basingstoke: Palgrave Macmillan, 2010), p. 2.

23 West-Pavlov, *Spaces of Fiction*, p. 3.

24 Anna Fuchs, *Remarks on Deixis* (Heidelberg: Groos, 1993), p. 24.

25 West-Pavlov, *Spaces of Fiction*, p. 51.

26 See, for example, Celia M. Chazelle, 'Pictures, books, and the illiterate: pope Gregory I's letters to Serenus of Marseilles', *Word and Image*, 6:2 (1990), 138–53; Lawrence G. Duggan, 'Was art really the "book of the illiterate?"', in Marielle Hageman and Marco Mostert (eds), *Reading Images and Texts: Medieval Images and Texts as Forms of*

Communication: Papers from the Third Utrecht Symposium on Medieval Literary, Utrecht, 7–9 December 2000 (Turnhout: Brepols, 2005), pp. 63–107; and Madeline Caviness, 'Reception of images by medieval viewers', in Conrad Rudolph (ed.), *A Companion to Medieval Art: Romanesque and Gothic in Northern Europe* (Oxford: Blackwell, 2006; paperback 2010), pp. 65–85.

27 Herbert Kessler, 'Gregory the Great and image theory in northern Europe during the twelfth and thirteenth centuries', in Rudolph (ed.), *Companion to Medieval Art*, pp. 151–72, p. 160.

28 Michael Camille, 'The language of images in medieval England 1200–1400', in Jonathan Alexander and Paul Binski (eds), *The Age of Chivalry: Art in Plantagenet England 1200–1400* (London: Royal Academy of Arts, 1987), pp. 33–40, p. 33.

29 *Dives and Pauper*, ed. Priscilla Heath Barnum, EETS OS 275 (Oxford: Oxford University Press, 1976), vol. I, p. 91. All subsequent quotations refer to this edition and volume by page number.

30 Madeleine Gray, 'Images of words: iconographies of text and the construction of sacred space in medieval church wall painting', in Joseph Sterrett and Peter W. Thomas (eds), *Sacred Text, Sacred Space: Architectural, Spiritual, and Literary Convergences in England and Wales* (Leiden: Brill, 2011), pp. 15–34, pp. 18–19.

31 Gray, 'Images of words', p. 19.

32 Woodforde, *Norwich School of Glass Painting,* p. 184.

33 *Ibid.*, p. 194.

34 Miriam Gill, 'Preaching and image: sermons and wall paintings in later medieval England', in Carolyn Muessig (ed.), *Preacher, Sermon and Audience in the Middle Ages* (Leiden: Brill, 2002), pp. 155–80, p. 156.

35 David Freedberg, *The Power of Images: Studies in the History and Theory of Response* (Chicago: University of Chicago Press, 1989), pp. 306–7.

36 Freedberg, *Power of Images*, p. xxii.

37 *An Alphabet of Tales*, ed. Mary Macleod Banks, EETS OS 126–7 (London: Kegan Paul, Trench and Trübner, 1904–5), p. 238. All subsequent quotations refer to this edition by page number.

38 Rosewell, *Medieval Wall Paintings*, pp. 167 and 158.

39 See the select catalogue of angels in Norfolk churches in Appendix 1 in Ann Eljenholm Nichols, *The Early Art of Norfolk: A Subject List of Extant and Lost Art including Items Relevant to Early Drama* (Kalamazoo: Medieval Institute Publications, 2002), pp. 289–97.

40 For the Fairford angels, see Sarah Brown and Lindsay MacDonald, *Fairford Parish Church: A Medieval Church and its Stained Glass* (Stroud: Sutton Publishing, 2007), plates 21–4. For Norfolk examples, see the inventory in Adrian Rose, 'Angel musicians in the medieval stained glass of Norfolk churches', *Early Music*, 29:2 (2001), 186–217, pp. 198–217.

41 Alexandra Buckle, '"Of the finest colours": music in stained glass at Warwick and elsewhere', *Vidimus*, 46, December 2010, http://vidimus.org/issues/issue-46/feature/ [accessed 15 September 2016].
42 Brown and MacDonald, *Fairford Parish Church*, plate 15.
43 For a comprehensive overview of the Tutivillus tradition, see Margaret Jennings, 'Tutivillus: the literary career of a recording demon', *Studies in Philology*, 74:5 (1977), 1–95.
44 In a fifteenth-century macaronic lyric featuring Tutivillus, 'þes women þat sitteþ þe church about' are singled out as belonging to 'þe deuelis rowte'; see 'On Chattering in Church', in *Religious Lyrics of the XVth Century*, ed. Carleton Brown (Oxford: Clarendon Press, 1939), p. 277, lines 7–8.
45 'Warning against idle gossip': http://paintedchurch.org/idlegoss.htm [accessed 15 September 2016].
46 M. D. Anderson, *Drama and Imagery in English Medieval Churches* (Cambridge: Cambridge University Press, 1963), p. 174 and plate 24d.
47 Anderson, *Drama and Imagery*, pp. 173–4.
48 Jennings, 'Tutivillus', pp. 51–70.
49 *The Towneley Plays*, ed. Martin Stevens and A. C. Cawley, EETS SS 13 (Oxford: Oxford University Press, 1994), vol. I, p. 413, lines 430–8.
50 Laura Varnam, 'The crucifix, the pietà, and the female mystic: devotional objects and performative identity in *The Book of Margery Kempe*', *Journal of Medieval Religious Cultures*, 41:2 (2015), 208–37. Dan Hicks, 'The material-cultural turn: event and effect', in Dan Hicks and Mary Beaudry (eds), *The Oxford Handbook of Material Culture Studies* (Oxford: Oxford University Press, 2010), pp. 25–98, p. 30.
51 Richard Marks, *Image and Devotion in Late Medieval England* (Stroud: Sutton Publishing, 2004), p. 174.
52 *The Gesta Romanorum*, ed. Sidney J. H. Herrtage, EETS ES 33 (London: N. Trübner, 1879), p. 393.
53 George Shuffelton calls the tale 'The knight who forgave his father's slayer' in his edition of Ashmole 61 for TEAMS. See *Codex Ashmole 61: A Compilation of Popular Middle English Verse*, ed. George Shuffelton (2008) 'TEAMS Middle English Text Series': http://d.lib.rochester.edu/teams/publication/shuffelton-codex-ashmole-61 [accessed 22 September 2016].
54 Holly Johnson, 'Fashioning devotion: the art of Good Friday preaching in Chaucerian England', in Georgiana Donavin, Cary J. Nederman, Richard J. Utz (eds), *Speculum Sermonis: Interdisciplinary Reflections on the Medieval Sermon* (Turnhout: Brepols, 2004), pp. 315–34, pp. 316–17.
55 Robert Mannyng of Brunne, *Handlyng Synne*, ed. Idelle Sullens (Binghampton, New York: Medieval and Renaissance Texts and Studies, 1983), lines 3883–4 and 3896–3900. All subsequent quotations refer to this edition by line number.

56 *Speculum Sacerdotale*, p. xli.
57 *MED* 'sanctificacioun' (n.) a) and b).
58 *MED* 'reconcilen' (v.) 5c).
59 *MED* 'reconcilen' (v.) 7.
60 *MED* 'ouen' (v.) 4a).
61 *MED* 'foulen' (v.) 3.
62 Mary Douglas, *Purity and Danger: An Analysis of Concepts of Pollution and Taboo* (London: Routledge, 2003; first published 1966), p. 95.
63 Douglas, *Purity and Danger*, pp. 2–3.
64 Mircea Eliade, *The Sacred and Profane: The Nature of Religion*, trans. Willard R. Trask (Orlando: Harcourt, 1987), p. 11.
65 Julian of Norwich, *A Revelation of Love*, ed. Marion Glasscoe (Exeter: Exeter University Press, 1993), p. 38.
66 *MED* 'irken' (v.) 2a) and b).
67 Miriam Gill, 'Female piety and impiety: selected images of women in wall paintings in England after 1300', in Samatha J. E. Riches and Sarah Salih (eds), *Gender and Holiness: Men, Women, and Saints in Late Medieval Europe* (London: Routledge, 2002), pp. 101–20, p. 110 and figure 7.3.
68 *MED* 'tail' (n.) 1b) c).
69 Both can be found at http://paintedchurch.org/deadlysi.htm [accessed 15 September 2016].
70 Douglas, *Purity and Danger*, p. 41.
71 *MED* 'filen' (v.2) 1c), 2a) and b).
72 *MED* 'vilein' (n.).
73 *Over-Hippers and Skippers* in *John the Blind Audelay*, ed. Fein, p. 213, lines 1–7.
74 *MED* 'titlen' (v.) (Fein glosses 'tytild' as 'whispered' but the *MED* does not include this meaning).
75 *Virtues of the Mass* in *John the Blind Audelay*, ed. Fein, p. 88, line 293.
76 *Virtues of the Mass*, p. 88, lines 302–3.
77 *Ibid.*, p. 89, lines 335–6. *MED* 'assheler' (n.), pavement or masonry.
78 *Ibid.*, p. 89, lines 340–1. In the version in *Handlyng Synne*, the deacon's laughter at the fiend's misfortune causes him to destroy the evidence he has collected, he 'to drofe hyt wiþ hys fyste' in anger (9301). The church is cleansed by the sound of the laughter and the gossips in the story have a lucky escape.
79 *The Myroure of Oure Ladye*, ed. John Henry Blunt, EETS ES 19 (London: Kegan Paul, Trench, and Trübner, 1873), p. 54.
80 Michael Camille, 'The devil's writing: diabolic literacy in medieval art', in Irving Lavin (ed.), *World Art: Themes of Unity in Diversity* (University Park, PA: Pennsylvania State University Press, 1989), vol. II, pp. 355–60, p. 356.
81 Geoffrey Chaucer, *The Riverside Chaucer*, ed. Larry D. Benson et al. (Oxford: Oxford University Press, 1987; paperback 1988), p. 196, lines 464 and 470.

82 *The Riverside Chaucer*, p. 196, lines 480–1.
83 *The Book of Vices and Virtues*, ed. W. Nelson Francis, EETS OS 217 (London: Oxford University Press, 1942), pp. 53–4. All subsequent quotations refer to this edition by page number.
84 See Nigel Saul, *English Church Monuments in the Middle Ages: History and Representation* (Oxford: Oxford University Press, 2009), especially chapter 6, 'Function and Meaning', pp. 120–42.
85 For example, the Last Judgement window at Fairford, see Brown and MacDonald, *Fairford Parish Church*, plate 15, and 'The Ladder of salvation' wall painting at Chaldon, Surrey, Rosewell, *Medieval Wall Paintings*, p. 73.
86 *MED* 'fermen' (v.1).
87 Douglas, *Purity and Danger*, p. 3.
88 Mircea Eliade, *Patterns in Comparative Religion*, trans. Rosemary Sheed (London: Sheed and Ward, 1958), pp. 14–15.
89 René Girard, *Violence and the Sacred*, trans. Patrick Gregory (London: Continuum, 2005), p. 32.
90 *The Testament of Dan John Lydgate* in *The Minor Poems of John Lydgate*, ed. Henry Noble MacCracken, EETS ES 107 (London: Kegan Paul, Trench, Trübner and co, 1911), pp. 329–62, pp. 357–62, lines 761, 825, and 873, respectively.
91 Girard, *Violence and the Sacred*, p. 273.
92 *Ibid.*, p. 271.
93 *Ibid.*, p. 8.
94 *Ibid.*, p. 8.
95 *MED* 'mende' (n.) 2) 'mendes making'.
96 *MED* 'minde' (n.1).
97 *MED* 'fresh' (adj).
98 *Book of Margery Kempe*, p. 286.
99 I discuss this episode in more detail in Varnam, 'The crucifix, the pietà, and the female mystic', pp. 219–29.
100 MED 'fresh' (adj.) 2a). *Richard Morris's Prick of Conscience: A Corrected and Amplified Reading Text*, ed. Ralph Hanna and Sarah Wood, EETS OS 342 (Oxford: Oxford University Press, 2013), p. 147, lines 5305–7.
101 Caroline Walker Bynum, *Wonderful Blood: Theology and Practice in Late Medieval Northern Germany and Beyond* (Philadelphia: University of Pennsylvania Press, 2007), pp. 1–2.
102 See http://paintedchurch.org/rothdoom.htm [accessed 16 September 2016].
103 Bynum, *Wonderful Blood*, p. 16.
104 *MED* 'prive' (n) 2a) 'a privy'; 1c) 'private parts, genitals'.
105 Bettina Bildhauer, *Medieval Blood* (Cardiff: University of Wales Press, 2006), p. 21.
106 *Minor Poems of John Lydgate*, pp. 216–21, lines 86–8.

107 Caroline Walker Bynum notes that thirteenth- and fourteenth-century moralised Bibles 'frequently drew parallels between the birth of Eve from Adam's side and the birth of the Church from Christ's body', *Fragmentation and Redemption: Essays on Gender and the Human Body in Medieval Religion* (New York: Zone Books, 1992), p. 97 and figure 3.6.
108 *MED* 'bildinge' (ger.) 4b).
109 Johnson, 'Fashioning devotion', p. 316. On the *Improperia* and religious lyrics, see Douglas Gray, *Themes and Images in the Medieval English Religious Lyric* (London: Routledge and Kegan Paul, 1972), pp. 139–45.
110 *Abide, Ye Who Pass By* in *Religious Lyrics of the XIVth Century*, ed. Carleton Brown, second edition revised by G. V. Smithers (Oxford: Clarendon Press, 1957), pp. 59–60, lines 1–6.
111 *Abide, Ye Who Pass By,* lines 7–12.
112 *Ibid*., lines 13–18.
113 *MED* 'affiaunce' (n.) 1a) and 2.
114 *Thou Sinful Man that by Me Goes* in *Religious Lyrics of the XVth Century*, ed. Brown, pp. 151–6, lines 9 and 15.
115 *Nicholas Love: The Mirror of the Blessed Life of Jesus Christ*, ed. Michael G. Sargent (Exeter: University of Exeter Press, 2004), p. 174.
116 Christ also speaks the words of the *Improperia* from the cross in the York Crucifixion Play, see *The York Corpus Christi Plays*, ed. Clifford Davidson (Kalamazoo: Medieval Institute Publications, 2011), p. 300, lines 253–64.
117 Sarah McNamer, *Affective Meditation and the Invention of Compassion* (Philadelphia, University of Pennsylvania Press, 2010), p. 12.
118 McNamer, *Affective Meditation*, p. 12.
119 *Religious Lyrics of the XIVth Century*, ed. Brown and rev. Smithers, p. 114.
120 See Anne Marshall, 'The doom, or last judgement, and the weighing of souls: an introduction', http://paintedchurch.org/doomcon.htm [accessed 16 September 2016].
121 Shannon Gayk, *Image, Text, and Religious Reform in Fifteenth-Century England* (Cambridge: Cambridge University Press, 2010), pp. 117 and 118.
122 The inscriptions from Long Melford are transcribed by J. B. Trapp in his article, 'Verses by Lydgate at Long Melford', *Review of English Studies*, n.s. 6.21 (1955), 1–11, p. 5. Ellipses are original and indicate loss of text in the inscription.
123 Gail McMurray Gibson, *The Theater of Devotion: East Anglian Drama and Society in the Late Middle Ages* (Chicago: University of Chicago Press, 1989), p. 87.
124 Trapp, 'Verses by Lydgate', p. 6.

125 *MED* 'graven' (v.) 3a) and 3e). Also 'emprenten' (v.) 1 and 4.
126 McNamer, *Affective Meditation*, p. 135.
127 *Ibid.*, p. 136.
128 *Ibid.*
129 Suzannah Biernoff, *Sight and Embodiment in the Middle Ages* (Basingstoke: Palgrave Macmillan, 2002), p. 3.
130 Biernoff, *Sight and Embodiment*, p. 3.
131 *Ibid.*, p. 4, 'looking in the Middle Ages entailed a physical encounter between bodies'.
132 *Ibid.*, p. 137.
133 Henri Lefebvre, *The Production of Space*, trans. Donald Nicholson Smith (Oxford: Blackwell, 1991), p. 44.

4
What the church betokeneth: Placing the people at the heart of sacred space

In the Middle English translation of the compendium for Lollard preachers, the *Rosarium Theologie*, the entry for 'edifiyng' asks: 'wilt þou belde þe house of God?' If so, the reader is instructed to proceed as follows:

> Giffe to trewe pore men warof þei may liffe and þou has edified a resonable house to God. Men forsoþ duelleþ in beledyngz, God forsoþ in holi men. Wat kynez þerof be þai þat spoilez men & makeþ edifyngz of martirez? Þei made habitacions of men and sturbiliþ habitacions of God.[1]

The *Rosarium* sets up an opposition between the dwelling place of God (holy men) and the dwelling place of man (material buildings). Charitable giving to true, poor men edifies a 'resonable house to God', and the word 'resonable' here is at the heart of the late medieval debate on the material church. Its meaning ranges from wise and sensible to moderate and fair, appropriate, proportionate, and crucially, not excessive.[2] For Lollard sympathisers, the 'resonable' house of God was built by nourishing the poor, the living stones of the church (1 Peter, 2.5), not by wasting vital sustenance on elaborately ornamented buildings, crammed with richly decorated but ultimately lifeless statues of the saints. In the entry for 'ecclesia', the *Rosarium* laments, 'O vanite of vanitez', invoking Bernard of Clairvaux's famous *Apologia*, 'þe chirche schyneþ in þe walles and haþ nede in pouer men, it cloþeþ his stonez wiþ golde and forsakeþ his childer naked; of the costage of pouer men it is serued to þe eien of riche men' (p. 67). The eyes not only of rich men but of the entire parish community were trained on the visible, material church in the fifteenth century. It was the building that, as Henri Lefebvre argues, offered 'each member of society an image of that membership, an image of his or her social visage', and parishioners could increasingly contribute to that image, donating decorations such as stained glass windows, and funding much-needed restoration and rebuilding work.[3] The materiality of the church could not be ignored. Indeed, it was subject to serious scrutiny from a wide range of writers who debated the opportunity and the threat that the material church posed to the parish community.

The texts under discussion in this chapter are drawn from a diverse range of traditions but what all of them have in common is a desire to establish what the church 'betokeneth' and, importantly, to determine the relationship that the church building has, or ought to have, with the people housed within it. The texts construct, refashion, or attempt to dismantle the 'House of God' as a material building and I will explore what is at stake for sacred space and communal identity when they do so. I will begin with the most important and influential understanding of church architecture in the Middle Ages, the thirteenth-century *Rationale divinorum officiorum* by William of Durandus. The *Rationale*'s allegorical reading of the church builds the Christian community into the architecture from the pavement to the roof and it was the foundation of late medieval thinking about the material church. A section of the text was translated into Middle English as *What the Church Betokeneth* in the mid-fifteenth century, and this translation was not only linguistic but also spatial as the image of the 'church' that emerges is shaped by the pastoral care material that I examined in Chapter 3. Durandus's ordered and idealised image of the church building, in which every member of society has their place and is vital to the strength and integrity of the structure, found renewed significance in the face of the challenge posed by Lollard writers in the fifteenth century, such as the polemicist of the *Lanterne of Liȝt*, a text that represents the 'fullest exemplification of the Wycliffite concept of church'.[4] Paying careful attention to the vocabulary and rhetorical strategies of a range of vernacular Lollard texts, from sermons to treatises, I will show how the fifteenth-century church is not only presented as a dead space of costly and 'curious' materials but that the very nature of the church as a community is deliberately and painstakingly divorced from its material representation, the church building. The Lollard texts discussed reimagine the idea of the church but, as keen as such writers are to sever the dependence of medieval Christians on the material building for their understanding of value, sanctity, and community, the building still remains a dynamic and vividly imagined textual presence with the potential to edify its audience.

According to one anonymous Lollard writer, 'it is litel deynte of [there is little value in] a gay churche and a false curate', but as the depiction of the churches of the religious orders in *Pierce the Ploughman's Crede* demonstrates, this fails to account for the edificatory value of narrative critique and satire.[5] Bruce Holsinger has recently argued that the *Crede* is an ekphrastic poem that is 'able to beguile its readers with the aesthetic mimesis of poetry – prosody, diction, alliteration, metaphor, syntax – while using this beguilement to instil a critical awareness of clerical wealth and the idolatry of visual culture'.[6] The *Crede* translates the polemic of the *Lanterne of Li3t* into narrative, and I will explore what happens when the ordinary layman is brought face to face with the 'curious' churches that the Lollards feared would distract and even destroy them. All of the texts in this chapter tell stories about how the material church was read, how it should be read, and how it could be 'imagined otherwise' by late medieval communities.[7] In his book *Material Culture and Text*, the archaeologist Christopher Tilley approaches the paradox of writing about objects and translating three-dimensional materiality into words:

> No archaeological text is anything more or less than a flood of words so the question becomes which ones are deemed desirable as metaphoric transformations of the material reality being studied. You seem to think that telling stories is not my proper purpose but I regard any attempt to understand the past as fundamentally involving narrative. Narrative is not an option, it is an ontological status: we all live narratives.[8]

This chapter is about the 'desirable' narratives of the material church that were produced by Middle English writers for whom the building and its decorations were not only a fundamental part of everyday life, but a vital stake in some of the most important debates of the age: debates about community, charity, poverty, and devotional intention. The words used by these writers are those which were deemed 'desirable as metaphoric transformations of the material reality' that they too were studying and debating. And what constituted a 'desirable narrative' of the material church to the translator of *What the Church Betokeneth* was a very different story than for the Lollard polemicist of *The Lanterne of Li3t*.

In Chapter 3, I argued that the sanctity of the church was made manifest by miracles of animation and purification that relied upon the material culture of the church for their efficacy: graves that expelled the sinful dead, images that miraculously responded to the devotions of the laity, churches built from ill-gotten gains that fell to the ground and crumbled. The profane challenge of lay misbehaviour was, paradoxically, necessary because it reinforced the sanctity of the church and kept it alive. The relationship between the people and the building was integral to its status as a sacred space. In the texts under discussion here, however, that visible, material, and animate sanctity is called into question. In *What the Church Betokeneth*, the sanctity of the church resides in order, in a highly schematic representation of a building in which every member of society has their place and pastoral teaching stands unchallenged. In the texts of Lollard ecclesiology, the church as the congregation of the predestined is no longer harmoniously aligned with the material church. Rather than supporting and nourishing communal identity, the material church is an excessively ornamented distraction and a direct threat to the poor, who depend upon the church community for charity. The true church is the community of the saved, not the material building on earth. The material church is not alive but dead, not the house of God but a house of lime and stone. And it is essential that this division between the community and the material building is recognised if the church is truly to be reformed.

But where Durandus and the Lollard writers take pains to locate and place the Christian community, whether inside or outside the church building, the systematic and seemingly straightforward classifications that they produce risk neglecting the very real, lived experience at the heart of parish life. The church is not simply the house of God on earth in one formulation and a house of lime and stone in the other. The final section of this chapter will analyse the vigorous debate over the state of England's 'fayre chirchys' in *Dives and Pauper* in order to show that the fifteenth-century church was a sacred space in the parish because the laity cared deeply for it and it signified in multiple, interlocking ways. In his 1999 article, Paul Binski recognised that the parish church has not been sufficiently studied in terms of its place in the emotional landscape of late medieval religious practice and to conclude this chapter, I will show how the material evidence of church-building, restoration, and decoration in the period reveals that the church should be thought of not only as a lived and practised space of experience, but as a space of feeling and emotion too.[9] Drawing on Shelley Hornstein's discussion of architecture as both material and emotional, I will show how the medieval church is a physical entity and an 'architecture of the heart'.[10] The image of the heart recurs time and again within the texts in this chapter as the location of devotional feeling and practice. The sanctity of the church resides within an 'architecture of the heart' that is both the material church and the body of the devout Christian.

What the church betokeneth: Allegorical architecture and community

The *Rationale divinorum officiorum* by the thirteenth-century bishop of Mende, William of Durandus, was the most influential text for understanding 'what the church betokeneth' in the Middle Ages. Durandus's allegorical interpretation of church architecture was the culmination of a long tradition that taught medieval Christians not only how to read the church building but also how its community ought to be constructed. The text was edifying in both senses of the word. It taught the community and built them into the structure at the heart of their pastoral education. Part of the proliferation of didactic material produced in the wake of the Fourth Lateran Council in 1215, by the end of the fifteenth-century the *Rationale* had become 'one of the most widely disseminated treatises of its kind in Western Europe'.[11] Its continued importance is evidenced by the fifteenth-century translation *What the Church Betokeneth*, which will be my focus here, but its influence can also be seen in the architectural metaphors of a range of Middle English texts. Durandus interpreted the pillars of the church, for example, as the 'bishops or teachers who spiritually hold up the temple of God' and this metaphor is used of St Thomas Becket in *Þe Simonie* in the Auchinleck manuscript: Becket is 'a piler ariht to holden up holi cherche'.[12] Catherine of Siena similarly refers to the 'two goostly fadris' whom God 'has lente to me for my kepyng and doctryne' as 'two pilers' in *The Orcherd of Syon*.[13] More significantly, in *The Book of Margery Kempe*, Christ refers to Margery, a laywoman, as 'a peler of Holy Cherch', and the red ink annotator confirms this designation by drawing a pillar in the margins of the manuscript.[14] Here the architectural metaphor invokes the authority with which Durandus endowed bishops and teachers to position Margery at the heart of her community as a strong supporter of the parish church.[15]

The architecture of the church was, as Paul Binski argues, 'in part a vehicle of communication' and in the *Rationale*, William of Durandus shows how church architecture communicates an ideal, pastoral community.[16] The text as a whole is divided into eight books which cover a diverse range of topics including the symbolism of the church building and its furniture, the consecration ceremony, the sacraments, ecclesiastical vestments, the mass, feast days and holy days, the office of the dead, and the liturgical calendar. Durandus laments that 'nowadays most of those priests who manage the Church's affairs and conduct its worship on a day-to-day basis have little or no understanding of what the Divine Offices signify or why they were instituted' and he positions his 'rationale' as a remedy for this ignorance.[17] *What the Church Betokeneth* is a Middle English translation of passages from Book I on the church building and its furniture, augmented with pastoral material taken from Edmund of Abingdon's *Speculum Ecclesie*. The text's editors states that it contains a 'highly selective sequence of sentences or ideas, with little original material' from Durandus, but although *What the Church Betokeneth* does represent a much reduced series of extracts from the *Rationale*, a close comparison of the two texts reveals originality in the subtle adaptation of the material for a lay audience.[18] It is my suggestion that *What the Church Betokeneth* deliberately situates Durandus's ideal church in the late medieval parish through a small set of additions to the *Rationale* that focus on the lay audience and their spiritual lives. The *Rationale*'s modern editor and translator, Timothy M. Thibodeau, comments of the original text that the 'windows, lattice work, pavement, choir and vaulted ceilings of the Gothic cathedrals of Durandus's epoch' are evident throughout the work.[19] I want to suggest that the linguistic translation of the text from Latin to Middle English is paralleled by the spatial translation of the church into the English parish and it is to this reimagining of Durandus's ideal architecture that I will now turn.

The primary additions that *What the Church Betokeneth* makes to the *Rationale* concern the relationship between the laity and their parish priests. In the explanation of the chancel, for example, the Middle English text follows the *Rationale* in reading the chancel as the 'hed of the churche' that 'betokenyth the mekenes that shulde be in the clergye and in the prelatis of the Churche' (p. 88). But it elaborates on Durandus's comment that the 'choir signifies the separation of the celestial from the terrestrial realm' in architectural and parochial terms:

> The particion betwene the queer and the book [nave] of the churche betokenyth that the myndis of the spiritualte shulde be departid in especialle fro alle erthelye thyngis, lyke as thaye be departid fro the laye people bodely in tyme of Goddis seruyce. (p. 88)[20]

The architectural division of the community is foregrounded here, reproducing the ideal state of the parish church outlined in my first chapter. The importance of the church as a pastoral space is also highlighted in another addition to the *Rationale*, the explanation of the white cloth that covers the altar. Drawn from Book I's discussion 'On the Altar', *What the Church Betokeneth* explains that the white cloth signifies the soul made white with good works, but this is then developed with reference to priests and bishops acting as a good example for the laity:

> At alle tymes oure werkis shulde be white and clene, and moost speciallye the busshops and the preestis that mynyster vpon the auter the holye bodye of oure lorde Ihesu Cryste, þaye aught to be clene fro synne and made white with good werkis to the gode ensample of the laye people. (p. 90)

Just as the altar cloths are white and clean, so too should the ministers of the church be pure and virtuous if they are to set a good example to their congregation. That this 'aught' to be the case may, perhaps, be a subtle reference to criticisms of the clergy, most notably by the Lollards, or, more realistically, a recognition of the rigours of the position. The material culture of the mass is pressed into service here not only to betoken the didactic role of the priest in teaching his congregation but also to construct an ideal moral order in the church.

What the Church Betokeneth similarly develops the *Rationale*'s reading of the pews in the church to create the impression of a parish church with a lay congregation. Durandus explains that the stalls 'signify the contemplatives who remain at rest in God without offense, who, on account of their great holiness and the clarity of the eternal life they contemplate, are compared to gold'.[21] In *What the Church Betokeneth*, the pews similarly 'betokenyth contemplatyfe men' but they are then glossed to apply to the entire congregation: 'lyke as we rest in the pewys, right so in the churche we shulde rest in mynde fro alle worldelye besynesse, and onlye to entende to please God and to rest in hym by holye meditacions, for the churche is the place of prayer' (p. 88). In Chapter 3, I showed how priests were constantly battling against the 'worldelye besynesse' of their congregations, so the additional reading of the pews as a place of refuge, an escape from worldly distraction, contributes to the text's reconstruction of the church as an ideal space for their pastoral work.

The reading of the crucifix at the centre of the church is the final addition to the Middle English text that presents its church as a building in the late medieval parish. The *Rationale* states:

> In many places a triumphal cross is placed in the middle of the church to denote that we love our redeemer from the depth of our heart, who, according to Solomon, offered his body, with deep charity (Song, 3.10), on account of the daughters of Jerusalem; and thus, all who see this sign of victory sing: 'Hail, salvation of all the world, tree of life!' And this is done so that the love of God that dwells in us – our God, who in order to redeem His servants, handed over His only son – will never be handed over into oblivion, but rather we will imitate Christ's cross. Moreover the cross is held high to designate Christ's victory.[22]

The cross here is a symbol of victory and its placement at the centre of the church is a symbol of the depth of love for Christ. In *What the Church Betokeneth*, however, the middle of the church betokens the middle of the heart, a space that I will argue at the end of this chapter is a crucial locus for the emotional connection that parishioners are encouraged to cultivate with their parish churches:

> The crucyfixe that is sette in the myddis of the churche betokenyth that, lyke as oure lorde died for oure redempcion in the myddis of the worlde, so we shulde haue euer Cryste in lyke remembraunce in the myddis of oure hertis, euer thankyng hym for the grete grace and godenes that he hath shewid to vs at alle tymes. And also he is set in the churche that we shulde ofte beholde whate payne and passhion he suffrid for vs to brynge vs oute of the feendis bondis. And for cause of that victory the crosse is set on hie, for we shulde alwaye dresse oure mynde vpwarde to God and remembre that we haue no grace but onlye of hym. (p. 89)

As Christ died in Jerusalem, the centre of the world in the Middle Ages, the crucifix is 'sette' at the centre of the church to signify that we should have Christ 'in lyke remembraunce in the myddis of oure hertis'.[23] The verb 'sette' is especially resonant here because in addition to meaning placed or positioned, 'setten' also means to construct or build, to consecrate, and to ornament.[24] The association of 'sette' with ornamentation is relevant to the second use of the verb in the passage, when Christ is described as being 'set in the church that we shulde ofte beholde what payne and passhion he suffrid for vs'. This refers to the artistic representation of Christ on the crucifix; his image is set in the church like a precious stone so that we can behold the pain and passion that he suffered. The addition of ‘payne and passhion’ in *What the Church Betokeneth* is also another indication of the translation of Durandus’s church into the late medieval English parish because of the ubiquity of images of the suffering Christ in the medieval wall paintings and stained glass, as I discussed in Chapter 3. The suffering Christ replaces the triumphant Christ of the *Rationale*. The image additionally signifies Christ’s deliverance of mankind ‘oute of the feendis bondis’, which also reminds us of the presentation of the church in the literature of pastoral care as a space in which fiends have jurisdiction over sinners but the virtuous break free of their shackles and gain salvation. In this passage, then, the suffering Christ at the centre of the parish church finds a place in the ‘architecture of the heart’ cultivated by the laity. The church is folded into the heart of the believer and the symbiotic relationship between the body of the congregation and the building in which they worship forms the basis of the entire text’s construction of the ideal Christian community.

What the Church Betokeneth opens by asserting that the church ‘betokenyth ij thyngis, that is the place where the seruyce of God is saide and songe and þer is gadryng place togeder of alle true cristen people and þerin to serve God with one wylle in loue and charyte, for the churche is the specyalle place ordeynid for prayer’ (p. 87). This establishes the church as a space of ritual practice, as I’ve argued elsewhere, and privileges the function of the church as a ‘specyalle place ordeynid for prayer’.[25] The church is ‘specyalle’ in the sense that it is an extraordinary or distinctive space as a result of the consecration ceremony, alluded to in the use of the verb ‘ordeynid’.[26] The three uses of the word ‘place’ signal the three elements in the traditional understanding of the church. The church is a physical location ‘where the seruyce of God is saide’, the place where ‘true cristen people’ gather, and a sacred or special place. Having established this tripartite definition as the foundation for what the church ‘betokeneth’, the text then proceeds in a highly structured manner to explain the key elements of the church’s architecture and material culture, introducing each item with the same formula, ‘what x betokenyth’. The verb ‘bitoknen’ in Middle English means to ‘represent symbolically’ and it is related to the noun ‘token’ which means ‘a physical concept that by virtue of a physical or conceptual similarity is used to represent an action, a concept, state’, ‘a visible indicator of an inward state’, and ‘evidence, proof, a confirming detail’.[27] The material church is a ‘token’ of the community, a physical embodiment of the congregation of the faithful, and each element of the architecture betokens a specific group in a highly organised manner.

The congregation is built into the church in a strictly hierarchical schema from the foundations to the roof. The pavement, for example, betokens 'the pore people of Cryste in spirite':

> For though þaye ben lowe, here whate sayeth Cryste of them: Blessid be pore men in spirite, for the reame of hevyn is theris. And also the pament signyfieth the comyn people that holye Churche is susteynid by moost. (p. 88)

The beams or wooden timbers of the church 'betokenyth the pryncis of this worlde and the prechours that kepe þe pees of hoolye Churche' and the roof represents 'the prechours in hooly Churche that liften vp the thoughtis of men into þe ioye of hevyn' (p. 88). The pillars, a popular motif in later texts, as we saw, betoken 'the bysshops and doctours that maynten the feythe of hooly Churche' (p. 87), and the chancel betokens the meekness of the clergy and their separation from the laity in the church. Placement in the vertical axis of the church indicates authority, both ecclesiastical and social; the laity are at the bottom and the priests and princes of the world are at the top, and proximity to the high altar in the horizontal axis denotes sanctity.

This is an idealised, ordered, and structured image of the church community. It is also an image that is underpinned by important architectural metaphors from scripture. For example, 'the dore of the churche is Cryste, for by hym we shal entre into the blysse of hevyn after this lyfe' (p. 87, cf. John, 10.9). The 'light in the churche betokenyth Criste, for he is the very light of alle the worlde as he sayeth himself: *Ego sum lux mundi* [I am the light of the world]' (p. 89 cf. John, 8.12). The image of church lights is extended to include the 'apostlis and oþer hooly doctours' for 'þaye shulde be the light of the comyn people, as oure lorde sayeth: "*Vox estis lux mundi* [You are the light of the world] *et bonorum operum exempla*"' (p. 89, cf. Matthew, 5.14). Here the translator adds '*et bonorum operum exempla* [and examples of good works]', further contributing to the presentation of the church and its community as an exemplary space for edifying parishioners. The text thus builds scriptural quotations into the church in the same way as the consecration ceremony, materialising the word of God and making it integral to the fabric of sacred architecture.

A major element in the consecration ceremony is ritual purification, and *What the Church Betokeneth* includes a definition of holy water that builds this process into the textual church:

> Furst the hooly water dryveth awaye alle wyckid and vnclene spiritis oute of alle placis where it is caste and oute of the hertis of true cristen people. And also holye water doith awaye alle venyalle synnes whan it is mekelye and devoutelye receyuid. And the halowyng of the hooly water euery Sondaye is blessid in remembraunce of oure baptym, and we shulde cast it into euery place of oure howsis, and we shulde saye whan we caste it aboute: *Asperges me Domine*, &c, and than alle oure housis shalle be kepte oute of the power of alle wyckid spiritis. And therefore we shulde caste holye water vpon vs as ofte as we can haue it, for it doith aweye oure euery dayes venial synnes as often as we take it mekelye with charite. (p. 93)

This passage is also important because it aligns the church with the heart as holy water drives away wicked spirits from 'alle *placis* where it is caste and out of the *hertis* of true cristen people' (italics mine). The explanation of holy water is a chance to teach the reader about its sacred properties, for example its ability to keep domestic dwellings safe from the power of the fiend if we 'cast it into euery place of oure howsis'.[28] But the passage also encourages us to 'caste holye water vpon ys as often as we can haue it' which is a subtle encouragement to enter the church as often as we can, for the church is, of course, where it is kept. The text's reading of church bells also stresses their qualities of protection, singling out the weather which was a major concern for congregations restoring the damage it caused to their churches:

> Whye bellis ben ordeynid to ryng in the churche. For by the ryngyng of bellis true cristen people ben called togeders into the churche to saye þer there deuocions in praysing of almyghty God and in heryng devyne seruyce to the helthe of there souls. And þereby the frutis and the cornys on erthe ben savid and the power of the gostelye enemyes is put fro them, and by the ryngyng of halowid bellis thondryng, lightnyng and other tempestis ben put awaye fro vs. (p. 91)

The sound of the church bells puts to flight 'gostelye enemyes', protects against thunder and lightning, and safeguards crops, which would have been especially welcome in rural communities. In the *Rationale*, the windows are also interpreted as repelling the wind and rain but *What the Church Betokeneth* reads their defensive qualities more abstractly.[29] The windows represent 'the scripture of

God that puttith awaye and defendith fro vs alle evils that noyen vs' (p. 87), deploying the plural pronoun to include the reader in this protective space. The image of the church that emerges from *What the Church Betokeneth* is of a building that not only represents but protects its community.

The windows of the church also signify the five wits or senses and in Durandus, they are both open and closed: 'the five corporeal senses are also signified by the windows, which must be *well structured on the outside*, lest they allow in the vanities of the world; and they are *open within* to acquire more freely the spiritual gifts'.[30] *What the Church Betokeneth* betrays an anxiety about the permeability of the windows and states instead that 'by þe glasse wyndowis is vnderstonde oure v wyttis whereby we shulde *kepe oute* of soules al evils and vanytees, and by Goddis grace to *kepe within* vs mekelye loue and charitie and oþer vertues' (p. 87, italics mine). Here the windows aim to keep out evils and vanities and they act as a barrier preventing virtues from escaping the soul. In the context of the pastoral care narratives I discussed earlier, it is easy to understand this anxiety as the parish church is frequently presented as dangerously open to violation, sacrilege, and sin in the shape of demons entering the church as a result of parishioners unable to control their wits. This might also explain why the entry for the church door in *What the Church Betokeneth* is so overwhelmingly positive, stressing that 'we entre into þe churche to praye God to haue foryevenes of oure offencis' and 'by the dore, that is Cryste, alle gode thoughtis and offeryngis ben borne into the churche' (p. 87). Recalling narratives such as the proud woman who brought a throng of demons into the church, hitching a ride on her elaborate headdress, the door as the entry point for 'alle gode thoughtis and offeryngis' is clearly an idealised picture. But this is precisely the aim of the text, to construct a sacred image of the church building: at one with its community, protected, strong, and embodying Christian teachings without question.

With this aim in mind, the remainder of *What the Church Betokeneth* furnishes the church with everything that is required for the liturgical practice that guarantees its continued sanctity after the consecration ceremony. The text describes and explains the priest's vestments for mass (pp. 91–3), the bearing of the cross in procession, bell-ringing, and the use of incense (pp. 93–5), and then runs through the crucial elements of the liturgy, including the kyrie eleison (p. 95), the collect (p. 95), the gospel reading (p. 98), and the creed (p. 99). The hours of evensong, compline, matins, and lauds are explained (pp. 101–2) and rituals such as breaking bread (p. 101), eating fish during fasting (p. 103), and the consecration of the font (p. 104) are examined. The text then includes a selection of basic pastoral material from Edmund of Abingdon's *Speculum Ecclesie* and Archbishop Pecham's Constitutions, all of which edifies the congregation and keeps the sacred space of the church free from sin. The material includes the Ten Commandments (pp. 105–7), the Seven Deadly Sins (pp. 107–9), the Seven Virtues (pp. 109–10 and 111–12), the Twelve Articles of the Faith (p. 112), the Seven Sacraments (pp. 113–14), the Cardinal Virtues (p. 115), and the Seven Works of Mercy (pp. 115–17, both corporal and spiritual). This constitutes the fundamental pastoral instruction that every member of the congregation needs to ensure their own salvation and every priest needs to ensure the smooth running of his parish church. Good Christian teaching leads to good behaviour, which in turn protects sacred space. As I have argued throughout this book, the sanctity of the church is in large part produced by the people, and the church that is constructed in *What the Church Betokeneth* contains all the objects, tools, teachings, and rituals required to produce and maintain sacred space in an ideal state.

The sanctity of the church is also sustained by and contained within the text's rhetorical strategies, as Christiania Whitehead has argued. Discussing the *Rationale* but equally applicable to the Middle English translation, Whitehead comments that the allegorical reading of the building and its objects gives to the 'places and liturgical operations the same authority and depth as the narratives of scripture themselves'.[31] Biblical exegesis and 'the sacredness associated with it' is translated 'from the scriptures to the contemporary spatial domain', in this case the domain of the English parish church, as I have shown.[32] The church and its material culture 'begin to seem inspired, divinely ordained, heavenly in design, virtually incontestable'.[33] The systematic and structured *reading* of the material church sanctifies it by endowing it with sacred meaning. If the church building does not *mean* anything, if it does not betoken anything beyond its own material fabric, it is no longer truly sacred. Indeed, if the meanings constructed here, which to Durandus are fixed and immutable, are contested, then the very significance and value of the word 'church' is at stake. And in the fifteenth century, that contestation was levelled clearly and rigorously by the Lollards across a range of vernacular texts that reimagined the 'church' as a community by dividing it from its material representation, the church building.

Lollard attitudes to the material church: Divide and conquer

In direct contrast to the allegorical tradition that united the church building with its community, the dominant strategy of Lollard ecclesiology was to divide the church into its constituent parts: the congregation of the saved and the material building on earth. This division is established in the church dedication sermon based on the gospel story of Zacchaeus the tax collector (Luke, 19.1–10). Dedication sermons were usually an opportunity to reinforce the relationship between the people and their church that was established during the consecration ceremony, so the alternative argument that is presented here is all the more striking. When Christ decides to dwell in Zacchaeus's house, he is criticised by the people who claim that Zacchaeus is a sinful man. But Zacchaeus defends himself, declaring 'Lo! Þe half of my godis, Sire, Y ȝyue to pore men', setting a good example of which the Lollards would no doubt approve.[34] Surprisingly, Zacchaeus's charity is not emphasised by the sermon, which focuses instead on the nature of the church:

> Þis gospel is red in ȝeris whanne þe chirche is halewid, for no feeste ne masse is wrþ but ȝif þe gospel conferme it. And, as Zachee reseyuede Crist, so chirchis reseyuen cristen men. But heere shulden men vndirstonde þat þe chirche is takun on many maners: first for men þat shulden be sauyd, whiche Crist clepiþ Abrahams sones; aftir, for þe hous of lym and stoon, þat conteyneþ siche men. We taken no heede to oþere wittis, þat þe chirche sumtyme bitokeneþ þes two þingis gederid togidere, on what maner þat it be. þe firste chirche is Goddis spouse, in what plase euere it be; þe toþer chirche is halewid and maad as oþir plasis ben; and þes wittis ben dyuerse, to speke þus of þe chirche. For no drede God is not spousid wiþ þis lyym and þis stoon; but to sich plasis gaderen men, boþe gode and yuele, for to here Goddis word and to reseyue þer sacramentis.[35]

The sermon is forthright in its rejection of the 'oþer wittis, þat þe chirche sumtyme bitokeneþ', reading the church firstly as signifying the saved, God's spouse 'in what plase euere it be', and secondly the house of lime and stone, that is 'halewid and maad as oþir plasis ben'. The first is placeless; the second is constructed and sanctified by mankind. 'As oþir places ben' downplays the special status that the consecration ceremony usually confers; it might be a hallowed space but that does not make it unique. The sermon does not deny the efficacy of the consecration ceremony but it does make sure to link its celebration back to scripture, reminding us that 'no feeste ne masse is wrþ but ȝif þe gospel conferme it'. As we saw in Chapter 1, the consecration ceremony relied on scriptural quotation for its efficacy but whereas the liturgy for consecration united the congregation, building, and scriptural quotations in its performance, here the exegesis of the gospel passage seeks to separate the material church from its congregation. The 'church' has two separate manifestations, the spiritual and the material, and this separation is even more emphatic when the sermon asserts that God is not 'spousid wiþ þis lyym and þis stoon'. The deixis creates a proximity to the material building that the statement itself undercuts; God is not married to *this* physical building, the sermon declares decisively. The material church is merely a vessel that contains man ('þe hous of lym and stoon, þat conteyneþ siche men'), it is not the house of God.

Another Lollard sermon deploys the container metaphor to explain why presence in the material building is no guarantee of salvation or membership of the church of the saved. Exploiting the precision afforded by prepositions, the sermon explains with reference to the parable of the fishing net in Matthew, 13.47–50, that 'on two manerus ben men in þis chirche':

> Somme men ben in þis chyrche and eke of þis chyrche; and þes men may not wende ouȝt of þis net. And oþre men ben only in þis chyrche and not of þis chyrche; and þes men wendon out.[36]

The sermon adapts the 'þis chyrche' formula that is crucial for establishing loyalty between congregation and parish church and uses it to emphasise that true membership of the church belongs only to the predestined. The saved are 'in and of' this church, but the damned are 'in but *not* of' this church, able to enter the material church physically but lacking membership of the true spiritual church. This ties in to the dedication sermon in which the first definition of the church is 'men þat shulen be saved'. While on earth, the predestined mingle with the damned in the material church which, rather than a sacred space, is merely a place where 'boþe gode and yuel' gather, as the dedication sermon states. There is a clear distinction, then, between the 'visible, institutional church and the invisible community of those who will be saved', as J. Patrick Hornbeck argues.[37] And although Lollard sermons are often quick to assert that we should not boast 'þat we ben membris of holy chyrche' because 'hit is hyd from vs wheþur we schulle be sauyd', a considerable amount of rhetorical energy is devoted to dividing the saved from the damned.[38] In another sermon, based on the miraculous catch of fish in Luke, 5.1–11 the two groups are even described as belonging to separate churches: 'holy chirche or chirche of God, þat on no maner may be dampnyd; and þe chirche of þe feend, þat for a tyme is good and lasteþ not, and þis was neuere holy chirche ne part þerof'.[39] Here the word 'chirche' is no longer inherently sacred; it must be qualified as holy or belonging to God before it can be securely identified as the true community of Christians.

The drive to divide and categorise the different churches is established in the entries for 'ecclesia' and 'edifiyng' in the Middle English translation of the *Rosarium Theologie*. An alphabetical compendium of Lollard teaching for the use of preachers, the *Rosarium* provides a short summary of key beliefs and its influence has been seen in texts such as *The Lanterne of Liȝt* and the *Apology for Lollard Doctrine*.[40] The entry for 'ecclesia' asserts that 'holi chirche, is seid many maners': 'a material temple halowed of þe bischope' and then three manners of 'noumbour'. The 'noumbour of chosen bi þamself, or for noumbour of reproued be þamself, or medely for noumbour of þam to be saued & reproued togedere' (p. 66). The number of the saved and damned reside within the church, again drawing on the image of the fishing net: 'for as þe nette gederiþ al kynd of fiches of god & of yuel, so þis chirch conteneþ in it choson & reproued willes it walkeþ here' (pp. 66–7). The *Rosarium* then goes on to divide the church into three parts: the church 'trauelyng, slepyng, and ouercomyng' (p. 67), which corresponds to the church on earth, in purgatory, and in heaven. The travailing church is the 'body of predestinate men wilez it walkeþ here to þe contre, & þis sufferiþ many tribulacions', alluding to the Lollards' current state of persecution in the world (p. 67). The sleeping church is the saved suffering in purgatory and the overcoming church is 'þe congregacion of blessed men in þe contre of heuen' (p. 67). In contrast to *What the Church Betokeneth*, which presents a unified picture of the church, marrying architecture and congregation, the Lollard approach to the church is to divide and conquer. The material church is a container that holds both the saved and the damned but it is not until Judgement Day that the three churches will be united. The *Rosarium* explains that 'one gret chirche forsoþ schal be made of al þise in the day of dome. Þis chirch is þe misty body of Criste, & Criste is þe hede of þe same body' (p. 67). Those 'þat departeþ fro þe vnite of hym is noȝt a membre of his holy chirche' (p. 68) and this division in the earthly church is compounded by the assertion that while Christ is head of 'holi chirche', the devil is 'þe hede of wicked men, wiche bene in a maner his body to go wiþ hym into tourmentyng of ailastyng fire' (p. 68). As we will see in the *Lanterne of Liȝt*, the concept of the devil's church is deliberately constructed in Lollard texts in order to cleanse the 'true' church of the predestined from any association with wickedness. But, reimagining the pastoral concept of the devil's tavern, the devil's church becomes an independent space, brought to life by textual discussion and vying for the laity's attention.

Returning to the *Rosarium*, the entry for 'edifiyng' discusses the oppositional relationship between the material church and the spiritual church in more detail, drawing on Christ's experience at the temple in the gospels to establish an inversely proportionate relationship between sanctity and church building:

> Oure Lord entred into þe edifying of þe temple sekyng þe holynez of þe temple, but wen he fand noþing in þe temple þat was propre of þe temple he ȝede, goyng out of þe temple, for þe edifiyng forsoþ stode þat men reised, þe holinez forsoþ fel awey wiche God had ordeyned. Forwi þe temple of men is beldedyng of stones of fair makyng, þe temple of God forsoþ is congregacioun of chosene men lyuyng religiously. A man forsoþ is delited in beledyng of wallez, God forsoþ in conuersacion of sentis, seyng þe profete, 'Lorde, I haue luffed þe fayrnes of þi house.' Wiche fairnez? Noȝt wiche þe diuersite of schynyng marblez makeþ, but wiche þe variosnez or diuersenes of lyuyng grace giffeþ [...] þat for a tyme deceyueþ & iapeþ or bigiliþ þe eien, þis forsoþ wiþout end edifieþ þe vnderstandyng. (p. 70)

As the 'edifiyng' of men is raised, 'holinez' falls away; the increased materiality of the temple directly reduces its sanctity. This is all the more serious because the holiness has been 'ordeyned' (established or consecrated) by God himself, who dwells not in the temple built by man but in the living temple that is man ('chosene men lyuyng religiously'). The opposition between God and man's attitudes is further emphasised when the text explains that man 'delited in beledyng of wallez, God forsoþ in conuersacion of sentis'. The *Rosarium* then quotes Psalm, 25.8, 'Lorde I haue luffed þe fayrnes of þi house', and explains that true fairness is not 'þe diuersite of schynyng marblez' that 'deceyueþ & iapeþ or bigiliþ þe eien' but the 'diuersenes of lyuyng grace'. It is this that 'edifieþ þe vnderstandyng'. In the Vulgate, the passage reads *Domine, dilexi decorem domus tuae* [Lord, I have loved the *beauty* of your house] whereas in the Wycliffite Bible, fairness has been substituted for beauty because of the crucial importance of the concept in Lollard ecclesiology.[41] Rather than fair denoting beauty in outward appearance, for the Lollards church decoration was inherently *un*fair as the much-needed sustenance of the poor was translated into costly, dead materials.

The language of this critique is drawn from the Seven Corporal Works of Mercy, which encouraged parishioners to do good deeds such as feeding the hungry or clothing the naked. The anonymous Wycliffite work known as *How Satan and his Children* offers a systematic explanation of how 'sathanas & his children turnen werkis of mercy vpsodom & disceyuen men þer-inne & in here fyue wittis'.[42] The Works of Mercy are turned 'vpsodom' (upside-down) which, as the Middle English Dictionary explains, means to be transformed 'into a state of reversal or negation, into a contradiction of itself'.[43] For example, Christ 'comaundiþ men of power to fede hungry pore men' but the fiend teaches them to 'make costy festis & waste many goodis on lordis & riche men & to suffre pore men sterue & perische for hunger'.[44] Clothing the naked is reversed when money is spent on adorning images, or purchasing elaborate vestments and bridles for horses, the latter reminding us of Chaucer's Monk in the *General Prologue* whose bridle 'gynglen in a whistlynge wynd als cleere / And eek as loude as dooth the chapel belle.'[45] The Monk's bells are not a call to prayer in the church but a reminder of his secular concerns. *How Satan and his Children* explains that Christ teaches us to 'herbwre pore men' but the friars 'maken grete houses & costy & gaely peyntid' which forces the poor to 'lie wiþ-outen or geten houslewth at pore men or ellis perische for wederis & cold'.[46] Here the arrogant churches of the friars exclude the poor who are forced to endure the very weather against which the church building should offer protection. Christ is the good host, welcoming the poor inside, and what is additionally important about this text is that it is Christ himself who performs the Works of Mercy, rather than a pious parishioner, as we will see in a stained glass window that I will discuss in further detail at the end of this chapter. Charitable works are practised in imitation of Christ and they have the welfare of the poor at their heart.

Christ's example is again crucial in the sermon on the state of the church preached at St Paul's cross in 1406 by the Lollard William Taylor. Taylor complained that:

> Sum men anoon caren for susteynynge of greet bildyngis of tree and stoon, and recken not of þe susteynynge of þe hooly temple

> of God þat is man, þe which, glorified in body and soule, shal be euerlastynge tabernacle of God, for þe which to be repareilid Crist fro þe myddis of his herte shedde out his precious blood endelesly, lasse reckinge of sich costlew bilding.[47]

Here Taylor employs the traditional Lollard opposition between 'bildingis of tree and stoon' and the true image of God, which is mankind, but he does this with reference to the Pauline reading of man as the temple of God in 1 Corinthians, 3.16–7. This passage was the basis for Robert Grosseteste's influential treatise the *Templum Dei*, and here it is developed by Taylor to depict mankind as a building in need of restoration.[48] Taylor explains that Christ shed his blood 'fro þe myddis of his herte' so that man, the 'tabernacle of God', can be 'repareilid'. This verb means to 'restore to God's favour' and 'revivify' but also to rebuild (a city or temple).[49] Christ's blood is a spiritual and physical restorative that rebuilds the true temple of God, man, in direct contrast to the material restoration work underway in many fifteenth-century churches. Christ does not care about 'costlew building' but shed his blood from the middle of his heart to restore mankind. The image of the bleeding heart evokes the traditional relationship between the wound in Christ's side and the birth of the church but Taylor is careful to eschew any connection with the material church. In Lydgate's poem *Cristes Passioun*, that I discussed in Chapter 3, Christ declares that when 'blood & water went be my sides doun [...] þe bylding first began' but for Taylor, Christ's blood restores the allegorical tabernacle of God, not its material counterpart.[50] Taylor's Christ is a good Lollard who cares more for man than for 'susteynyng of greet bildyngis of tree and stoon'.

Taylor draws on the Biblical depiction of the temple when he contrasts the state of the contemporary church with the church in the time of Christ, and the response which the reader ought to have to it: 'certeyn, so haue we greet mater of weping if we biholden þe nobletee, glorie and clennesse of þe raþere [earlier] chirche in Cristis tyme and his apostlis' (p. 8). In his sermon, Taylor draws on the emotional response of the people to the new temple that was built after the Babylonian captivity; there was much rejoicing, but the people who had seen the original temple wept at the sight of its replacement (1 Esdras, 3.12–13). Taylor transfers this dual reaction on to contemporary Christians, commenting:

> Neþeles summe now as in þat tyme, not seynge þe abhomynacioun of þe desolacioun stondinge in þe hooly place, shynyngly arayed and

> delicatly fed wiþ poore mennys goodis, criynge areren up her vois in gladnesse – and summe wepen; and so þe vois of hem þat maken mirþe and þe vois of þe wepyng of þe puple ben medlid togidere. (p. 8)

Those who cry with gladness are unable to see ‘þe abomynacioun of desolacioun stondinge in þe hooly place’ that is clothed and fed with poor men’s goods. The Middle English Dictionary glosses this phrase in Wycliffite texts as denoting sacrilegious images, but ‘desolacioun’ is also used to indicate a state of distress or ruin, such as the desolation of a city or, in Higden’s *Polychronicon*, the desolation of the temple.[51] Both meanings come into play here: the people are unable to see either the image that is ‘shynyngly arayed’ or the fundamental desolation that stands at the heart of fifteenth-century holy places. The church is portrayed as a ruin, abject and empty, and it is the ability to recognise this desolation that *The Lanterne of Liȝt* teaches in its systematic delineation of the church in all its forms, both spiritual and material. It is only by truly recognising the desolation of the contemporary church that it can be reformed.

The Lanterne of Liȝt: Identifying the material church and the fiend’s church

The Lanterne of Liȝt, written between 1409–15, is an essential source for examining the Lollard position on the material church. Anne Hudson asserts that the *Lanterne* represents the ‘radical wing of Lollardy’, and certainly possession of the text saw the London currier John Claydon tried for heresy by Archbishop Chichele and burnt in Smithfield in 1415.[52] More recently, however, Nicholas Watson has argued that ‘it proves remarkably difficult to pinpoint any precise moment in the text where its radicalism can be shown to be strictly “heretical”’ and he suggests that we should reconsider the text within the ‘powerful English tradition of pastoral writing […] whose aim is to cultivate the piety of individual readers by telling them in detail how they can remove themselves from the world and cultivate a life of inner holiness in separation from the sinfulness of their surroundings’.[53] A major strategy in aiding this self-imposed exile is the text’s delineation of the church in all its forms so that through educated ‘discernment’, as Watson puts it, the reader can make the choice to ‘leeue þe fendis chirche & brynge ȝoure silf boþe bodi & soule in to þe chirch of Iesu Crist while grace & mercy may be grauntid’.[54]

The Lanterne of Liȝt begins by establishing what James M. Dean has called a 'crisis atmosphere', asking for God's mercy in 'þise daies of greet tribulacioun' in which the devil has 'marrid [corrupted] þis world' and broken the 'oonhed or vnite' of Christendom (p. 2).[55] After the opening five chapters that delineate the nature of the antichrist, the *Lanterne* turns its attention to the definition of the church, declaring that there are 'þre chirchis [...] and miche þei diuersen iche from oþir to hem þat taken good hede. But witles foolis ben marrid here þat wil not lerne to knowe iche atwynne' (p. 22). It is the aim of the text to teach the reader how to 'knowe' each church separately ('atwynne') as they are greatly divergent ('miche þei diuersen') from one another. The first church is the congregation of the saved and the second is the material church, following the definition given in the *Rosarium Theologie*, but the *Lanterne* adds a third church to its definition, the fiend's church. The text not only divides the congregation of the saved from the material building, it also attempts to separate them from the damned by housing the reprobate in the fiend's church and thereby purifying the true church of the saved. Ironically, as we shall see, this strategy endows the fiend's church with greater autonomy and imaginative power. Rather than sinful behaviour in the material church being an opportunity for the reinscription of sanctity, as we saw in the literature of pastoral care, in *The Lanterne of Liȝt*, the textual construction of the fiend's church establishes a rival profane space that is far more difficult to control.

The *Lanterne* begins by defining the name and likeness of the true church according to the scriptures (pp. 22–4). The church is 'clepid a litil flok' (Luke, 12.32), 'þe chosun noumbre of hem þat shullen be saued' (Ecclesiasticus, 3.1), 'a clene chaast maiden' (Ephesians, 5.25, 27) and 'Cristis spouse' (2 Corinthians, 11.2). It is then 'lickned' (likened) to 'a womman wiþ childe' (John, 16.21), 'a womman clad in þe sunne' (Revelation, 12.1), 'Petris litile boot þe whiche was in myddis of þe see' (Matthew, 14.24; Mark, 6.47; Luke, 8.22–3), and 'paradise' (Ezekiel, 31.8). At first, the text is keen to preserve a distinction between the specific names and likenesses of the church, but the chapter then unifies the diversity by declaring:

> But how euere we speken in diuerse names or licknessis of þis holi chirche þei techen nouȝt ellis but þis oo name. Þat is to seie þe congregacioun or gedering togidir of feiþful soulis þat lastingli kepen feiþ & trouþe in word & in dede to God & to man & reisen her lijf in seker hope of mercy & grace & blisse at her ende and ouer-coueren

> or hillen þis bilding in perfite charite. Þat schal not faile in wele ne in woo. Of þis spak seint Poul to þe Corinthis & in hem to alle oþir seiyng Cor. iii '*Templum enim dei sanctum est quod estis vos*.' Þe temple of God is holi & þat ben ȝe & bi þis we vndirstand þat þe soule of a riȝtwise man is þe seet of God. (p. 25)

Each of the names and likenesses signifies the congregation of faithful souls who 'reisen' or elevate their lives in the hope of salvation and 'ouer-coueren or hillen þis bilding in perfite charite'. The reference to 'þis bilding' here is surprising and the passage seems to suggest that the congregation 'ouer-coueren or hillen' the material building with their virtuous actions. But the quotation that follows from Corinthians suggests that 'þis bilding' is the temple of God which is the soul, rather than the material church, but the use of the verb 'hillen' reinforces the material aspect of the comparison. 'Hillen' means 'to cover' and is used both of clothing and of the shelter provided by a roof.[56] It is used in this way in *Pierce the Ploughman's Crede*, for example, when describing the cloister 'pilered and peynt [...] all y-hyled with leed lowe to the stones'.[57] Despite wanting to separate the people from the material church in its first definition, the *Lanterne*'s vocabulary betrays a lingering reliance on material imagery.[58]

Having established the church as a community based on scriptural quotation and allegory, the *Lanterne* then moves on to its definition of the second church, entitled 'what is þe material chirche wiþ hir honourmentis':

> The secounde chirche dyuerse from þis is comyng togiddir of good & yuel in a place þat is halowid fer from worldi occupacioun for þere sacramentis schullen be tretid & Goddis lawe boþe radde & prechid. Of þis chirche spekiþ þe prophet Dauiþ & seiþ. Ps. Lxvii '*In ecclesijs benedicite deo domino*.' In chirchis blesse ȝe to þe Lord God. In þis place oure graciouse God heeriþ oure preiers in special manere & bowiþ his eere to his seruauntis in forme as he grauntid Salamon III Re. ix II Paral. vii '*Oculi quoque mei erunt aperti & aures mee erecte ad orationem eius qui in loco isto orauerit*'. Myn iȝen seiþ God schullen be open & myn eeris schullen be lefte vp to þe preiour of him þat haþ iustli preid in þis place & þis is clepid a material place for it is made bi mannes crafte of lyme of tymbre & of stoon wiþ oþir necessarijs þat longen þerto. (pp. 35–6)

There is much here that accords with the definition of sacred space in my earlier chapters and that could be considered orthodox or at least traditional. The church is 'halowid fer from worldi occupacion' for the performance of the sacraments and the preaching of God's law and the text draws on the scriptural reference to God having his eyes and ears trained upon the church that is employed in *The Book of the Foundation of St Bartholomew's Church* (1, Kings 8.29; 2 Chronicles, 7.15). But where the *Book* declared that as a result of God's special attention 'the asker yn hit schall resceyue, the seker shall fynde, and the rynger or knocker shall entre', for the *Lanterne*-author it is the prayers 'of him þat haþ *iustli* preid in þis place' that are heard.[59] 'Iustli' here means righteously and honestly but also, I would argue, with justice and fairness.[60] In the Wycliffite Bible prologue to the Book of Esther, the author declares that 'God helpith hem that tristen in him and lyuen *iustli* in the drede of him', and I have already discussed the discourse of social justice that runs through Lollard accounts of the material church.[61] God will hear the prayers that are fairly and honestly offered in 'þis place', and 'þis place' is very clearly a material location in the passage. It is 'clepid a material place' because it is made 'bi mannes crafte' out of lime, timber, and stone, foregrounding the materials and skill involved in its construction. But in Lollard texts, emphasising the 'construction' of a place does not contribute to its sanctity, it is a reminder of its earthly status and its difference from the corporeal temple of God which is man.

The *Lanterne* asserts that this second, material church is 'dyuerse', that is, separated, from the church of the saved previously described, and this is because although the material church is 'halowid', it is a place in which good and evil come together. This church is not purged of the sinful by virtue of its sanctity, like the material church in the literature of pastoral care; that church expelled the sinful and performed miracles to ensure the continued efficacy of its consecration. The material church of the *Lanterne* is just that, a material building. And it is a material building with none of the sacred defences that pastoral care texts came to rely on for their teaching. The *Lanterne* emphasises this by declaring that the place has no power to sanctify man: 'Man bi vertu of Goddis word halowiþ þis place but þis place mai not halowe man' (p. 36). This argument is evidenced with reference to heaven, the 'moost hooli place', and paradise, the 'moost miriest place':

> Alas what woodnes is þis to boost of hooli placis & we oure silf to be suche viciouse foolis. Lucifer was in heuene & þat is moost hooli place but for his synne he fel to helle. Þe place myȝt not holde him. Adam was in paradise, þe moost miriest place & for his synne he was dryuen out, þe place miȝt not defende him. Þou þat art neiþir in

> heuene ne in paradise but in þis wrecchid world where wenest þou to fynde a place to halowe þee þat leuest not þi synne? (pp. 36–7)

It is madness to boast of holy places when Lucifer was not held by heaven and Adam was not defended by paradise. Both were expelled for their sin. This is a very different understanding of 'holy' places to that of *The Book of the Foundation*, for example, which boasts that 'trewly God is yn this place And though ther be non place with-owte hym [...] nat for the place these be done only but for man for the whiche *bothe man & place is reuerencid*.'[62] Popular devotional practice held that the church could, in fact, protect the individual from sudden death, for example, through the sight of a wall painting of St Christopher (figure 3) or presence in the church during the elevation of the host.[63] The *Lanterne*-author would disagree that the 'place miȝt [...] defende' the individual, and his text, rather than supporting the sanctity and protective qualities of the material church, aims to educate the reader in understanding the 'true' church as the predestined faithful instead.

The *Lanterne* then turns to the traditional Lollard critique of elaborate ornamentation, commenting that 'miche peple demen it a medeful werke to iape mennes iȝen wiþ curiouse bilding & manye veyn staring siȝtis in her chirches but Ierom forbediþ þis þing to be don & dampneþ it vttirli for greete synne' (p. 37). Rather than a 'medeful' or spiritually beneficial work, 'curiouse' building is, emphatically, a 'greete synne' (p. 37). 'Crist oure pore Lord haþ halowid þe hous or þe chirche of oure pouerte', the *Lanterne* counters, 'bere we þe cros of Crist & richesse acounte we as cley' (p. 38). Christ has consecrated the house of our poverty, not richly decorated material buildings. This redeploys the concept of consecration and the metaphor of the house to support the Lollard emphasis on poverty.[64] The *Lanterne* then quotes William of St Amour who argues that 'suche men semen to turne þe breed of pore men in to stoones & in þis þei ben more cruelar þan þe deuel þat axid stoones to be turned into bred' (p. 38). The allusion here is to Christ's temptation in the wilderness by the devil (Matthew, 4.1–4) but the image of the transformation of bread into stones is additionally powerful because of its reversal of the life-giving power of the Eucharist. Rather than feeding the poor both in the flesh and in the spirit as Christ's body, the bread becomes imprisoned in its physical state and concretised as sterile stone. The church is no longer built out of the living stones of the congregation; its material form is a cruel trick that starves the poor of their physical and spiritual food.

The *Lanterne* offers four additional reasons against the excessive decoration of churches, beginning with the argument that we have seen earlier that 'bisines aboute suche costious bilding wiþ manyfold worldli occupacioun to reparailen hem whanne þei peyren & holde hem vp in þis same forme bringeþ in necligence of goostli maners, quenching vertues & good þewis' (p. 40). 'Loweli housis & pore refreynen þe coueitise of oþir' and set a good example, but more importantly, the *Lanterne* argues that:

> We owen raþir to mervaile in þe siȝt of heuene þan in þe siȝt of bilding of mannes handiwork & miche more schulde we mervaile þe greet werkis of God þan þe werkis of deedli men þat duren but a while. (p. 41)

The 'mervaile', which is such a characteristic response to and part of sacred space, is here redeployed to the works of God and the sacred space of heaven. The church should not be an attempt to replicate heaven on earth, it should set an example of poverty and humility, and our marvel should be reserved for the space that is truly sacred and eternal, heaven, rather than the works of men 'þat duren but a while'.

The next chapter of the *Lanterne* deals with the coming together of good and evil in the material church using the parable of the net, a popular image in Lollard ecclesiology:

> Þe secounde chirche here in erþe is lijke to a nett sent into þe see for as þe see ebbiþ & flowiþ so þis chirche now riseþ & falliþ to preise & lake [blame] as wawis of þe see þat risen feel siþes [many times] ouir menes miȝt. (p. 44)

Here the static, lifeless material church is replaced with the fluid, changing image of the church as a net in the sea which rises and falls. The sea is interpreted as the Seven Deadly Sins: the waves are pride that 'al dai men bollen [puff up] in hiȝenes of herte', the bitterness of the water represents envy, the storms signify wrath, and so on (p. 44). The fish in the sea represent men on earth and the fishermen are the angels at Judgement Day when good and evil are finally divided. Having submerged the material church in the sea of allegory, the *Lanterne* moves on to the chapter on 'discrecioun', that is, the ability to distinguish between good and evil:

> Noon may discryue þise twoo parties verrili iche from oþir wandiryng in þis secounde chirche for licknessis þat þei vsen and also þei han in

> comune mani heuenli þingis. For oure Lord haþ in his chirche laburers about his vintre boþe fastars, preiars & also wakears. Almisdoars ben in þis chirche wiþ prechours & redars of lessouns & singars traueilen here also wiþ minastrars of sacramentis wiþ studiars in Goddis lawe & men þat maken louedaies and like seruauntis haþ þe fende in þe þridde chirche but þei don her seuyse in a straunge manere. Neþeles þei ben hard to knowe þerfore we schal marke hem how wondirfulli þei varien in þise forseide condiciouns. (p. 48)

Distinguishing between good and evil in the material church is difficult because 'þei han in comune mani heuenli þingis', which the text defines as the offices and ritual practices of the church: fasting, keeping vigils, preaching, singing, administering the sacraments, for example. The primary difference is that they are performed in the third church, which belongs to the fiend, 'in a straunge manere'. 'Straunge' here emphasises the foreignness of this practice and the *Lanterne* tries to distance such evil practitioners from the second church by containing them in the third church that belongs to the fiend.[65] But as the opening of the chapter reminds us, all of these activities take place 'in þis secounde chirche', that is, the material church. Because they are 'hard to knowe', the author declares that 'we schal marke hem how wondirfulli þei varien [deviate] in þise forseide condiciouns' (p. 48). The use of the verb 'marke' is significant here because its meanings are primarily spatial. To 'mark' means 'to set the boundaries or limits' of a place and also to make marks on stone such as marks of measurement for architectural planning and for the purpose of identification.[66] It also means to 'take note mentally' and the spatial, architectural, and mental meanings come together here as the *Lanterne* endeavours to mark out a space for the fiend's church that keeps it far away from the church of the saved and simultaneously constructs a recognisible representation of that church to enable the text's readers to identify it. This section of the text is clearly pastoral in its aim of teaching the laity and it betrays a desire to cleanse both the first church of the saved and the material church by keeping the profane practices of the devil's church in a safe space elsewhere. But by delineating in such detail the workings of the fiend's church, the text risks bringing it to life in textual form. Just as the *Lanterne* offers a blueprint for the true church of the saved, it also provides a detailed outline of a profane church and its practices through a principle of opposition.

This is achieved by contrasting each practitioner in Christ's church with their opposite in the fiend's church. Fasters in Christ's church 'abstynen hem from lustis for to tempir þe coragenes of þe reble fleishe & kepe her bodi clene chast & suget to her soule'; fasters in the fiend's church 'fasten for vngroundid cause, summe fasten for ypocrisie [...] summe wiþdrawen from her wombe boþe mete & drink to spare her purse' (pp. 48–9). Men who pray in Christ's church do so with 'deuocioun wiþ al þe strengþe of her herte & her mouþe', invoking the imagery of the heart that we saw earlier, but men who pray in the fiend's church, on the other hand, 'maken miche noise mumling wiþ her lippis' (p. 50), familiar imagery from pastoral care exempla featuring lazy monks who neglect their prayers. In this section, the author exclaims, 'Lord! Whanne þi body is in þe chirche and þi herte in þe world [...] art þou not þanne wrechidli diuidid in þi silf?' (pp. 50–1). This imagery of division returns to one of the key ideas in the text and the reference to a non-specific church, 'þe chirche' rather than the fiend's church or Christ's church, reminds us that *both* the sacred and profane church are to be found in the material church of lime and stone; the difference is the location of the heart. If the heart is in the world, the material church is the fiend's church; if the heart is fully present at worship, the material church has the potential to become a sacred space. The sanctity of the church is therefore entirely reliant upon the heart of the individual.

The chapter continues with contrasting archetypes of the officers of Christ and the fiend's churches. Alms-doers in Christ's church 'releuen in dwe tyme wiþ þe plente of her catel hem þat suffren nede' (p. 53), unlike the 'curious' church-builders that are such a constant in Lollard polemic on the material church. Preachers in Christ's church 'prechen treweli to edifie þe peple in vertu' (p. 55); preachers in the fiend's church, rather like Chaucer's Pardoner, preach 'vndir colour for to take ȝiftis' (p. 55). Readers, singers, administrators of the sacraments, students, and peacemakers in each of the churches follow. This delineation of sacred and profane roles ties in with my argument that sacred and profane space is produced by human practice but while the *Lanterne* claims that both good and evil are to be found in the material church, the clear divisions in the text between the activities of Christ's and the fiend's officers belies this. The constant repetition of 'in Cristis chirche' and 'in þe fendis chirche' strongly suggests that the two churches are separate spaces and in this respect the fiend's church is indebted to the idea of the tavern as the fiend's church in the literature of pastoral care, an alternative space that individuals frequent instead of attending their parish church. This endows the fiend's church with a dangerous autonomy. It is it given the same imaginative space in the text as Christ's church and, moreover, there is no mechanism for the fiend's church to be destroyed or for its power to be redirected towards the sanctification of Christ's church, as we saw with the helpful devils and demons in Chapter 3. In fact, in the final chapter of the *Lanterne*, the fiend's church gains further independence as the text endows this profane inversion of sacred space with its own allegorical interpretation.

The fiend's church is built out of sin and its congregation are sinners. The foundation of the church is 'in glotenye & leccherie' (p. 128), the 'hilling' or covering of the church is 'pride & hiȝenes of liif' (p. 129) and night and day, 'wickidnesse schal cumpasse aboute þis chirche vpon hir wallis & traueile in middis of it & vnriȝtwisnesse & okir-julling [usury] and treccherie haþ not stinted in þe weies of hir' (p. 129). The allegorical edifice of the fiend's church turns the true church upside down, to recall the method of inversion employed by *How Satan and his Children*. The temple of God that was 'hillen [...] in perfite charite' (p. 25) is now covered with pride and 'hiȝenes of liif', reminding us of the equation of height with sin in Lollard ecclesiology. Where Christ was at the heart of the church in *What the Church Betokeneth* and the consecration ceremony enclosed the building in sanctity through ritual procession, here wickedness shall 'cumpasse aboute þis chirche vpon hir wallis & traueile in middis of it'. The members of this profane church are 'sclaundirars & blasfemars', 'glosears' (flatterers), 'bacbitears' (backbiters), 'robbars and extorcioneris, tyrauntis, & oppressours' (p. 131). They are merchants and taverners, usurers and deceivers, men who puff themselves up and wear fashionable clothes, with pinched-in bellies and long-pointed shoes (p. 132). They are 'þoo [those]' that paint their faces and wear elaborate headdresses 'to make hemsilf salle-kene [eager] to synne & setten abrood her pappis to cacche men wiþ her lymȝerdes' (p. 132). Although 'pappis' can refer to the breast, regardless of sex, it is likely that the *Lanterne*-author is referring to women's fashions here, especially given the reference to 'gigge-haltiris' and 'honycombis', which Swinburn interprets as elaborate collars and headdresses.[67] The seductive appeal of such clothing as a snare to sin reminds us of Margery Kempe's penchant for vain apparel before her conversion. Her cloaks were 'daggyd [ornamentally slashed]' and underlaid with 'dyvers colowrs betwen the daggys, that it schuld be the mor staryng [ostentatious] to mennys sygth and hirself the mor ben worshepd' (p. 57). Margery's clothing is deliberately used to attract the attention and worship of men, a strategy which the literature of pastoral care recognises as a particular danger of the presence of women in church. The *Lanterne*'s comparison of such self-promotion to a 'lymȝerde' snare (a stick smeared with birdlime for catching birds) recurs in a similar context of the enticing yet sinful appeal of visual excess in the poem to which I will now turn, *Pierce the Ploughman's Crede*, but with reference to the church building rather than its female congregation.

Pierce describes the great churches of the friars as 'heyghe helle-hous of Kaymes [Cain's] kynde' and he laments the negative effect that the visual display of these buildings has upon the individual who enters the church to hear a mass:

> His sight schal so be set on sundrye werkes,
> The penounes and the pomels and the poyntes of scheldes
> With-drawen his deuocion and dusken his herte;
> I likne it to a lym-yerde to drawen men to hell,
> And to worchipe of the fend to wraththen the soules. (561–5)

The excessive, secular decoration darkens the heart and acts as a 'lym-yerde' to draw men to hell and the worship of the devil, producing the very fiend's church that the *Lanterne of Liȝt* educates the reader to recognise and abjure. In *Pierce the Ploughman's Crede*, the ordinary layman in search of pastoral education comes upon the concrete materialisation of the *Lanterne*'s fiend's church in his encounter with the great houses of the friars. The fiend's church is not located within the material churches of the parish in this poem, but stands in direct competition, not only draining the financial resources of the laity but endangering their spiritual lives. The *Lanterne* declares that 'þe fendis chirche pursueþ Cristis chirche in malice bi weye of sclaundir & sleeyng' but Christ's church 'purswеþ yuel lyuars in charite bi weye of amendement' (p. 133). Amendment is a keyword in *Pierce the Ploughman's Creed*. The friars try to trick the narrator into 'amending' their houses by making financial donations, a purely material interpretation of amendment that compounds their church's capacity to 'dusken' the devoted heart. But, just like the reader of the *Lanterne*, the *Crede*-narrator goes through a didactic process that enables him to recognise the fiend's church and avoid being caught by the 'lym-yerde' in its sticky trap.

Pierce the Ploughman's Crede: Entering the fiend's church

The narrator of *Pierce the Ploughman's Crede* has one goal, to complete his pastoral education by learning his creed, and the poem charts his journey through the great houses of the friars in his quest to do so. This alliterative poem, in the *Piers Plowman* tradition, stages a narrative encounter between a poor layman and the very worst examples of the sinful material churches discussed thus far. The critical difference, however, is the genre in which these churches appear. *Pierce the Ploughman's Crede* is not a sermon or treatise, it is a narrative poem and it places an individual in direct contact with material buildings and shows how those buildings might be read by an ordinary layperson seeking religious instruction. Like the pilgrims in the *Canterbury Interlude*, with which I began this book, the narrator enters the church but unlike the Miller and the Pardoner, he is a proficient reader of the space around him. He is, in fact, the ideal reader that the author of the *Lanterne of Liȝt* hoped to produce: able to discern when he finds himself in the fiend's church and to act accordingly. The *Lanterne* concludes by urging the reader to 'leeue þe fendis chirche' (p. 136) and the *Crede*-narrator does precisely this and as a result, meets the only person truly able to teach him the Creed, Pierce the Ploughman. The narrator completes his quest for the creed on a road in the company of a poor man and his destitute family, with Pierce praying that God, of his great might, should 'amende' all of the false friars (848). The poem has produced a 'desirable' narrative of the church building, to return to Christopher Tilley, in which the layman is able to recognise the fiend's church masquerading as the house of God. But the vision of the material buildings that the narrator has encountered remains in the reader's mind; the effect that sinful buildings have on sacred space is bleak and pessimistic. This is space without the sanctity. Buildings that are barren of good works. Houses that do not contain the presence of God but instead harbour the pride, hypocrisy, and greed of man.

The catalyst for the poem is the narrator's admission that 'all myn A.b.c. after haue y lerned/And patred in my pater-noster iche poynt after other' (5–6). He has also learned his Ave Maria, but 'all my kare is to comen for y can nohght my Crede' (8). He fears that 'the prest wil me punyche and penaunce enioyne' (10) and he seeks out the four orders of friars in turn but none of them are able to help him; instead they criticise each other and offer him absolution in return for money and donations to their churches. Before I turn to the details of his experience, it is worth reflecting on the nature of the narrator's quest and his choice of how to pursue it. The Creed makes up the trinity of basic knowledge for the laity, alongside the Pater Noster and the Ave Maria, and as John Mirk explains in his

Instructions for Parish Priests, the responsibility for delivering that knowledge lay with the parish priest:

> The pater noster and þe crede,
> Preche þy paresche þou moste nede;
> Twyes or þryes in þe ȝere
> To þy paresche hole and fere. (404–7)

That the narrator of *Pierce the Ploughman's Crede* is lacking this knowledge may be an implicit criticism of the parish clergy. He should not need to seek instruction from the friars as he should have learned the Creed at home in his parish. The poet does not pursue this, admittedly literal, line of argument but it is linked to the competitive and often hostile relationship between the secular clergy and the friars as a result of the latter being granted the ecclesiastical privileges of preaching, confession, and burial.[68] This meant that the laity had an alternate source of teaching and indeed absolution, one that John Mirk tried to discourage when he instructs parish priests that a man may not confess to a priest outside the parish without express permission or a very good reason.[69] In the *Fifty Heresies of the Friars*, the Lollard author asserts that the friars 'maken dissencioun bitwix curatis and hor gostly childer', not only by enticing the laity to confession and burying the rich, but by claiming that 'þei haf more power þan þo curat' himself.[70] The threat posed by the friars to the parish was material as well as didactic and spiritual, however. The great churches of the friars were in direct competition with parish churches and they were frequently criticised in Lollard texts for ruining established churches by diverting funds away from the parish.

De Officio Pastorali, for example, declares that the 'costly chirchis of þes ordris & oþere housis þat þey han destrien olde pariȝs chirchis'.[71] *Of the Leaven of Pharisees* asserts that if the orders say that 'grete chirchis ben worschipful to god', they should be asked 'what charite it is to laten parische chirchis fallen doun for defaute, where þe peple schulde heere goodis worde, goddis seruyce, and resceyue here sacramentis, and to maken newe chirches as castelis wiþ outen nede'.[72] Here the author compares the new churches to castles, using secular vocabulary to indicate their worldly rather than sacred nature, a feature that is also found in *Pierce the Ploughman's Crede*, as we shall see. The parish church suffers for 'defaute', that is, need and poverty.[73] There is no charity in such churches. Indeed, *Of the Leaven of Pharisees* continues that while 'men suffreden resonable cost of chirchis whi schulde þei suffre so grete cost of kechenes and ȝate housis and wast chambris for lordis and ladies and riche men, and a frere to haue a chambre for an erl or duk or a kyng whanne he is bounden to þe pouert of crist, siþ þis cost is geten bi beggen of pore men and disceit of riche mennus almes'.[74] The 'resonable' house of God is contrasted here with the additional buildings that the friars erect, dedicated to entertaining the rich, guarding the orders ('ȝate housis'), and filling the stomachs of the friars and their visitors ('kechens'). The text also makes a link between gluttony and architecture in an earlier passage in which the friars are imagined tempting people away from their devotions on holy days through a mixture of fables, visual display, and luxurious food and drink:

> Ȝif þei maken hem besi on þe holy day to preche fablis and lesyngis to þe peple and not þe gospel, and gon fro place to place and fro man to man to begge of pore men for here false lesyngis, and letten men fro here deuocioun; þei kepen not wel here holiday. Ȝif þei drawen þe peple in þe holiday by coryouste of gaye wyndownes and colours and peyntyngis and babwynrie fro conpunccion of here synnes and fro mynde of heuenely þyngis, and fede riche men wiþ pore mennus goodis, wiþ costly metis and wynes and wast spicerie to glotonye, dronkennesse, lecherie, and weiward takis, and suffren pore men hungry and þristi and in gret mischef; þei kepen euyl here holyday and letten oþere men to kepen it.[75]

This is the fiend's church built on foundations of sin, as we saw in the *Lanterne of Liȝt*, but the text develops the typical Lollard emphasis on visual excess by depicting the friars stuffing the rich with food and the people with lies and fables. This is an important connection that is also evident in *Pierce the Ploughman's Crede* in the representation of the Dominican friar in the refectory, who becomes a human 'babywynrie', a grotesque ornamentation, or in modern terms, a gargoyle.[76]

The first of the four orders that the *Crede*-narrator meets on his journey is a Franciscan, who, after criticising the virtue of the Carmelites, asserts that 'we Menures most scheweth/The pure apostelles life with penance on erthe' (103–4). His claims for the Minorites' virtue is undercut, however, when he states that 'in pouertie' they 'praien for alle oure parteners/That gyueth vs any good god to honouren' (113–14). They pray for those who are 'partners' (i.e. have paid to joined a confraternity) and who give them goods, such as 'bell other booke or breed to our fode' (115). Spiritual reward is clearly presented as a commodity available to purchase; 'money or money-worthe, here mede is in heven' (117). The Minorite then directly begs for money from the narrator by describing the convent that they are currently building and offering him a place within it:

> For we buldeth a burwgh— a brod and a large—
> A chirche and a chapaile with chambers a-lofte,
> With wide windows y-wrought and walles well heye,
> That mote bene portreid and paynt and pulched ful clene,
> With gaie glittering glas glowing as the sonne.
> And myghtestou amenden vs with money of thyn owne,
> Thou chuldest cnely bifore Crist in compas of gold
> In the wide windowe westward wel nighe in the mydell,
> And seynt Fraunces himself schall folden the in his cope,
> And presente the to the trynitie and praie for thy synnes.
> Thi name schall noblich ben wryten and wrought for the nones,
> And, in remembrance of the y-rade ther for euer. (118–29)

The friar uses a vocabulary of spaciousness here: 'brod', 'large', and 'wide' (used twice). This, however, collocates with the pejorative terms 'heye' and 'gaie' and with a focus on material decoration, in particular the 'portreid and paynt and pulched [polished]' surfaces, indicating that the abundance of space should not be read positively. This is also implied by the Minorite's use of the verb 'amenden' when he asks for a donation from the narrator. 'Amenden' is a keyword in the poem, used eight times in total: five by the friars themselves (123, 321, 369, 396) and three times by Pierce at the end of the poem (838, 843, 848). When it is used by the friars it collocates with 'oure hous' in lines 321 and 396, and here the association is similar. The Minorite asks the narrator to 'amenden vs with money of thyn owne' (123) in order to purchase a place in the stained glass window, kneeling before Christ. 'Amenden' has a range of meanings in Middle English, including to repair a building, to restore (a ruined city), to reform or strengthen (an institution), and these are the meanings that the friars employ with reference to their houses.[77] 'Amenden' also means to improve the quality or appearance, to adorn or embellish, and this for the friars would be the result of the narrator's donation to the stained glass window in the quotation above.[78] Later in the poem the Carmelite friar states that he will 'clene the assoile', despite the fact that the narrator does not know his Creed, if he will 'amenden our hous with money other ells, / With some katell other corne or cuppes of siluer' (396–7). Once again wealth, property, and high-status objects such as silver cups are the price for absolution, but the immorality of this exchange is implied if we recall that 'amenden' also means to improve spiritually or morally, and to save the soul.[79] The friars commodify absolution and do not understand what it truly means to amend the souls of the laity or indeed themselves. Indeed, the Carmelite friar is oblivious of the irony when he criticises the Dominicans and asks 'where ben thei pryue with any pore wightes, / That maie not amenden her hous ne amenden hemseluen?' (368–9). Pierce is the only person in the poem to grasp the spiritual dimensions of the term when he states that 'for *amending* of thise men [the friars] is most that I write' (838, italics mine). He uses the word again when humbly asking 'all maner men this matere amende, / Iche a word by him-self and all, yif it nedeth' (844–5), and finally he attributes the power of amending to God himself in his final prayer:

God of his grete myghte and his good grace
Saue all freres that faithfully lybben,
And alle tho that ben fals fayre hem amende,
And yiue hem wijt and good will swiche dedes to werche
That thei maie wynnen the lif that euer schal lesten! Amen. (846–50)[80]

This is far removed from the friars' understanding of what it means to 'amend'. Returning to the Minorite's description of their convent, the building would be amended or 'improved in standing' by the proliferation of secular signs and secular writing, rather than by spiritual restoration. This is evident from the initial assertion that they are building a 'burwgh', a word that encompasses a range of secular dwellings, including fortified strongholds, palaces, and castles, the latter a popular description of the friars' great churches, as we saw in *Of the Leaven of the Pharisees*.[81] The worldliness of the convent is also signalled by the Minorite's comment that 'thi name schall *noblich* ben wryten and wrought for the nones' in the window (117, italics mine). The narrator is on a quest for a spiritual text, the Creed; the Minorite offers him an alternative text which will increase his social rather than sacred standing. But luckily the narrator has the 'wit' that Pierce prays for at the end of the poem. When he parts from the Minorite, he perceptively identifies the friar's individual sin and that of his order. 'Here semeth litel trewthe: / First to blamen his brother and bacbyten him foule' (138–9), and we might remember that the occupations of the fiend's church in the *Lanterne of Liȝt* include such sins of the tongue as backbiting. He also recognises the sin of covetousness underlying the friar's proffered deal: 'y sey coueitise catel to fongen, / That Crist hath clerliche forboden and clenliche destruede' (146–7). He decides then to proceed to question the Dominicans and here he encounters the first material buildings of his quest.

The narrator has been primed for the kind of building he is likely to see when he hears the Minorite's description of their imagined convent, but this does not prepare him for the sight of the Dominican house. As Shannon Gayk and Bruce Holsinger have discussed, the narrator is beguiled by the visual extravagance and sensory splendour of the buildings and this is recreated ekphrastically in the poetic textures of the poem itself. As Gayk states:

> We do not only 'see' the scene with the narrator, we hear it as we linger on the images emphasised by the alliteration: the 'bild bold y-buld' and the 'pilers … y-peynt and pulched'. The author masterfully appeals to multiple senses.[82]

The narrator's progress through the Dominican house is worth following in detail:

> Ich highede to her house to herken of more;
> And whan y cam to that court y gaped aboute.
> Swich a bild bold, y-buld opon erthe heighte
> Saw I nought in certeine siththe a longe tyme.
> Y yemede vpon that house and yerne theron loked,
> Whough the pileres were y-peynt and pulced ful clene,
> And queynteli i-coruen with curiouse knottes,
> With wyndowes well y-wrought wide vp o-lofte
> And thanne y entrid in and even-forth went,
> And all was walled that wone though it wid were. (155–64)

The narrator is overcome by the visual display and like the Canterbury pilgrims, 'goglyng with hir heedes' in the *Interlude*, he 'gaped aboute'.[83] He looks and 'yemede' (pays attention to) the house and that looking is 'yerne', which means eager and enthusiastic.[84] The Canterbury pilgrims look with similar intensity but perhaps surprisingly with more scrutiny: they 'pyred fast and poured highe oppon the glase' and attempt to read the imagery in the stained glass, as I discussed in my introduction.[85] The *Crede*-narrator, on the other hand, although he employs the keywords of the Lollard critique of material decoration – 'heighte', 'queynteli', 'curiouse' – he focuses on 'whough' (how) the pillers are painted and polished and carved. His attention is not on *what* is depicted, but *how* it has been achieved, on the craftsmanship itself rather than what it signifies. The Lollard position on imagery often points out that such objects are 'maade be werkyng of mannys hand' and therefore should not be worshipped, but the narrator's forensic inspection of the craftsmanship almost slips into this very adoration.[86]

Fortunately, the narrator's reading of the Dominican house quickly improves as he penetrates further into the group of structures that make up the site. He develops what Bruce Holsinger has termed a form of 'critical gazing' as he shifts from focusing on the craftsmanship of particular architectural features to an assessment of their value.[87] Holsinger suggests that the poet endeavours to remind his readers 'even in the midst of its own ekphrastic performance of the social conditions that make this performance possible'.[88] For example, the narrator comments:

> The pris of a plough-lond of penyes so rounde
> To aparaile that pyler were pure lytel. (169–70)

As Helen Barr points out, the comparison highlights the 'manual labour conspicuously absent from the description of the friars in the poem' and it also reminds us of the poor men, such as the narrator, whose honest work has provided the money to 'aparaile' the Dominican house in such a lavish manner.[89] What is additionally important here, however, is the architectural feature that the narrator chooses to assess: a pillar. As I discussed above, in the allegorical tradition of *What the Church Betokeneth*, pillars 'betokyn the bysshops and doctors that maynten the feythe of hooly Church by the doctrine of God' and who should be fulfilled with the gifts of the Holy Spirit 'so that oþer men maye take gode ensample by them' (p. 87). The Dominicans were especially known for their preaching and learning and so it is especially regrettable that the pillars of their house betoken surface decoration and the social cost of their elaborate buildings. The pillar cannot be pressed into service as symbolising the Dominicans' sacred mission to preach, it is purely a material sign of their degeneration.

The narrator continues to explore the Dominican complex, discovering a range of buildings and architectural features that further emphasis the distinct lack of sanctity at work. We saw earlier that *Of the Leaven Pharisees* criticised the additional buildings that the friars construct, and they are clearly evident here:

> Thanne walked y ferrer and went all abouten,
> And seigh halles full hyghe and houses full noble,

Chambers with chymneyes and chapels gaie:
And kychens for an hyghe kinge in castells to holden,
And her dortour [dormitory] y-dighte with dores ful stronge
Fermery [infirmary] and fraitur [refectory] with fele mo houses,
And all strong ston wall sterne upon heithe,
With gaie garites and grete and iche hole y-glased
And othere houses y-nowe to herberwe the queene.
And yet thise bilderes wilne beggen a bagg-full of wheate
Of a pure pore man that maie onethe paie
Half his rente in a yer and half ben behynde. (207–18)

Despite this catalogue of buildings appropriate for royalty, the Dominicans – here denigrated to mere 'bilderes' – still beg for a bagful of wheat from the poor. The buildings and the entire complex are walled with strong stone, reflecting the Lollard criticism of the friars that they retreat into their houses which 'as Ierusaleem was wallyt aȝenys Crist and hise apostles, so þese religiows today ben wallyd aȝen cristene men'.[90] The walls do not prevent the friars from escaping for their own pleasure, however, as the narrator observes 'posternes in pryuytie to pasen when hem liste; / Orcheyardes and erberes euesed well clene' (165–6), which evokes the trysts that take place in the secular gardens of romance. When the narrator finally enters the church, he is assailed once more with secular imagery and crafty carvings:

With arches on eueriche half and belliche y-corven,
With crochetes on corners with knottes of golde,
Wyde wyndowes y-wrought y-written full thikke,
Schynen with schapen scheldes to schewen aboute,
With merkes of marchauntes y-medled bytwene,
Mo than twenty and two twyes y-noumbred.
Ther is none heraud that hath half swich a rolle,
Right as a rageman hath rekned hem newe. (173–80)

Gayk comments that the ekphrastic catalogue at the beginning of this passage 'reads like contemporary mercantile catalogues – describing and listing the worth of the various parts of the building'.[91] This focus on secular and financial assessment once again reminds us of the lack of sacred meaning here. This decorated building does not betoken the house of God, its windows do not depict holy exempla for the laity to imitate; it is a house of donors whose windows' only function is to advertise their social standing. As Gayk points out, these images are 'self-referential signs, referring only to their own creation and maintenance' and as such I would argue that they cannot produce sacred space, they can only reinforce the worldly materiality of their construction.[92] They are not generative of sanctity, they are sterile, secular signs.

But under the narrator's 'critical gaze', such signs can function as a negative exemplum and therefore teach the reader what the church and its decorations should *not* betoken. For example, the narrator compares the density of names in the window to a 'ragemen' or document that records accusations and offences.[93] In *What the Church Betokeneth*, the windows signify the scriptures (p. 87) but here that meaning is replaced by a secular text, although one that is similarly edificatory. It accuses the rich donors of being more concerned with their public reputation but it also stands as evidence for the friars' greed, usury, and deceit. *Of the Leaven Pharisees* claims that the friars '*disceyuen riche men* in makyng restitucioun of extorcions and euyl geten goodis, and suren hem of al perel ȝif þei maken siche costly houses and wast paleises to men'.[94] The narrator also turns his critical gaze on the tombs of knights that are found in the church. The distinguishing feature of their visual display is again secular; the narrator notes their coats of arms and 'conisantes' or emblems by which a knight is identified.[95] The narrator's judgement on this spectacle is key: 'all it semed seyntes y-sacred opon erthe' (186), they *seemed* to be saints sanctified upon the earth. Gayk argues that the material culture of the house promotes the power of the friars but 'teach[es] little else' and in contrast with the didactic meaning of the architectural forms set out in *What the Church Betokeneth*, this is certainly the case.[96] But there is still a lesson to be learned from looking at a space that produces overtly secular rather than sacred identity. When used in this way, the material church does not strengthen and confirm the living, breathing sanctity of the space it encloses, it highlights its absence.

This is nowhere more evident than in the depiction of the Dominican friar that the narrator finally meets. Significantly, he is not in the church but in the refectory, a space concerned not with feeding the soul but the body. The friar is described as follows:

> A greet cherl and a grym, growen as a tonne,
> With a face as fat as a full bledder
> Blowen bretfull of breth and as a bagge honged
> On bothen his chekes, and his chyn with a chol lollede,
> As greet as a gos eye growen all of grece;
> That all wagged his fleche as a quyk myre. (221–6)

In this memorable passage, the friar is compared to a series of containers: he is built like a 'tonne' or barrel, his face is fat like a 'full bledder' and a bag. As Helen Barr argues:

> The Dominican is full, not of spiritual 'bread' but of 'breath' – physical air without substance. He is puffed up with his own pride and gluttony. As his physique amply testifies, he is empty of 'charite', 'corpus' without Christ.[97]

The friar embodies the 'abhomnacyon of desolacioun' that William Taylor feared was haunting the sacred space of the church. In Lollard texts, the alternative sacred space to the material church is the body of mankind, the true *templum dei*. But here the body of the friar is a container fit only for bodily waste and hot air. In pastoral care literature, the bag or sack is associated with sloth as the demon Tutivillus fills it with the over-skipped syllables of the liturgy. In *De Officio Pastorali*, the bag is the receptacle for the friars' ill-gotten gains, as Christ urges them not to 'go fro hous to hous [...] and bere not vpon þer backis *baggis* ne sachels to begge þus'.[98] The bloated friar is the embodiment of the damning criticism of the friars in the *Fifty Heresies* which declares that they are 'a swolowhe of symonye, of usure, of extorsiouns, of raveyns, and of thefftis'.[99] A 'swolwe' is defined by the Middle English Dictionary variously as a pit or chasm, a flood or outpouring, or in bodily terms, the throat.[100] The Dominican friar in the *Crede* is just such a 'swolwe' of sin. He is not a pillar of holy church or the temple of God, and he cannot produce even a whiff of sanctity with which to 'amend' this space. When he does speak to the narrator, he criticises the Austin friars and promotes his own order as 'of gretest degre', but the narrator rebukes him vehemently: 'here fynde y but pride; / Y preise nought thi preching but as a pure myte' and 'angerlich' he leaves (266–8). This is the first time that the narrator's response to what he encounters is emotional as well as analytical. In her chapter on Lollard 'tales' in *Feeling like Saints*, Fiona Somerset argues that 'narrative is for Lollards an important tool for evoking and sustaining appropriate emotion, as a means to train the will towards living in virtue'.[101] Here, it could be argued that the narrator's discernment of pride leads him to commit another sin, wrath, but his righteous anger is part of an emotional journey that leads to his encounter with Pierce the Ploughman himself. When the narrator has met with representatives of the two remaining orders, the Austins and the Carmelites, he walks on and 'talked to my-selue /

Of the falshede of this folk' (418–19). It is while wandering thus that 'be the waie wepynge for sorowe' he meets Pierce. His tears for the absence of sanctity in the four orders prepares the way for the chance encounter with the ploughman, who finally teaches him his Creed, rather like a hermit appearing in the forest in a romance narrative.

That the narrator's tears pave the way for the achievement of his spiritual quest is suggested by a comparison with the *Tractatus de Pseudo-Freris* which explains why the buildings of the friars are not 'shapen bi lore of crist'.[102]

> When men loken on heere castelis þei hauen matere to *wepe*, boþe þise ordris & seculeris, but specialliche þe pore peple. For ȝif we loken to cristis lif, he forsok sich bildyng, & lokyng on þe citee, þat he seyde was aȝen þe apostlis, *he wepte* þer upon for greet synne þat it hoordede.[103]

The *Crede*-narrator is right to weep at the sin that is 'hoordede' in the friars' churches. He has experienced first-hand that the friars absolve men 'for monee, & not for deuocioun', as the *Tractatus* puts it, and he has shown quite clearly that the ornaments of their churches are 'toolis to bigyle þe peple, & to feede here bodiliche eye, & robbe þe eye of heere soule'.[104] The narrator's eye has been 'bigyled' but he has survived his journey through the material churches of the friars and emerged on to the highway in the appropriate frame of mind to meet Pierce and finally learn his Creed. Barr comments that the final performance of the Creed is 'strikingly de-institutionalised', recited as it is in a muddy field, and that the text as a whole has 'seriously weakened the importance of the material church on earth as a site for authorised meanings'.[105] Certainly the material church of the friars has undergone irreparable damage. In no possible way can such churches be rehabilitated as sacred space. The architecture is stubbornly material rather than spiritual, it is a house of bloated friars intent on deceiving rich and poor alike. But the narrator's experience has produced a discerning reader of the material church who, as the *Lanterne of Liȝt* advocates, has learned to 'know', to mourn, and most importantly, to 'leeue þe fendis chirche' (p. 136) of his own accord. To be able to read a church that purports to be a sacred space, and to find it wanting, is the most important lesson that the medieval layperson can learn.

'So many fayre chirchys': The state and value of the material church in fifteenth-century England

The final declaration of the *Twelve Conclusions of the Lollards*, pinned to the door of Westminster Hall in 1395, sums up the Lollard position on church decoration that found its most extreme expression in *Pierce the Ploughman's Crede*: 'Þe multitude of craftis nout nedful, used in our chirche, norsschith michel synne in wast, curiosite, and disgysing'.[106] Unnecessary craft fosters the three types of sin that the religious houses of the friars amply demonstrated in the *Crede*: 'wast' (excessive or needless consumption), 'curiosite' (idle or vain interest), and 'disgysing' (new-fangled or elaborate alteration in fashion, cognate with 'disgisen' meaning to disguise or dissemble).[107] But hidden in this dogmatic pronouncement is an acknowledgement that the Lollards remain deeply invested in the church and what it betokens. These sinful crafts are used in 'oure chirche'. The possessive pronoun stakes a claim to the church and reminds us that the relationship between the people and their churches is more complex than the polemic of the *Crede* or the *Lanterne* would have us believe. In this final section, I will show that the lived experience of the late medieval parish church was dynamic, active, and involved all levels of society, from the rich donors who could afford to fund stained glass windows to the everyday laypeople who left money in their wills for the upkeep of the church fabric. The parish church was not simply a building to be read, or a sign of orthodox belief, or an indictment of contemporary corruption, it was a crucial part of a living, breathing community. Not only was the parish church at the very heart of religious life, it had a place in the heart of its parishioners.

Dives and Pauper, the fifteenth-century treatise on the Decalogue, exemplifies the rich variety of responses to the material church. The text's dialogue form enables us to see the debate on the state of England's churches from multiple viewpoints in a way that acknowledges but complicates the binary approach of the more schematic and polemical texts that I have discussed so far. Rather than operating in the 'grey area' between orthodoxy and heresy, *Dives and Pauper* represents the reality of lived experience and as such, is a productive space in which to explore not only what the church betokens but also what the medieval laity felt about it.[108] How does the church building fit into the devotional *and* emotional lives of parishioners, and how might this contribute to our understanding of what it means for a church to be sacred to its community?

Dives and Pauper begins its discussion with a bold declaration of national pride in the thriving state of England's churches. Dives declares:

> God is in non lond so wel seruyd in holy chyrche ne so mychil worchepyed in holy chyrche as he is in þis lond, for so many fayre chirchys ne so good aray in chyrchis ne so fayr seruyce, as men seyn, is in non oþir lond as is in þis lond.[109]

The defining qualities of England's churches in this positive assessment are that they are numerous and fair, in good order or 'aray', and that they perform fair services. Both fairness and 'aray' are key words here. When applied to buildings, 'fair' means attractive and pleasing to look upon, and the word is also frequently used of the Virgin Mary and of angels. It also means 'accordant with truth, reason, approved practice', the latter meaning applicable to the services performed there.[110] Fairness in all its forms is crucial to the Lollard critique of church buildings, as we have seen, but here it also signifies the quality of the liturgical practices ('fayr seruyce') performed in the church. The churches themselves are in 'good aray' and 'aray' refers to 'arrangement, order, sequence', so to be in 'good aray' is to be well placed and well formed.[111] England's churches are thus superlative. They are well built and arranged, fair in appearance and integrity, and well-served by ritual practice.

But Pauper questions this idealised picture and articulates the major anxiety about the churches of 'þis lond':

> ȝif þe makyng of chirchis and þe ornamentys and þe seruyse in þis lond were don principaly for deuocion and for þe worchepe of God, Y trowe þis lond pasyd alle londis in worchepynge of God and of holy chirche. But Y drede me þat men don it mor for pompe and pride of þis world, to han a name and a worchepe þerby in þe contre or for enuye þat o town hat to an oþre, nouȝt for deuocion but for þe worchepe and þe name þat þey sen hem han be þe aray and ornamentys in holy chyrche, or ellys be sley couetyse of men of holy chyrche. (pp. 188–9)

Pauper fears that the 'makyng of chirches' is motivated more by the 'pompe and pride of þis world' than by devotion to God, as we saw in the *Crede*, and historical evidence can be found to support his concerns. Instructions for the carving of rood screens, for example, that request that they be 'carven and wrought in every form of woorkemanship or better' than that found in a neighbouring parish evidences Pauper's unease about the 'enuye þat o town hat to an oþre'.[112] There were tensions between parishes over bell-ringing schedules, each community keen to make themselves heard above their neighbours.[113] Stained glass windows featuring donor portraits contributed to an individual's 'name and worchepe' in 'þe contre', as Pauper points out. In the Works of Mercy window at All Saints North Street in York, for example, the most striking feature is not the works themselves but the distinctive bearded figure that performs them, Nicholas Blackburn senior, whom the window commemorates (Figure 5).[114] But Pauper's anxiety, and my reading of the evidence here, is rather one-sided. In practice, it is impossible to assign single, uncomplicated motives to church

5 Nicholas Blackburn feeding the hungry. 'The Works of Mercy', stained glass panel, All Saints North Street, York, n 4.

builders and donors; indeed, it is misguided. The high quality of a rood screen made a visible statement about the community's regard for their church, as well as a desire to keep up with their neighbours. Nicholas Blackburn's good works were an example of local piety in action that his fellow parishioners could and should aspire to emulate. Secular 'worchepe' and the worship of God are not so easy to separate.

The Works of Mercy window also encapsulates another cause for concern that *Dives and Pauper* highlights: the social impact of expensive church decoration. In the window, Nicholas Blackburn feeds the hungry, gives drink to the thirsty, and clothes the naked, but of course the money that his family donated for the window is not directly helping the poor because it has been invested in the window instead. Dives muses that:

> Me þynkith þat it were betere to ȝeuyn money to þe pore folc, to þe blynde and to þe lame wose soulys God bouȝte so dere, þan so to spendyn it in solempnyte and pride and makynge of heye chyrchis, in riche vestimentys, in curyous wyndowys, in grete bellys, for God is nouȝt holpyn þerby and þe pore folc myȝte ben holpyn þerby wol mychil. (pp. 189–90)

The 'opportunity cost' of church decoration is relieving the suffering of the poor and in this passage Dives employs the vocabulary that we have encountered in Lollard critiques of the church: the adjectives 'heye', 'riche', 'curyous', and 'grete', contrasted with the 'pore' folk in need of charity. The economic impact on the poor is also weighed against Christ's sacrifice: he 'bouȝte' their souls 'so dere'. Funding elaborate church decoration was seen as detrimental to the ideals of charity represented by the Works of Mercy. As one Lollard treatise explains, the laity 'tristus vtterly in þes deade ymagis, and louen God and hese comandementis þe lesse, for men skateren þere loue in siche stokkis and leeuen precious werkis of mercy vndone til here pore neȝeboris, whiche ben Cristis ymagis'.[115] Illustrating charitable activity in stained glass windows is no substitute for getting out in the community and helping the poor directly.

It was not just the objects of lay devotion and financial support that came under scrutiny, however, it was the very intent with which they were undertaken. Pauper argues that 'God takyth mor hede to a manys herte þan to his ȝifte and mor to his deuocioun þan to his dede' (p. 188), but medieval parishioners did put their hearts and souls into their churches. The objects that they commissioned, the money they donated to repair bell-towers or maintain the nave, embodied and materialised their devotional feeling. As I have shown elsewhere, devotional identity in the late Middle Ages was produced through performative practices and those practices typically included deeds of patronage for the material fabric, from rich and poor alike.[116] In his study of medieval Norwich, Norman Tanner has shown that 95 per cent of the laity left money to at least one parish church in their wills, most often specifically directed towards the fabric of the church and its repair.[117] But as Katherine French points out, 'it is easier to see the priorities of the wealthy than those of the poor' when it comes to church-building and church decoration.[118] Donor portraits in stained glass windows are a case in point. A small number of such portraits even depict the donors holding a model of the church in question.[119] A lost example from the east window of Elsing church, Norfolk, featured Hugh de Hastings and his wife Margery on their knees holding up a miniature version of their church.[120] At York St Denys, Robert Skelton holds up a miniature of the stained glass window that he donated to the church in 1340.[121] Such images, although relatively rare, advertise the good deeds of the donors but also indicate the potential for a personal and material connection between the individual and the church. The donors hold the church in their hands and while the miniature scale of the building does imply that they are in a position of power over it, the kneeling posture, in which they present the object, indicates their devotion to and respect for the building or window that they are offering up to God.[122]

It is this intimate and physical connection between the individual and the material building that I want to highlight here as a crucial part of the sanctity of the church for its parishioners. When Pauper states that God takes 'no gret hede how mychil man or woman ȝeuyth or offerith in holy chirche, but he takith hed of *how mychil deuocioun and of what herte* he ȝeuyth or offeryth', that 'offering' can be emotional and spiritual as well as financial (p. 188, italics mine). It is my suggestion that the 'herte' and the building are integrally related and that it is this relationship that is at stake when the material church is critiqued and dismantled in Lollard texts. In his influential article on the English parish church in 1999, Paul Binski commented that there had been a lack of focus on 'a history of subjectivity and even, though here we are on more tendentious grounds, of the emotions' when it comes to the parish church and its art.[123] In the scholarship of the 1980s and 1990s, Binski found a 'lack, even perhaps a kind of refusal, of what it might have been to have been human in the context of religious life, practice, and feeling', but current scholarship on the history of emotions and the work of medievalists such as Sarah Stanbury encourages us to be more alert to the ways in which objects and buildings are imbricated in the emotional lives of their parishioners.[124] The place of the church in the emotional landscape of the parishioner can be most clearly seen in *The Book of Margery Kempe* when Margery's parish church, St Margaret's in Lynn, is threatened by fire.[125]

A 'hydows fyer and grevows' has already burnt down the Guild Hall in Lynn and the *Book* tells us that it was 'ful lekely to a brent the parysch cherch dedicate in the honowr of Seynt Margarete, a solempne place and rychely honowryd, and also the town, ne had grace ne myracle ne ben' (p. 307). The high status of the church in the town is evident from the description. It is 'rychely honowryd' by the community, 'rychely' here meaning both magnificently and lavishly.[126] It is also a 'solempne' place which means that it is sacred in the sense of consecrated, produced with 'due religious ceremony or reverence'.[127] It is a sacred space because of the rituals that have been performed there *and* because of the support, both spiritual and financial, of the townspeople who hold it to be sacred. Margery weeps and prays to God and 'notwythstondyng in other tymes thei myth not enduryn hir to cryen and wepyn', the townspeople encourage Margery's outpourings 'for enchewyng of her [their] *bodily perel*' (p. 307, italics mine). The threat to the church is conceived as a threat to the social body, but it is also a threat to Margery's body. She prays to God, 'Good Lord, make it wel, and sende down sum reyn er sum wedyr that may thorw thi mercy qwenchyn this fyer and *esyn myn hert*' (p. 308, italics mine). The danger that the fire poses to the material church is felt by Margery in her heart and this emotional reaction equates her body with the church itself. 'Esen' in Middle English means to relieve from danger or oppression, to be freed from anxiety and care.[128] If the church building is under attack, Margery herself is under attack. And as a direct result of Margery's prayers from her anxious heart, God sends a miraculous snowstorm to extinguish the flames and the church is saved. God takes heed, to return to *Dives and Pauper*, 'of how mychil deuocioun and of what herte' Margery gives her support to her parish church and he protects the building as a result.

This episode in *The Book of Margery Kempe* shows how deeply the heart can be enmeshed with the material church for lay parishioners. In her book *Losing Site: Architecture and Place*, Shelley Hornstein explores our emotional connection to material buildings through the image of the heart. She argues that architecture always exists in two, interrelated forms, firstly as a 'physical entity' and secondly, 'beyond the physical site in our recollection of it':

> We function always with what I call, an 'architecture of the heart', or a place within us that holds onto the emoting memory of a place. That place is the symbolic construction that connects our idea or image of a place to its physicality.[129]

The 'emoting memory of a place' is crucial for the sanctity of the church because if the parishioners do not think and feel a place to be sacred, they will not richly honour it like the people of King's Lynn. *What the Church Betokeneth* strengthened the architecture of the heart by cementing the community into the building so that their bodies truly are the living stones of the church. *The Lanterne of Liȝt*, on the other hand, aimed to disengage the heart from the architecture, to reduce the church building to its material parts as purely a physical entity that no longer represents the community but instead inspires feelings of hostility and outrage that lime and stone should be honoured above the poor and needy. In an emotional outburst, the anonymous Lollard treatise on images and pilgrimages aims to stir up our righteous anger against church decoration, declaring: 'Dere Lord! What almes is it to peynte gayly dede stones and rotun stokkis wiþ sich almes þat is pore mennus good and lyfelode, and suffir pore men perysche for hungor, for cold and oþer many meschefis, in presoun and in oþere placis?'[130] Elaborate visual display has fatal consequences not only for the poor but for the emotional integrity of the laity; the treatise explains that they are so distracted that 'þei may not fynde at her herte to gif þere almes to quicke ymagis of God, þat ben pore folc'.[131] In this formulation, the material church deadens the source of charitable feeling, the heart.

The image of the heart recurs in *Dives and Pauper* when Pauper explains why prayer is 'betere in holy chyrche with þe comounte' than in a domestic chamber or oratory:

> Synguler preyere of on persone is good in chambre & in oratorie and betere in chirche, but comoun preyere of a comonte in chirche is beter þan synguler preyere, for Crist seyth in þe gospel (Matthew, 18.20) þat ȝif two or thre be gaderyd togedere in his name þat is charite, þer is he in þe myddys of hem, þat is to seyne, in here hertys to helpyn hem in here preyere. (p. 196)

Gathering together in communal prayer in the church ensures Christ's presence in the community, 'in þe myddys of hem, þat is to seyne, in *here hertys* to helpyn hem in here preyere' (italics mine). Prayer, in particular, is seen as an activity that takes place in the heart and as we saw in the previous chapter, one of the primary reasons for church consecration was the creation of an efficacious space for communal prayer. Pauper explains the best method of prayer with reference to Christ's assertion in Matthew, 6.6 that when a man prays he should 'gon into his chambre and schettyn þe dore' (p. 195). Pauper reads this allegorically, arguing that it teaches us 'nout only wher we shuldyn preyyn but *principaly* he techith us *how* we schuldyn preyyn, for þe chambre we schuldyn entryn is *oure herte*' (p. 195, italics mine). Praying in the chamber of the heart while in attendance in the church facilitates Christ's presence which is, of course, essential for the church to be a truly sacred space. Each parishioner who prays in the church becomes a miniature house of God as they are filled with the presence of Christ in their hearts and this brings Christ into the church as a whole.

This presentation of the church does not mean, however, that all parishioners were as devoted to their sacred architecture as Margery Kempe. To return to Christopher Tilley's formulation, it represents a 'desirable' narrative that could then be used to influence parishioners' behaviour – for example, to encourage church attendance. Prayer together as a community is better than prayer at home alone, as Pauper explains. But he admits that there is room for improvement, lamenting that 'þe peple þise dayys is wol indeuout to God and to holy chirche' (p. 189). Unlike Margery Kempe, such parishioners are 'loth to comyn in holy chyrche whan þey are boundyn to comyn þedyr and wol loth to heryn Godys seruyse. Late þey comyn and sone gon aȝen awey' (p. 189). Pauper fears that the people are more interested in listening to secular narratives in the tavern than sacred liturgy in the church: 'þey han leuer gon to þe tauerne þan to holy chirche, leuer to heryn a tale or a song of Robyn Hood or of som rybaudye þan to heryn messe or matynys or onyþing of Goddis seruise or ony word of God' (p. 189). Cultivating an attachment to the church that went beyond parochial duty was essential both for the spiritual health of parishioners and the material health of the church itself. Margery Kempe prayed to God to protect her church from physical damage but not all parishes were as lucky in their patrons. The church existed as a 'physical entity' in the first instance, as Hornstein argues, and that entity loomed large in the late medieval imagination. Creating desirable narratives of the church's sanctity and spiritual efficacy was a crucial strategy in stimulating the interconnected emotional and financial support for England's churches.

Such strategies were clearly effective, as the fifteenth century became known as the great age of church building. The construction and reconstruction of the 'idea' of the church in the texts I have been discussing exists in a symbiotic relationship with the physical restoration and enlargement of material church buildings. This building work meant that the material form and composition of the church was constantly in the public eye and that the meaning and motivation behind decorative and practical building projects was continually being discussed and assessed. In a medieval proverb in the literature of pastoral care, the image of the church is of a building that is steadfast, permanent, and stable. Used as an excuse not to go to church by a glutton who is too full to get out of bed, the proverb declares, 'þe chirche is noon hare; he wol abide me wel'.[132] The quick, darting hare is contrasted to the constant, enduring church and in the version in *Jacob's Well*, the glutton adds, 'þere men leve it, þey may fynde it'.[133] But this image of longevity and stability is, to some extent, misleading. The church will not scamper away into the hedgerows like a hare, but its material form was far more fluid and mobile than this monolithic statement would suggest.

In reality, late medieval churches were in constant need of material attention and support. In the fifteenth century, many were the focus of significant building work simply because they were falling apart and needed repair in order to carry out their basic parish functions. Richard Morris notes as a representative case the visitation of churches in the diocese of Salisbury in 1405 which found that only 27 per cent of churches and chapels were free from disrepair.[134] In some parishes, the deterioration was almost fatal. Morris cites the case of Willesdon in Middlesex where parishioners complained of the chancel that 'a boy might easily overthrow the walls. Robbers have entered and carried off goods. Mass cannot be celebrated at the High Altar. Owls and crows fly in by day and by night and pollute the church.'[135] Damage from the weather, especially water and severe winters, took its toll on medieval churches.[136] Margery Kempe herself was the victim of the fragility of her own parish church when a stone and beam fell from the roof of St Margaret's on to her back during mass and nearly killed her (pp. 82–3). Indeed, documentary evidence from Lynn confirms that the bell tower at St Margaret's was in such poor condition that bell-ringing was prohibited until the repairs could be carried out.[137] The material state of the church simply could not be ignored.

The fifteenth century also saw considerable architectural development as parishes took the opportunity to extend and enlarge their churches. Most churches had reached their 'maximum areal extent' at the end of the previous century, so many began to grow upwards rather than outwards.[138] As Richard Morris explains, 'porches became more substantial, and may be of two storeys. Much effort is now directed upwards: into clerestories, pinnacle roofscapes and steeples.'[139] This increase in the height of the church improved its visibility in the landscape and the spire could become an important identifying feature for a church. In the 'Pricke of Conscience' window at All Saints North Street, in York, for example, the image for the seventh day at the end of the world is All Saints itself, distinguished by its distinctive spire toppling to the earth (Figure 6). But the increased height of medieval churches could be read as a symbol of pride, evidenced by the frequent use of the adjective 'hegh', which in the context of architecture connotes pride and ostentation.[140] It appears readily in Lollard texts but also, as we saw above, in *Dives and Pauper* when Dives worries about the effect on the poor of spending money in the 'makynge of *heye* chyrchis, in riche vestimentys, in curyous wyndowys, in grete bellys' (pp. 189–90, italics mine). Dives does not disapprove of the material objects themselves so

6 All Saints North Street church falling down. 'The Prick of Conscience', stained glass panel, All Saints North Street, York, n 3.

much as the message that their scale is sending about the community's priorities.

The rebuilding and remodelling of churches in this period took time and could result in what T. A. Heslop has called a 'compositional "hybridity"' of style, a factor that again called attention to the materiality of the church and its physical construction.[141] Building projects could evolve piecemeal over time, sometimes delayed by lack of funds, such that churches often appeared as a patchwork of different architectural styles. The church of St Peter and St Paul at Swaffham in Norfolk is a representative example. As Heslop has shown, there is a range of different window styles in the south aisle that may have been the result of different masons working on the project at different times, as well as the varying preferences of the windows' different donors.[142] At Swaffham, the nave was extended upwards in the fifteenth century by reusing the thirteenth-century supporters and Heslop reads this as a materialisation of the metaphor used by St Paul in 1 Corinthians: 'as a wise architect I have laid the foundation, and another buildeth thereon' (1 Corinthians, 3.10).[143] The material church was subject to many material and personal exigencies and it was always a work in progress that was available for the next devout parishioner to build upon and develop.

Such projects could also alter the appearance of the church in a way that reimagined the power dynamic in the parish, foregrounding the social capital represented by the form and appearance of the material church. The nave was the responsibility of the laity in the Middle Ages and in a number of cases the enthusiastic enlargement of the nave overshadowed the chancel, the space controlled by the clergy and the most sacred space in the structure. The chancel of the church at Methwold in Norfolk, for example, is overpowered by the great fifteenth-century nave and spire and, similarly, at Yatton in Somerset, the nave was rebuilt in such 'spectacular style' that, as Katherine French has argued, it must have required all the 'economic sacrifice, commitment, and the resources' that the rural congregation could muster.[144] In such cases, control of the 'social visage' of the community, to recall Lefebvre's phrase, was firmly in the hands of the laity. The church was an advertisement for the congregation and for some wealthy patrons, for their own piety. At Long Melford in Suffolk, for example, the donations of John Clopton, his family, and associates are famously commemorated in inscriptions around the outside of the church that both petition the community for prayers and stake a claim to the material architecture itself.[145]

All of this building work meant that the material fabric of the church was a constant but changing presence in the medieval imagination. Parishioners would have seen builders, masons, and artists at work, installing stained glass and rood screens, painting murals, and shoring up the fragile foundations with all the tools and materials of their trade. Direct contact with the material fabric was not necessarily reserved for specialist craftsmen and masons, however. Recent research on medieval graffiti by Matthew Champion suggests that parishioners regularly and enthusiastically made their own mark on their churches, scratching all manner of designs into the paintwork, from devotional symbols (such as crosses and signs representing the Virgin Mary) to merchant's marks, images of ships to apotropaic signs designed to protect the church and ward off evil.[146] A small number of images even show the church building itself reproduced on the walls and the back of rood screens, suggesting that the building was not just a physical entity, to return to Hornstein, but an image that could be claimed and replicated in miniature.[147] The surface of the church was available for parishioners of all backgrounds to inscribe their own priorities and concerns, demonstrating that, as Champion concludes, 'the medieval church was a far more interactive space than we may once have believed [...] It was a building that you were meant and required to interact with on a number of different levels, and one of the most fundamental of those levels was the physical.'[148]

As well as reflecting the everyday lives of parishioners, the increased decoration and expansion of the material church is imbricated in the religious controversies that produced many of the texts in this chapter. Andrew Brown has explored the relationship between the increase in Lollardy and the increase in church building work in the diocese of Salisbury. He notes that 'most of the places in the diocese where Lollardy was found after Wyclif also saw their parish churches extensively rebuilt' and he goes on to suggest that later Lollardy was 'fuelled by a continuing opposition to the pious practices of the majority'.[149] Practices that we might characterise as 'orthodox' or 'Lollard' did of course take place concurrently and Robert Lutton has explored this complex intersection in his study of Tenterden in Kent, whose parishioners engaged in a 'rich variety of orthodox as well as heterodox piety'.[150] Rather than seeing increased church building leading to an increase in Lollard heresy, it is possible that the influence went in the other direction. Building projects and church decoration may have been stimulated by individuals wanting to push back against criticism of the material church, to demonstrate their devotional intent and to assert their orthodoxy in the traditional manner. Richard Marks has made this argument regarding the proliferation of devotional imagery that he suggests was given 'renewed impetus by the early fifteenth-century campaign by the English ecclesiastical hierarchy to combat the Lollard heresy by an "increase of devotion"' that included new feasts and elaboration of liturgical practices.[151] Certainly writers such as John Mirk were provoked to reassert an orthodox position on imagery, proclaiming dismissively that 'crosses and oþer ymages ben necessary in chyrches, whatteeuer þeis Loleres seyne'.[152] Rather than reinforcing the binary opposition, however, it is more profitable to think of these impulses as part of a network of interconnected ideas and motivations that become 'desirable' narratives of the church at different stages of a community's life cycle.

The depiction of the church in the Lollard treatise *On the Twenty Five Articles* demonstrates the need for careful attention to be paid to the ways in which a text's arguments might operate in the context of lived experience. *On the Twenty Five Articles* puts forward the argument that 'men owen not raþer for to pray in chirche þen in oþer placis' because 'in iche place where a man is he owes for to pray God in spirite and treuthe, þat is, wiþ wille and devocioun and clennes of lyvynge'.[153] The author laments the state of churches which have become 'dennus of thefis and habitationis of fendis' due to sins such as simony, extortion, swearing, and lechery.[154] But the text also concedes that there are churches where 'prestis bene gode and clene, and Gods word wele tauȝt, ande sacramentis frely mynistrid, not solde for money'; when this is the case, 'Cristen men willen devoutely comyn to þo chirche.'[155] The state of the reader's local church and their feelings towards it will determine which elements of the description are most resonant. But the reader is encouraged, either way, to look inward, to cleanse the soul and the conscience, and 'mak redy to þe a privey place in pes of þine hert, willynge to pray; pray þou in þi selfe, and do so, broþer, þat þou be þo temple of God'.[156] The place of the people in relation to the church, and the place of the church within the hearts of the people, was a core concern of late medieval religious experience. It is no surprise that the mid-fifteenth century saw the translation into Middle English of the sections of Durandus's *Rationale* that dealt with this very relationship and formed the foundation of medieval thinking about architecture, community, and sanctity. *What the Church Betokeneth* is a text whose renewed relevance shows just how inseparable the material building and its congregation really were and it provides the enthusiastic supporters of England's fair churches with a very real reason to keep investing in their parish churches. It showed them what they were truly building when they contributed to the funds for the church roof or a new bell or rood screen. They were not just making practical adjustments to the building or advertising their own individual piety, they were supporting the structure that symbolised their own communal identity. They were building an ordered and sacred house of God in which Christ was eternally present, listening to their devout prayers.

The place of the parish church at the heart of the community is nowhere more evident than in the fifteenth-century stained glass window at All Saints North Street, York, known as the 'Prick of Conscience' window. The window (Figure 6) illustrates and contains quotations from the Middle English poem of the same name and it depicts the fifteen events at the end of the world. The donors kneel in supplication at the foot of the window, with looks of terror on their faces as they behold what is to come. On the seventh day, the window declares that 'howses mon fall / Castels & towres & ilk a wall' but the image that accompanies this pronouncement is not a secular building or a fortification. It is the church of All Saints itself, recognisable from its distinctive spire toppling to the ground. Like the poem, the window teaches its audience to repent their sins before it is too late. It would be the end of the world indeed if the parish church were to fall to the ground, depriving the congregation of their gateway to salvation and their treasured sacred space.

Notes

1 *The Middle English Translation of the Rosarium Theologie*, ed. Christina von Nolcken (Heidelberg: Carl Winter Universitätverlag, 1979), p. 69. All subsequent quotations refer to this edition by page number.

2 *MED* 'resonable' (adj.2) 1, 2, 3 and 4.

3 Henri Lefebvre, *The Production of Space*, trans. Donald Nicholson Smith (Oxford: Blackwell, 1991), p. 220.

4 Anne Hudson, *The Premature Reformation: Wycliffite Texts and Lollard History* (Oxford: Clarendon Press, 1988), p. 318. I want to offer a brief note on my use of the term 'Lollard'. As Mishtooni Bose and J. Patrick Hornbeck II comment, in recent years there has been a 'crisis of nomenclature' with regard to the term 'Lollard'; see their introduction, Mishtooni C. A. Bose and J. Patrick Hornbeck II (eds), *Wycliffite Controversies* (Turnhout: Brepols, 2011), pp. 1–11, pp. 2–3.

The terms 'Lollard', 'lollard', 'Wycliffite', 'heretic' and 'dissenter' are discussed at length by Hornbeck, Andrew Cole and most recently Fiona Somerset. See J. Patrick Hornbeck II, *What is a Lollard?: Dissent and Belief in Late Medieval England* (Oxford: Oxford University Press, 2010), pp. 1–24; Andrew Cole, *Literature and Heresy in the Age of Chaucer* (Cambridge: Cambridge University Press, 2009), pp. 25–45; and Fiona Somerset, *Feeling like Saints: Lollard Writings after Wyclif* (London: Cornell University Press, 2014), pp. 12–18. Michael G. Sargent has argued that we should think instead about so-called 'Lollard' and 'orthodox' texts performatively, investigating 'the many different kinds of work that they do in the cultural economy in which they are situated'; see 'Censorship or cultural change? Reformation and renaissance in the spirituality of late medieval England', in Vincent Gillespie and Kantik Ghosh (eds), *After Arundel: Religious Writing in Fifteenth-Century England* (Turnhout: Brepols, 2011), pp. 55–72, p. 67. I agree with Sargent in this reading but because both *The Lanterne of Liȝt* and *Pierce the Ploughman's Crede* set themselves up as oppositional texts, I have deliberately chosen to capitalise 'Lollard' in order to foreground the difference of opinion. In her discussion of language in the *Piers Plowman* tradition, Helen Barr argues that key Lollard vocabulary, such as true/false, is 'actively constituted in difference; and a difference that is antagonistic' and while I will suggest that *The Lanterne of Liȝt* and the *Crede* are reliant on the imagery and reading practices of orthodox texts such as Durandus's *Rationale*, their oppositional stance and cultivation of difference are essential to their polemic. See Helen Barr, *Signes and Sothe: Language in the Piers Plowman Tradition* (Woodbridge: D.S. Brewer, 1994), p. 100.

5 Oxford, Bodleian Library MS Bodley 288, folio 47vb, quoted in Hudson, *The Premature Reformation*, p. 321.

6 Bruce Holsinger, 'Lollard ekphrasis: situated aesthetics and literary history', *Journal of Medieval and Early Modern Studies,* 35:1 (2005), 67–89, p. 83.

7 Fiona Somerset suggests that for Lollard writers, showing 'their readers how to feel differently, and how to imagine their world otherwise' is as important 'as telling their readers what they need to know and do'; see *Feeling like Saints*, p. 7.

8 Christopher Tilley, *Material Culture and Text: The Art of Ambiguity* (London: Routledge, 1991), pp. 174–5.

9 Paul Binski, 'The English Parish Church and its art in the late Middle Ages: a review of the problem', *Studies in Iconography*, 20 (1999), 1–25, p. 3.

10 Shelley Hornstein, *Losing Site: Architecture, Memory, and Place* (Farnham: Ashgate, 2011), p. 3.

11 *The Rationale Divinorum Officiorum of William Durand of Mende: A New Translation of the Prologue and Book One*, trans. Timothy M. Thibodeau (New York: Columbia University Press, 2007), p. xxii.

12 Durandus, *Rationale*, p. 19. Line 39 of 'Þe Simonie' in *The Auckinleck Manuscript*, ed. David Burnley and Alison Wiggins, National Library of Scotland, 5 July 2003, http://auchinleck.nls.uk/ [accessed 21 July 2016].
13 *The Orcherd of Syon*, ed. Phyllis Hodgson and Gabriel M. Liegey, EETS OS 258 (Oxford: Oxford University Press, 1966), p. 242.
14 *The Book of Margery Kempe*, ed. Barry Windeatt (Cambridge: D. S. Brewer, 2000), p. 97. All subsequent quotations refer to this edition by page number.
15 For a more detailed discussion of this passage, see Laura Varnam, 'Church', in Marion Turner (ed.), *A Handbook of Middle English Studies* (Chichester: Wiley-Blackwell, 2013), pp. 299–314, pp. 303–4.
16 Binski, 'The English Parish Church', p. 18.
17 Durandus, *Rationale*, p. 2.
18 *What the Church Betokeneth*, in *Supplementary Lives in Some Manuscripts of the Gilte Legende*, ed. Richard Hamer and Vida Russell, EETS OS 315 (Oxford: Oxford University Press, 2000), pp. 85–128, p. 85. All subsequent quotations from the text refer to this edition by page number.
19 Durandus, *Rationale*, p. xix.
20 *Ibid.*, p. 20.
21 *Ibid.*
22 *Ibid.*, p. 22.
23 See Chapter 1 for the symbolism of the church as Jerusalem in the consecration ceremony.
24 *MED* 'setten' (v.) 1 and 2a), 4a) and 4c), 12a) and b).
25 See Varnam, 'Church', p. 303.
26 *MED* 'speciale' (adj.) 1a) and 1c), and 'ordeinen' (v.) 4g): invested in holy orders.
27 *MED* 'bitoknen' (v.) 1 and 'token' (n.) 1a), 3a) and 4a).
28 This recalls the miracles I discussed in Chapter 2 in which the material culture of the church is shown to protect domestic dwellings in the urban environment.
29 Durandus, *Rationale*, p. 18.
30 *Ibid.*, p. 19. Italics mine.
31 Christiania Whitehead, *Castles of the Mind: A Study of Medieval Architectural Allegory* (Cardiff: University of Wales Press, 2003), p. 52.
32 Whitehead, *Castles of the Mind*, p. 54.
33 *Ibid.*, p. 53.
34 *English Wycliffite Sermons*, ed. Anne Hudson, vol. III (Oxford: Clarendon Press, 1990), p. 304.
35 *English Wycliffite Sermons*, ed. Hudson, vol. III, pp. 304–5.
36 *English Wycliffite Sermons*, ed. Pamela Gradon, vol II (Oxford: Clarendon Press, 1988), p. 170.
37 J. Patrick Hornbeck II, 'Barn of unity or the devil's church? Salvation and ecclesiology in Langland and the Wycliffites', in Seeta Chaganti and

Penn R. Szittya (eds), *Medieval Poetics and Social Practice: Responding to the Work of Penn R. Szittya* (New York: Fordham University Press, 2012), pp. 33–52, p. 44.

38 *English Wycliffite Sermons*, ed. Anne Hudson, vol. I (Oxford: Clarendon Press, 1983), p. 341.

39 *English Wycliffite Sermons*, ed. Hudson, vol. I, p. 303.

40 Von Nolcken discusses the influence of the Latin *Rosarium* and the earlier, longer version known as the *Floretum*; see *Rosarium Theologie*, pp. 34–7.

41 See Shannon Gayk's discussion of the word 'fair' in *Image, Text, and Religious Reform in Fifteenth-Century England* (Cambridge: Cambridge University Press, 2010), p. 41.

42 *How Satan and his Children*, in *The English Works of Wyclif Hitherto Unprinted*, ed. F. D. Matthew, EETS OS 74 (London: Trübner and co, 1880), pp. 209–18, p. 210.

43 *MED* 'up-so-doun' (adv. phr.) 2b).

44 *How Satan and his Children*, p. 210.

45 *Ibid.*, and Geoffrey Chaucer, *The Riverside Chaucer*, ed. Larry D. Benson et al. (Oxford: Oxford University Press, 1987; paperback 1988), p. 26, line 170.

46 *Ibid.*, p. 211.

47 *The Sermon of William Taylor*, in *Two Wycliffite Texts*, ed. Anne Hudson, EETS OS 301 (Oxford: Oxford University Press, 1993), pp. 3–23, p. 18. All subsequent quotations refer to this edition by page number.

48 Robert Grosseteste, *Templum Dei*, ed. Joseph Goering and F. A. C. Mantello (Toronto: Pontifical Institute of Medieval Studies, 1984). The *Templum Dei* was translated into Middle English; see the edition by Cornelius, entitled *Templum Domini* in Roberta D. Cornelius, *The Figurative Castle: A Study in the Mediaeval Allegory of the Edifice with Especial Reference to Religious Writings* (Pennsylvania: Bryn Mawr, 1930), pp. 90–112.

49 *MED* 'repareilen' (v.) 2a) and 1b).

50 *Cristes Passioun*, in *The Minor Poems of John Lydgate,* ed. Henry Noble MacCracken, EETS ES 107 (London: Kegan Paul, Trench, Trübner and Co., 1911), pp. 216–21, lines 87–8.

51 *MED* 'desolacioun' (n.) 1a) and 1b).

52 Husdon, *Premature Reformation*, p. 213 and p. 211.

53 Nicholas Watson, 'Vernacular apocalyptic: on *The Lanterne of Liȝt*', *Revista Canaria de Estudios Ingleses*, 47 (2003), 115–17, p. 118 and p. 122.

54 Watson, 'Vernacular apocalyptic', p. 123. *The Lanterne of Liȝt*, ed. Lilian M. Swinburn, EETS OS 151 (London: Kegan Paul, Trench, and Trübner, 1917), p. 136. All subsequent quotations refer to this edition by page number.

55 James M. Dean, ed., *Medieval Political Writings* (Kalamazoo: Medieval Institute Publications, 1996), p. 40.
56 *MED* 'hillen' (v.) 1d).
57 *Pierce the Ploughman's Crede*, in *The Piers Plowman Tradition,* ed. Helen Barr (London: Dent, 1993), pp. 60–97, lines 193–4. All quotations refer to this edition by line number.
58 D.S. Dunnan notes that despite setting up a tripartite schema, 'the Lollard writer does not make a clear distinction between the church as a physical building and the "human beings that make up the actual congregation"', 'A note on the three churches in *The Lanterne of Liȝt*', *Notes and Queries*, n.s. 38 (1991), 20–3, p. 20.
59 *The Book of the Foundation of St Bartholomew's Church*, ed. Norman Moore, EETS OS 163 (Oxford: Oxford University Press, 1923), p. 5. Italics mine.
60 *MED* 'justli' (adv.) 1a) and 1b).
61 *The Holy Bible containing the Old and New Testaments, with the Apocryphal Books, in the Earliest English Versions made from the Latin Vulgate by John Wycliffe and his Followers*, ed. Josiah Forshall and Frederic Madden (Oxford: Oxford University Press, 1950), vol. II, p. 636.
62 *The Book of the Foundation*, p. 32. Italics mine.
63 Rosewell, *Medieval Wall Paintings*, p. 70 and *Instructions for Parish Priests by John Myrc*, ed. Edward Peacock, EETS OS 31 (London: Trübner, 1868), p. 10. All subsequent quotations refer to this edition by line number.
64 See Kate Crassons, *The Claims of Poverty: Literature, Culture, and Ideology in Late Medieval England* (Notre Dame: University of Notre Dame Press, 2010), especially chapters 2 and 3, pp. 89–176.
65 *MED* 'straunge' (adj.).
66 *MED* 'marken' (v.) 1a) and 3a) and b).
67 *MED* 'pappe' (n.) 1f) the breast, regardless of sex, and 1a) a woman's breast. Swinburne, p. 152, note to line 11.
68 Penn R. Szittya, *The Antifraternal Tradition in Medieval Literature* (Princeton: Princeton University Press, 1986), p. 8.
69 *Instructions for Parish Priests*, pp. 25–7, lines 813–62.
70 *Fifty Heresies of the Friars*, in *Select English Works of John Wyclif*, ed. Thomas Arnold (Oxford: Clarendon Press, 1871), vol. III, pp. 366–401, pp. 374–5.
71 *De Officio Pastorali*, in *The English Works of Wyclif*, ed. Matthew, pp. 405–57, p. 448.
72 *Of the Leaven of Pharisees*, in *The English Works of Wyclif*, ed. Matthew, pp. 1–27, p. 14. Compare *The Fifty Heresies of the Friars*, in which common roads as well as parish churches suffer: 'also freris bylden mony grete chirchis and costily waste housis, and cloystris as hit were castels, and þat wiþoute nede, where-thorw parische chirchis and comyne weyes ben payred, and in mony placis undone', *Fifty Heresies of the Friars*, p. 380.

73 *MED* 'defaute' (n.) 1c).
74 *Of the Leaven of Pharisees*, p. 15.
75 *Ibid.*, p. 8.
76 *MED* 'babewinrie' (n.).
77 *MED* 'amenden' (v.) 2a) and 6.
78 *MED* 'amenden' (v.) 8b).
79 *MED* 'amenden' (v.) 8c) and 12.
80 The word is also used in a spiritual sense in the *Fifty Heresies of the Friars*, 'þese errours schulen nevere be *amendid*, til freris be brouȝt to fredome of þo gospel, and clene religioun of Jesus Crist', p. 401.
81 *MED* 'burgh' (n.) 3.
82 Gayk, *Image, Text, and Religious Reform*, p. 32.
83 *The Canterbury Interlude* in *The Canterbury Tales: Fifteenth Century Continuations and Additions*, ed. John M. Bowers (Kalamazoo: Medieval Institute Publications, 1992), p. 64, line 163. Compare the congregation 'gapyng oloft' in *Images and Pilgrimages*, in *Selections from English Wycliffite Writings*, ed. Anne Hudson (Cambridge: Cambridge University Press, 1978), pp. 83–8, p. 85.
84 *MED* 'yerne' (adv.).
85 *The Canterbury Interlude*, ed. Bowers, p. 64, line 149.
86 From the confession of Hawsia Moone; see *Selections from English Wycliffite Writings*, ed. Hudson, pp. 34–7, p. 36.
87 Holsinger, 'Lollard ekphrasis', p. 82.
88 *Ibid.*
89 Barr, *Signes and Sothe*, p. 220.
90 *English Wycliffite Sermons,* ed. Hudson, vol. I, p. 328. This comparison is also made by Helen Barr in *Signes and Sothe*, p. 125. A further Lollard sermon comments similarly, 'for ȝif a man be closud in cloistre, what profiȝtuþ he by Cristus ordenaunce to make liȝt to his broþur, þat feluþ not of his profiȝt?' See *English Wycliffite Sermons*, ed. Gradon, vol. II, p. 150.
91 Gayk, *Image, Text, and Religious Reform*, p. 33.
92 *Ibid.*, p. 31.
93 Barr, *Signes and Sothe*, p. 221.
94 *Of the Leaven of Pharisees*, p. 14. Italics mine.
95 *MED* 'conissaunce' (n.) 2a).
96 Gayk, *Image, Text, and Religious Reform*, p. 31.
97 Barr, *Signes and Sothe,* p. 87.
98 *De Officio Pastorali*, p. 443. Italics mine.
99 *Fifty Heresies of the Friars*, p. 390.
100 *MED* 'swolwe' (n.) c), e), and a).
101 Somerset, *Feeling Like Saints*, p. 139.
102 *Tractatus de Pseudo-Freris,* in *The English Works of John Wyclif*, ed. Matthew, pp. 294–324, p. 321.
103 *Tractatus de Pseudo-Freris*, p. 321. Italics mine.
104 *Ibid.*, p. 323.

105 Barr, *Signes and Sothe*, p. 48 and p. 99.
106 *The Twelve Conclusions of the Lollards*, in *Selections from English Wycliffite Writings*, ed. Hudson, pp. 24–9, p. 28.
107 *MED* 'waste' (n.1) 3a) 'curiousite' (n.) 2b); 'disgising' (ger.) 1a), compare 'disgisen' (v.) 2a) and 2c).
108 For a recent discussion of the 'grey area' between heresy and orthodoxy, see Jill C. Havens, 'Shading the grey area: determining heresy in Middle English texts', in Helen Barr and Ann M. Hutchison, *Text and Controversy from Wyclif to Bale: Essays in Honour of Anne Hudson* (Turnhout: Brepols, 2005), pp. 337–53.
109 *Dives and Pauper,* ed. Priscilla Barnum, EETS OS 275 (London: Oxford University Press, 1976), vol. I, p. 188. All subsequent quotations refer to this edition and volume by page number.
110 *MED* 'fair' (adj.) 1a) and 10.
111 *MED* 'arrai' (n.) 2a) and 3.
112 The parishioners of Hackington, Kent, referring to the rood screen in the parish church of the Holy Cross in Canterbury. See Eamon Duffy, 'The parish, piety, and patronage in late medieval East Anglia: the evidence of rood screens', in Katherine L. French, Gary G. Gibbs and Beat A. Kümin (eds), *The Parish in English Life 1400–1600* (Manchester: Manchester University Press, 1997), pp. 133–67, pp. 146–7. Duffy finds similar instructions from the parishioners of Morebath in Devon, p. 147.
113 French, *The People of the Parish,* p. 46. I discuss the competition between churches in *The Book of the Foundation of St Bartholomew's Church* in Chapter 2.
114 Ellen K. Rentz argues in her discussion of the window that 'even as it celebrates the charity of a fellow parishioner whose benevolence knocks down barriers between rich and poor, the window ultimately reinforces the divide by reminding the viewer of Blackburn's prominence'; see *Imagining the Parish in Late Medieval England* (Columbus: Ohio State University Press, 2015), pp. 138–41, p. 141.
115 *Images and Pilgrimages*, p. 87. Italics mine.
116 See Laura Varnam, 'The crucifix, the pietà, and the female mystic: devotional objects and performative identity in *The Book of Margery Kempe*', in which I argue that devotional objects such as the crucifix and pietà provided an opportunity for the performance of religious identity, especially for women; see *Journal of Medieval Religious Cultures*, 41:2 (2015), 208–37. The parish church as a whole also provides such an opportunity, through financial and spiritual patronage and support.
117 Norman Tanner, *The Church in Late Medieval Norwich, 1370–1532* (Toronto: Pontifical Institute of Medieval Studies, 1984), p. 126.
118 French, *The People of the Parish,* p. 143.
119 See Richard Marks, *Stained Glass in England during the Middle Ages* (London: Routledge, 1993), p. 12.

120 Christopher Woodforde, 'The medieval glass in Elsing church, Norfolk', *Journal of the British Society of Master Glass-Painters*, 4:3 (1932), 134–36. A knight of the Drayton family holds a micro-church in a mid-fourteenth century window at Lowick, Northamptonshire, as does William de Ferrers in a window at Bere Ferrers in Devon; see Marks p. 12 and for images, see *Corpus Vitrearum Medii Aevi*: www.cvma.ac.uk/index.html [accessed 17 March 2017]. John, the third Lord Cobham, also holds a church in his fourteenth-century brass at Cobham, Kent, where he refounded the parish church as a chantry college. See Peter Fleming, 'Cobham family (per. c1250-c.1530)', *Oxford Dictionary of National Biography* (Oxford University Press, 2004); see www.oxforddnb.com/view/previous/52781/2004–09 [accessed 29 September 2015].

121 For the image, see *Corpus Vitrearum Medii Aevi*: www.cvma.ac.uk/index.html [accessed 17 March 2017].

122 For a discussion of miniature objects, identity and power, see Stephanie M. Langin-Hooper, 'Fascination with the tiny: social negotiation through miniatures in Hellenistic Babylonia', *World Archaeology*, 47:1 (2015), 60–79.

123 Binski, 'The English Parish Church', p. 3.

124 Binski, 'The English Parish Church', p. 3. See for example Sarah Stanbury, *The Visual Object of Desire in Late Medieval England* (Philadelphia: University of Pennsylvania Press, 2008), especially chapter 7, 'Arts of self-patronage in *The Book of Margery Kempe*', pp. 191–218, and the forthcoming essay collection edited by Stephanie Downes, Sally Holloway and Sarah Randles, *Feeling Things: Objects and Emotions through History* (Oxford University Press).

125 I discuss this episode in further detail in my article on St Margaret's church, 'The importance of St Margaret's church in *The Book of Margery Kempe*', *Nottingham Medieval Studies*, forthcoming 2017.

126 *MED* 'richeli' (adv.) 1a) and b).

127 *MED* 'solempne' (adj.) 1a).

128 *MED* 'esen' (v.) 4a) and 3.

129 Hornstein, *Losing Site,* p. 3.

130 *Images and Pilgrimages*, p. 85.

131 *Ibid.*

132 *The Book of Vices and Virtues: A Fourteenth Century English Translation of the Somme le Roi of Lorens d'Orleans*, ed. W. Francis Nelson, EETS OS 217 (London: Oxford University Press, 1942), p. 47.

133 *Jacob's Well*, ed. by Arthur Brandeis, EETS OS 115 (London: Kegan Paul, Trench, and Trübner, 1900), p. 141.

134 Richard Morris, *Churches in the Landscape* (London: Dent, 1989), pp. 322–3.

135 Morris, *Churches in the Landscape*, p. 323.

136 See *Ibid.*, chapter 8, 'Time and Tide', pp. 316–59.

137 Dorothy Owen, *The Making of King's Lynn: A Documentary Survey* (London: Oxford University Press for the British Academy, 1984), p. 27 and document 133, p. 141.
138 Morris, *Churches in the Landscape,* p. 277.
139 *Ibid.*
140 *MED* 'heigh' (adj.) 1a) and 5a).
141 T. A. Heslop, 'Swaffham parish church: community building in fifteenth-century Norfolk', in Christopher Harper-Bill (ed.), *Medieval East Anglia* (Woodbridge: Boydell, 2005), pp. 246–71, p. 255.
142 Heslop, 'Swaffham parish church', p. 266.
143 *Ibid.*, p. 256.
144 French, *The People of the Parish,* p. 152. For Methwold, see Colin Platt, *The Parish Churches of Medieval England* (London: Secker and Warburg, 1981), p. 97, figure 69.
145 On bay six of the south aisle, for example, the inscription reads: 'pray for the soulle of John pie & Alys his wyf of whos good[es] this arch was made & thes twey[n] wy[n]dowys glasid'; see David Dymond and Clive Paine (eds), *Five Centuries of an English Parish Church: The State of Long Melford, Suffolk* (Cambridge: EAH Press, 2012), p. 178.
146 Matthew Champion, *Medieval Graffiti: The Lost Voices of England's Churches* (London: Ebury Publishing, 2015).
147 Personal correspondence with Matthew Champion. A simple church with a tower and spire can be seen on a pillar in the north arcade at St Mary's, Ashwell, in Hertfordshire. See www.stmarysashwell.org.uk/church/graffiti_pillars.htm [accessed 30 August 2016].
148 Champion, *Medieval Graffiti*, p. 214.
149 Andrew Brown, *Popular Piety in Late Medieval England: The Diocese of Salisbury 1250–1550* (Oxford: Oxford University Press, 1995), p. 222.
150 Robert Lutton, *Lollardy and Orthodox Religious in Pre-Reformation England: Reconstructing Piety* (Woodbridge: Boydell, 2006), p. 1.
151 Richard Marks, *Image and Devotion in Late Medieval England* (Stroud: Sutton, 2004), p. 90.
152 *John Mirk's Festial*, ed. Susan Powell, EETS OS 334 (Oxford: Oxford University Press, 2009), vol. I, p. 157.
153 *On the Twenty Five Articles* in *Select English Works of John Wyclif*, ed. Arnold, pp. 454–96, p. 486.
154 *On the Twenty Five Articles*, p. 487.
155 *Ibid.*, p. 488.
156 *Ibid.*

Epilogue

By a Chapel as I came is a little-known fifteenth-century carol in which the narrator happens upon Christ, who is on his way to church:

> And By a chapell as y Came,
> Mett y wythe Ihũ to chyrcheward gone
> Petur and Pawle, thomas & Ihon,
> And hys desyplys Euery-chone.
>   Mery hyt ys in may mornyng,
>   Mery ways ffor to gonne.[1]

The narrator falls into step with Christ and his disciples as they make their way 'chyrcheward', and what they discover inside the chapel is truly marvellous: the saints are performing the liturgy.

> Sente Thomas þe Bellys gane ryng,
> And sent Collas [Nicholas] þe mas gane syng,
> sente Ihon toke þat swete offeryng,
> And By a chapell as y Came.
>   Mery hyt ys. (lines 5–8)

In this 'chanson d'aventure' we enter a wonderful space in which the saints have stepped down from the painted walls of the church to officiate the mass and ring the bells, calling the congregation to God's house on earth. Christ and the Virgin are in attendance, portrayed as prosperous donors offering up richly symbolic gifts:

> Owre lorde offeryd whate he wollde,
> A challes alle off ryche rede gollde;
> Owre lady, þe crowne off hyr mowlde,
> The sone owte off hyr Bosome schone.
>   Mery hyt ys. (lines 9–12)

Bestowed with Christ's golden chalice and the Virgin's own crown, the chapel gleams with sacred gifts. The Virgin herself illuminates the space as the sun, a symbol of her own Son and man's salvation, shines from her bosom. Finally, St George lights the candles in the chapel and the narrator's vision of this most sacred space is complete:

> Sent Iorge þat ys owre lady kny3te,
> He tende þe tapyrys fayre & Bryte—
> To myn y3e a semley sy3te,
> And By a chapell as y Came.
> Mery hyt ys. (lines 13–16)

The chapel with its flickering candles is a most 'semley sy3te' for the narrator, who miraculously encounters it one May morning. It is undoubtedly a sacred space, the house of God and his saints, a house of prayer. It has the multisensory, dynamic sanctity of a working chapel, chanced upon by a narrator like the knight of medieval romance who rides out in the hope of meeting a marvel.

This quality of 'aventure' can still be experienced in the twenty-first century. In the course of the research for this book, I 'came upon' the church of St Botolph in Slapton, Northamptonshire, whose surviving wall paintings offer a glimpse into the sacred world of the late medieval church. A rural church nestled beside a farm, a most 'semely sy3te' greets the visitor when they unlock the door and turn on the lights. Immediately visible on the south wall facing the entrance is a huge painting of St Christopher carrying the Christ child, who raises his hand in blessing, protecting the viewer from sudden death that day. At St Christopher's feet, a mermaid gazes into a mirror, smoothing her hair, while a series of comical fish look on, as if puzzled to find themselves on the walls of a medieval church (Figure 3). The arches immediately facing the door depict two contrasting scenes, the hanging of Judas to the left and the Annunciation on the right (Figure 7). At the back of the church, trying to keep a low profile, two gossiping women are dwarfed by the devil Tutivillus, who looms over them, pressing their heads together. Beneath the central arch into the nave, the resurrected Christ emerges from the tomb and displays his wounds to the kneeling figure of St Gregory. Just around the corner from the resurrected Christ, on the opposite side of the arch from Judas, St Francis receives the stigmata, his wounds directly linked to those of Christ on the crucifix by a series of black lines (Figure 8). In the nave itself, opposite St Christopher, a damaged painting shows St Michael the archangel weighing souls, with the Virgin Mary to his right assisting a soul by drawing the scales up towards

7 The hanging of Judas, St Christopher, and the Annunciation. Medieval wall paintings, St Botolph's, Slapton, Northamptonshire.

8 The Man of Sorrows, St Francis, Tutivillus and the gossiping women. Medieval wall paintings, St Botolph's, Slapton, Northamptonshire.

salvation (Figure 9). Above the Virgin is a fragmentary image of St George and a painting of what appears to be a building with an open archway and lattice windows, welcoming the viewer inside. Anne Marshall suggests that this hospitable architecture relates to the Weighing of Souls image below, depicting the 'apartments of Heaven into which the saved soul is about to pass'.[2] The golden archway may indeed represent the gate of heaven, the scriptural image that is so crucial to the identity of the church itself in the late Middle Ages. But the lattice windows in the wall painting bear a striking resemblance to the contemporary leaded lights in St Botolph's church and the modern visitor is reminded of the church's enduring sacred identity when they encounter a framed notice in the church porch that reads:

> 'This is none other but the House of God and this is the Gate of Heaven.' (Genesis, 28.17) Whosoever thou art that enterest this church, leave it not without one prayer to God for thyself, for those who minister, and for those who worship here.

The modern visitor is scripted into the community of worshippers at St Botolph's by this command. To pray for the congregation, the clergy, and indeed oneself is to enter into a performance that produces the identity of the church as a house of prayer as surely

9 The weighing of souls. Medieval wall painting, St Botolph's, Slapton, Northamptonshire.

as the medieval lyric's cast of saintly celebrants in *By a Chapel as I came*.

Visiting the church is an edifying experience. The wall paintings teach the viewer not to gossip in sacred space, to venerate the Virgin in the hope of her future intercession, and to see the church as a place of miracles, from St Francis receiving the stigmata to the appearance of the Man of Sorrows at the Mass of St Gregory. A visit to the church also incorporates the twenty-first century churchgoer into a community that has its roots in the medieval past but is still active and vibrant today. And this is true of many churches and cathedrals across England whose communities come up with ever more creative and playful ways to venerate their churches with projects that unite an interest in the medieval fabric of the church with twenty-first century modes of representation. At Durham, an accurate scale replica of the cathedral has been built with over three hundred thousand Lego bricks as a fundraising project for the cathedral's new 'Open Treasure' exhibition.[3] The model has taken three years to complete, and each brick represents a £1 donation to the project. Harnessing the imaginative power of the popular construction toy, the Lego cathedral has gained worldwide attention and is itself now a tourist attraction in the undercroft of the cathedral. The intricate miniature cathedral stands as testimony to the donations and support of a worldwide community who value the medieval cathedral and its sanctity. The Lego cathedral replicates the real cathedral, both as an image and a material object; the complexity of the model, the length of time it took to complete, and the essential support of the community playfully re-enact the original building process. The model reminds us of the sacred wonder of the building and the skill and devotion of those who created it, just as the Middle English translation of the foundation legend did for the community at St Bartholomew's. Even today sacred space relies upon an active, dedicated community if it is to continue to thrive.

Another twenty-first century project that shows parishioners reflecting upon and engaging with the materiality of their medieval churches is the 'Woolly Spires – Knitted Churches of Lincolnshire'.[4] Local knitting groups have crafted impressively detailed replicas of four churches in Lincolnshire in woollen form (St Mary and St Nicolas, Spalding; St Denys', Sleaford; St James' Louth; and St Botolph's church, Boston; Figure 10) and the choice of material is directly related to the history of the churches themselves, as they were funded by landowners whose wealth came from the wool trade.

10 Woolly Spires exhibition at St James Church, Louth, July 2015. Photo: Marion Sander.

As well as promoting their sacred spaces to a wider audience, such projects enable twenty-first century communities to think about the history, meaning, and importance of their churches in the same way as the medieval texts and images in this book. Whether it is adding a brick to a Lego cathedral or knitting a woolly church, these practical activities enable individuals and groups to get involved in their local sacred spaces and to show that they still represent an 'architecture of the heart' for their communities.[5] There is still wonder and marvel to be found in an encounter with sacred space. Whether the destination is a rural church, like St Botolph's, or a great cathedral like Durham or Canterbury, to go 'chyrcheward' is to embark upon a sacred 'aventure', to encounter Christ and the saints in his earthly house and to recognise that truly, God is in this place.

Notes

1 *By a Chapel as I came* in *Religious Lyrics of the XVth Century*, ed. Carleton Brown (Oxford: Clarendon Press, 1939), p. 183, lines 1–4 plus burden. All subsequent quotations refer to this edition by line number.

2 Anne Marshall, 'Slapton, Northants (Peterborough): weighing of souls', http://paintedchurch.org/slapweig.htm [accessed 13 September 2016].

3 www.durhamcathedral.co.uk/visit/what-to-visit/durham-cathedral-lego-build [accessed 13 September 2016].

4 www.facebook.com/woollyspires and www.artsnk.org/news/2016/06/woolly-spires-exhibition-coming-soon-to-st-mary-st-nicolas-spalding/ [accessed 13 September 2016]. Thanks to Marion Sander for kindly providing the photograph of the project.

5 Shelley Hornstein, *Losing Site: Architecture, Memory, and Place* (Farnham: Ashgate, 2011), p. 3.

Bibliography

Manuscripts

London, British Library, MS Cotton Vespasian B IX.

Primary Texts

An Alphabet of Tales, ed. Mary Macleod Banks, EETS OS 126–7 (London: Kegan Paul, Trench and Trübner, 1904–5).

'Annales Ricardi Secundi et Henrici Quarti, Regum Angliae', in *Johannis de Trokelowe et Henrici de Blaneforde, Monachorum S Albani, necnon quorundam anonymorum, Chronica et Annales, Regimantibus Henrico Tertio, Edwardo Primo, Edwardo Secundo, Ricardo Secundo, et Henrico Quarto*, ed. Henry Thomas Riley (London: Longmans, Green, Reader and Dyer, 1866).

Audelay, John, *John the Blind Audelay: Poems and Carols (Oxford, Bodleian Library MS Douce 302)*, ed. Susanna Fein (Kalamazoo: Medieval Institute Publications, 2009).

Bede, *The Ecclesiastical History of the English People; The Greater Chronicle; Bede's Letter to Egbert*, ed. and trans. Judith McClure and Roger Collins (Oxford: Oxford University Press, 1969).

The Book of the Foundation of St Bartholomew's Church, ed. Norman Moore, EETS OS 163 (Oxford: Oxford University Press, 1923).

The Book of the Foundation of the Church of St Bartholomew London, Rendered into Modern English from the Original Latin Version Preserved in the British Museum, Numbered Vespasian B IX, trans. E. A. Webb (London: Oxford University Press, 1923).

The Book of Margery Kempe, ed. Barry Windeatt (Woodbridge: Brewer, 2004).

The Book of Vices and Virtues, ed. W. Nelson Francis, EETS OS 217 (London: Oxford University Press, 1942).

The Canterbury Interlude in *The Canterbury Tales: Fifteenth Century Continuations and Additions*, ed. John M. Bowers (Kalamazoo: Medieval Institute Publications, 1992), pp. 60–79.

Chaucer, Geoffrey, *The Riverside Chaucer*, ed. Larry D. Benson et al. (Oxford: Oxford University Press, 1987; paperback 1988).

Chronique de la Traison et Mort de Richard Deux Roy Dengleterre, ed. and trans. Benjamin Williams (London: Aux dépens de la Société, 1846).

Codex Ashmole 61: A Compilation of Popular Middle English Verse, ed. George Shuffelton, TEAMS Middle English Texts Series (2008): http://d.lib.rochester.edu/teams/publication/shuffelton-codex-ashmole-61 [accessed 22 September 2016].

Dean, James M., ed. *Medieval Political Writings* (Kalamazoo: Medieval Institute Publications, 1996).

Dives and Pauper, ed. Priscilla Barnum, EETS OS 275 (London: Oxford University Press, 1976), vol. I.

Dugdale, William, *Monasticon Anglicanum*, ed. John Caley and Henry Ellis (London: James Bohn, 1846), vol. VI.

'An English translation of *Ordo benedicandam ecclesiam*: order to bless a church', in Brian Repsher (eds), *Rite of Church Dedication in the Early Medieval Era* (Lewiston, NY: The Edwin Mellen Press, 1998), pp. 139–69.

English Wycliffite Sermons, ed. Anne Hudson (Oxford: Clarendon Press, 1983), vol. I.

English Wycliffite Sermons, ed. Pamela Gradon (Oxford: Clarendon Press, 1988), vol. II.

English Wycliffite Sermons, ed. Anne Hudson (Oxford: Clarendon Press, 1990), vol. III.

Eulogium, ed. Frank Scott Haydon (London: Longman, Green, Longman, Roberts and Green, 1863), vol. III.

The Gesta Romanorum, ed. Sidney J. H. Herrtage, EETS ES 33 (London: N. Trübner, 1879).

Grosseteste, Robert, *Templum Dei*, ed. Joseph Goering and F. A. C. Mantello (Toronto: Pontifical Institute of Medieval Studies, 1984).

Historia Vitae et Regni Ricardi Secundi, ed. George B. Stow (Philadelphia: University of Pennsylvania Press, 1977).

The Holy Bible containing the Old and New Testaments, with the Apocryphal Books, in the Earliest English Versions made from the Latin Vulgate by John Wycliffe and *his Followers*, ed. Josiah Forshall and Frederic Madden (Oxford: Oxford University Press, 1950), vol. II.

How the Goode Wife Taught Hyr Doughter in *The Trials and Joys of Marriage*, ed. Eve Salisbury (Kalamazoo: Medieval Institute Publications, 2002), pp. 219–24.

Jacob's Well, ed. Arthur Brandeis, EETS OS 115 (London: Kegan Paul, Trench, and Trübner, 1900).

Julian of Norwich, *A Revelation of Love*, ed. Marion Glasscoe (Exeter: Exeter University Press, 1993).

Langland, William, *The Vision of Piers Plowman: A Complete Edition of the B Text*, ed. A. V. C. Schmidt (London: Dent, 1978).

The Lanterne of Liȝt, ed. Lilian M. Swinburn, EETS OS 151 (London: Kegan Paul, Trench, and Trübner, 1917).

Love, Nicholas, *Nicholas Love: The Mirror of the Blessed Life of Jesus Christ*, ed. Michael G. Sargent (Exeter: University of Exeter Press, 2004).

Lydgate, John, *The Minor Poems of John Lydgate*, ed. Henry Noble MacCracken, EETS ES 107 (London: Kegan Paul, Trench, Trübner and co, 1911).

Mannyng, Robert, *Handlyng Synne*, ed. Idelle Sullens (Binghampton, NY: Medieval and Renaissance Texts and Studies, 1983).

The Middle English Translation of the Rosarium Theologie, ed. Christina von Nolcken (Heidelberg: Carl Winter Universitätverlag, 1979).

A Middle English Treatise on the Ten Commandments: From St John's College, Oxford, MS 94 1420–1434, ed. James Finch Royster (University of Chicago, 1910–11).

Mirk, John, *Instructions for Parish Priests by John Myrc*, ed. Edward Peacock, EETS OS 31 (London: Trübner, 1868).

Mirk, John, *Mirk's Festial*, ed. Theodor Erbe, EETS OS 96 (London: Kegan Paul, Trench, and Trübner, 1905).

Mirk, John, *John Mirk's Festial*, ed. Susan Powell, EETS OS 334 (Oxford: Oxford University Press, 2009), vol. I.

Mirk, John, *John Mirk's Festial*, ed. Susan Powell, EETS OS 335 (Oxford: Oxford University Press, 2011), vol. II.

The Myroure of Oure Ladye, ed. John Henry Blunt, EETS ES 19 (London: Kegan Paul, Trench, and Trübner, 1873).

The Orcherd of Syon, ed. Phyllis Hodgson and Gabriel M. Liegey, EETS OS 258 (Oxford: Oxford University Press, 1966).

Pierce the Ploughman's Crede, in *The Piers Plowman Tradition*, ed. Helen Barr (London: Dent, 1993), pp. 60–97.

The Rationale Divinorum Officiorum of William Durand of Mende: A New Translation of the Prologue and Book One, trans. Timothy M. Thibodeau (New York: Columbia University Press, 2007).

Religious Lyrics of the XVth Century, ed. Carleton Brown (Oxford: Clarendon Press, 1939).

Religious Lyrics of the XIVth Century, ed. Carleton Brown, second edition revised by G. V. Smithers (Oxford: Clarendon Press, 1957).

Richard Morris's Prick of Conscience: A Corrected and Amplified Reading Text, ed. Ralph Hanna and Sarah Wood, EETS OS 342 (Oxford: Oxford University Press, 2013).

Selections from English Wycliffite Writings, ed. Anne Hudson (Cambridge: Cambridge University Press, 1978).

The Sermon of William Taylor, in *Two Wycliffite Texts*, ed. Anne Hudson, EETS OS 301 (Oxford: Oxford University Press, 1993), pp. 3–23.

'Þe Simonie', in *The Auckinleck Manuscript*, ed. David Burnley and Alison Wiggins, National Library of Scotland, 5 July 2003, http://auchinleck.nls.uk/ [accessed 21 July 2016].

Speculum Sacerdotale, ed. Edward H. Weatherly, EETS OS 200 (London: Oxford University Press, 1936).

St Erkenwald, ed. Clifford Peterson (University Park, PA: University of Pennsylvania Press, 1977).

Supplementary Lives in Some Manuscripts of the Gilte Legende, ed. Richard Hamer and Vida Russell, EETS OS 315 (Oxford: Oxford University Press, 2000).

Templum Domini, in Roberta D. Cornelius (eds), *The Figurative Castle: A Study in the Mediaeval Allegory of the Edifice with Especial Reference to Religious Writings* (Pennsylvania: Bryn Mawr, 1930), pp. 90–112.

The Testimony of William Thorpe, in *Two Wycliffite Texts*, ed. Anne Hudson, EETS OS 301 (Oxford: Oxford University Press, 1993), pp. 24–93.

The Towneley Plays, ed. Martin Stevens and A. C. Cawley, EETS SS 13 (Oxford: Oxford University Press, 1994), vol. I.

Usk, Adam, *The Chronicle of Adam Usk*, trans. C. Given-Wilson (Oxford: Clarendon, 1997).

de Voragine, Jacobus, 'The dedication of a church', in *The Golden Legend: Readings on the Saints*, trans. William Granger Ryan (Princeton: Princeton University Press, 1993), vol. II, pp. 385–95.

Walsingham, Thomas, *Thomæ Walsingham, Quoandam Monarchi S. Albani, Historia Anglicana*, ed. Henry Thomas Riley (London: Longman, Green, Longman, Roberts and Green, 1864), vol. I.

What the Church Betokeneth, in *Supplementary Lives in Some Manuscripts of the Gilte Legende*, ed. Richard Hamer and Vida Russell, EETS OS 315 (Oxford: Oxford University Press, 2000), pp. 85–128.

Wyclif, John, *Select English Works of John Wyclif*, ed. Thomas Arnold (Oxford: Clarendon Press, 1871), vol. III.

Wyclif, John, *The English Works of Wyclif Hitherto Unprinted*, ed. F. D. Matthew, EETS OS 74 (London: Trübner and co, 1880).

The York Corpus Christi Plays, ed. Clifford Davidson (Kalamazoo: Medieval Institute Publications, 2011).

Secondary Texts

Anderson, M. D., *Drama and Imagery in English Medieval Churches* (Cambridge: Cambridge University Press, 1963).

Ashley, Kathleen, and Wim Hüsken (eds), *Moving Subjects: Processional Performance in the Middle Ages and the Renaissance* (Amsterdam: Rodopi, 2001).

Aston, Margaret, *Thomas Arundel* (Oxford: Clarendon, 1967).

Balibar, Etienne, and Pierre Macherey, 'On literature as an ideological form', in Robert Young (ed.), *Untying the Text* (London: Routledge, 1990), pp. 79–99.

Barr, Helen, *Signes and Sothe: Language in the Piers Plowman Tradition* (Woodbridge: D.S. Brewer, 1994).

Barr, Helen, *Socioliterary Practice in Late Medieval England* (Oxford: Oxford University Press, 2001).

Barr, Helen, *Transporting Chaucer* (Manchester: Manchester University Press, 2014).

Barrett Jr., Robert, *Against All England: Regional Identity and Cheshire Writing, 1195–1656* (Notre Dame: University of Notre Dame Press, 2009).

Bell, Catherine, *Ritual Theory, Ritual Practice* (Oxford: Oxford University Press, 2009).

Biernoff, Suzannah, *Sight and Embodiment in the Middle Ages* (Basingstoke: Palgrave Macmillan, 2002).

Bildhauer, Bettina, *Medieval Blood* (Cardiff: University of Wales Press, 2006).

Binski, Paul, *Westminster Abbey and the Plantagenets: Kingship and the Representation of Power 1200–1400* (London: Yale University Press, 1995).

Binski, Paul, 'The English Parish Church and its art in the late Middle Ages: a review of the problem', *Studies in Iconography*, 20 (1999), 1–25.

Blick, Sarah, 'Reconstructing the shrine of St Thomas Becket, Canterbury cathedral', in Sarah Blick and Rita Tekippe (eds), *Art and Archaeology of Late Medieval Pilgrimage in Northern Europe and the British Isles* (Leiden: Brill, 2005), pp. 405–41.

Bose, Mishtooni C., and J. Patrick Hornbeck II (eds), *Wycliffite Controversies* (Turnhout: Brepols, 2011).

Brereton, Joel, 'Sacred space', in Mircea Eliade (ed.), *The Encyclopedia of Religion* (New York: Macmillan, 1987), vol. 12, pp. 526–35.

Brooke, Christopher, *London 800–1216: The Shaping of a City* (London: Secker and Warburg, 1975).

Brooks, Nicholas, 'The Anglo-Saxon cathedral and its community, 597–1070', in Patrick Collinson, Nigel Ramsay, and Margaret Sparks (eds), *A History of Canterbury Cathedral* (Oxford: Oxford University Press, 1995), pp. 1–37.

Brown, Andrew, *Popular Piety in Late Medieval England: The Diocese of Salisbury 1250–1550* (Oxford: Oxford University Press, 1995).

Brown, Peter, 'Journey's end: the prologue to the tale of Beryn', in Julia Boffey and Janet Cowen (eds), *Chaucer and Fifteenth-Century Poetry* (London: Centre for Late Antique and Medieval Studies, King's College, 1991), pp. 143–74.

Brown, Sarah, and Lindsay MacDonald, *Fairford Parish Church: A Medieval Church and its Stained Glass* (Stroud: Sutton Publishing, 2007).

Buckle, Alexandra, '"Of the finest colours": music in stained glass at Warwick and elsewhere', *Vidimus*, 46, December 2010, http://vidimus.org/issues/issue-46/feature/ [accessed 15 September 2016].

Bynum, Caroline Walker, *Fragmentation and Redemption: Essays on Gender and the Human Body in Medieval Religion* (New York: Zone Books, 1992).

Bynum, Caroline Walker, *Wonderful Blood: Theology and Practice in Late Medieval Northern Germany and Beyond* (Philadelphia: University of Pennsylvania Press, 2007).

Camille, Michael, 'The language of images in medieval England 1200–1400', in Jonathan Alexander and Paul Binski (eds), *The Age of Chivalry: Art in Plantagenet England 1200–1400* (London: Royal Academy of Arts, 1987), pp. 33–40.

Camille, Michael, 'The devil's writing: diabolic literacy in medieval art', in Irving Lavin (ed.), *World Art: Themes of Unity in Diversity* (University Park, PA: Pennsylvania State University Press, 1989), vol. II, pp. 355–60.

Camille, Michael, '"When Adam delved": labouring on the land in medieval art', in Del Sweeney (ed.), *Agriculture in the Middle Ages: Technology, Practice, and Representation* (University Park, PA: University of Pennsylvania Press, 1995), pp. 247–76.

Carruthers, Leo, '"Know thyself": criticism, reform, and the audience in *Jacob's Well*', in Jacqueline Hamesse (ed.), *Medieval Sermons and Society: Cloister, City, and University* (Louvain-le-Neuve: Fédération Internationale des Instituts d'Études Médiévales, 1998), pp. 219–40.

Carruthers, Mary, 'The poet as master builder: composition and locational memory in the Middle Ages', *New Literary History*, 24 (1993), 881–904.

Carruthers, Mary, *The Craft of Thought: Meditation, Rhetoric, and the Making of Images, 400–1200* (Cambridge: Cambridge University Press, 1998; paperback 2000).

Caviness, Madeline Harrison, *The Early Stained Glass of Canterbury Cathedral: c.1175–1220* (Princeton: Princeton University Press, 1997).

Caviness, Madeline Harrison, 'Reception of images by medieval viewers', in Conrad Rudolph (ed.), *A Companion to Medieval Art: Romanesque and Gothic in Northern Europe* (Oxford: Blackwell, 2006; paperback 2010), pp. 65–85.

de Certeau, Michel, *The Practice of Everyday Life*, trans. Steven Rendall (Berkeley: University of California Press, 1988).

Champion, Matthew, *Medieval Graffiti: The Lost Voices of England's Churches* (London: Ebury Publishing, 2015).

Chazelle, Celia M., 'Pictures, books, and the illiterate: pope Gregory I's letters to Serenus of Marseilles', *Word and Image*, 6:2 (1990), 138–53.

Clark, James G., 'The Augustinians, history, and literature in late medieval England', in Janet E. Burton and Karen Stöber (eds), *The Regular Canons in the Medieval British Isles* (Turnhout: Brepols, 2011), pp. 403–16.

Cohen, Anthony, *The Symbolic Construction of Community* (Chichester: Ellis Horwood, 1985).

Cole, Andrew, *Literature and Heresy in the Age of Chaucer* (Cambridge: Cambridge University Press, 2009).

Connerton, Paul, *How Societies Remember* (Cambridge: Cambridge University Press, 1989).

Connolly, Margaret, *John Shirley: Book Production and the Noble Household in Fifteenth Century England* (Aldershot: Ashgate, 1998).

Cownie, Emma, 'The cult of St Edmund in the eleventh and twelfth centuries: the language and communication of a medieval saint's cult', *Neuphilologische Mitteilungen*, 99 (1998), 177–97.

Cox, J. Charles, *Churchwardens' Accounts from the Fourteenth Century to the Close of the Seventeenth Century* (London: Methuen, 1913).

Crassons, Kate, *The Claims of Poverty: Literature, Culture, and Ideology in Late Medieval England* (Notre Dame: University of Notre Dame Press, 2010).

Dinn, Robert, '"Monuments answerable to mens worth": burial patterns, social status and gender in late medieval Bury St Edmunds', *Journal of Ecclesiastical History*, 46 (1995), 237–55.

Douglas, Mary, *Purity and Danger: An Analysis of Concepts of Pollution and Taboo* (London: Routledge, 2003).

Downes, Stephanie, Sally Holloway, and Sarah Randles (eds), *Feeling Things: Objects and Emotions through History* (Oxford: Oxford University Press, forthcoming)

Draper, Peter, 'Enclosure and entrances in medieval cathedrals: access and security', in Janet Backhouse (ed.), *The Medieval English Cathedral* (Donington: Shaun Tyas, 2003), pp. 76–88.

Duffy, Eamon, 'The parish, piety, and patronage in late medieval East Anglia: the evidence of rood screens', in Katherine L. French, Gary G. Gibbs, and Beat A. Kümin (eds), *The Parish in English Life 1400–1600* (Manchester: Manchester University Press, 1997), pp. 133–67.

Duffy, Eamon, 'Religious belief' in Rosemary Horrox and W. Mark Ormrod (eds), *A Social History of England 1200–1500* (Cambridge: Cambridge University Press, 2006), pp. 383–412.

Duggan, Lawrence G., 'Was art really the "book of the illiterate?"', in Marielle Hageman and Marco Mostert (eds), *Reading Images and Texts: Medieval Images and Texts as Forms of Communication: Papers from the Third Utrecht Symposium on Medieval Literary, Utrecht, 7–9 December 2000* (Turnhout: Brepols, 2005), pp. 63–107.

Dunnan, D. S., 'A note on the three churches in *The Lanterne of Liȝt*', *Notes and Queries*, n.s. 38 (1991), 20–3.

Durkheim, Emile, *Sociology and Philosophy*, trans. D. F. Pocock (London: Cohen and West, 1953).

Dymond, David, and Clive Paine (eds), *Five Centuries of an English Parish Church: The State of Long Melford, Suffolk* (Cambridge: EAH Press, 2012).

Eliade, Mircea, *Patterns in Comparative Religion*, trans. Rosemary Sheed (London: Sheed and Ward, 1958).

Eliade, Mircea, *The Sacred and Profane: The Nature of Religion*, trans. Willard R. Trask (Orlando: Harcourt, 1987).

Fairclough, Norman, *Language and Power* (London: Longman, 1989).

Finucane, Ronald C., *Miracles and Pilgrims: Popular Beliefs in Medieval England* (London: Macmillan, 1977).

Flanigan, C. Clifford, 'The moving subject: medieval liturgical processions in semiotic and cultural perspective', in Kathleen Ashley and Wim Hüsken (eds), *Moving Subjects: Processional Performance in the Middle Ages and the Renaissance* (Amsterdam: Rodopi, 2001), pp. 35–51.

Forshaw, Alec, and Theo Bergström, *Smithfield Past and Present* (London: Robert Hale, 1980).

Franklin, Jill A., 'The eastern arm of Norwich cathedral and the Augustinian priory of St Bartholomew's, Smithfield, in London', *The Antiquaries Journal*, 86 (2006), 110–30.

Freedberg, David, *The Power of Images: Studies in the History and Theory of Response* (Chicago: University of Chicago Press, 1989).

French, Katherine L., *The People of the Parish: Life in a Late Medieval Diocese* (Philadelphia: University of Pennsylvania Press, 2001).

French, Katherine L, 'Localized faith: parochial and domestic space', in John H. Arnold (ed.), *The Oxford Handbook of Medieval Christianity* (Oxford: Oxford University Press, 2014), pp. 166–82.

Foucault, Michel, 'Of other spaces', trans. Jay Miskowiec, *Diacritics* 18 (1986), 22–7.

Fuchs, Anna, *Remarks on Deixis* (Heidelberg: Groos, 1993).

Gayk, Shannon, *Image, Text, and Religious Reform in Fifteenth-Century England* (Cambridge: Cambridge University Press, 2010).

van Gennep, A. *The Rites of Passage* (London: Routledge and Kegan Paul, 1960).

Gibson, Gail McMurray, *The Theater of Devotion: East Anglian Drama and Society in the Late Middle Ages* (Chicago: University of Chicago Press, 1989).

Gibson, Gail McMurray, 'Blessing from sun and moon: churching as women's theatre', in Barbara A. Hanawalt and David Wallace (eds), *Bodies and Disciplines: Intersections of Literature and History in Fifteenth-Century England* (Minneapolis: University of Minnesota Press, 1996).

Gill, Miriam, 'Female piety and impiety: selected images of women in wall paintings in England after 1300', in Samatha J. E. Riches and Sarah Salih (eds), *Gender and Holiness: Men, Women, and Saints in Late Medieval Europe* (London: Routledge, 2002), pp. 101–20.

Gill, Miriam, 'Preaching and image: sermons and wall paintings in later medieval England', in Carolyn Muessig (ed.), *Preacher, Sermon and Audience in the Middle Ages* (Leiden: Brill, 2002), pp. 155–80.

Girard, René, *Violence and the Sacred*, trans. Patrick Gregory (London: Continuum, 2005).

Gray, Douglas, 'The five wounds of our lord II', *Notes and Queries*, 208 (1963), 82–9.

Gray, Douglas, *Themes and Images in the Medieval English Religious Lyric* (London: Routledge and Kegan Paul, 1972).

Gray, Madeleine, 'Images of words: iconographies of text and the construction of sacred space in medieval church wall painting', in Joseph Sterrett and Peter Thomas (eds), *Sacred Text, Sacred Space: Architectural, Spiritual, and Literary Convergences in England and Wales* (Leiden: Brill, 2011), pp. 15–35.

Hanawalt, Barbara, and Michel Kobialka (eds), *Medieval Practices of Space* (Minneapolis: University of Minnesota Press, 2000).

Hannam, U. C., 'The episcopal registers of Roger Walden and Nicholas Bubwith', *Transactions of the London and Middlesex Archaeological Society*, n. s. 11 (1954), 123–136.

Havens, Jill C., 'Shading the grey area: determining heresy in Middle English texts', in Helen Barr and Ann M. Hutchison, *Text and Controversy from Wyclif to Bale: Essays in Honour of Anne Hudson* (Turnhout: Brepols, 2005), pp. 337–53.

Hayes, Dawn Marie, *Body and Sacred Place in Medieval Europe 1100–1389* (London: Routledge, 2003).

Heslop, T. A., 'Attitudes to the visual arts: the evidence from written sources', in Jonathan Alexander and Paul Binski (eds), *The Age of Chivalry: Art in Plantagenet England 1200–1400* (London: Royal Academy of Arts, 1987), pp. 26–32.

Heslop, T. A., 'Swaffham parish church: community building in fifteenth-century Norfolk', in Christopher Harper-Bill (ed.), *Medieval East Anglia* (Woodbridge: Boydell, 2005), pp. 246–71.

Hicks, Dan, 'The material-cultural turn: event and effect', in Dan Hicks and Mary Beaudry (eds), *The Oxford Handbook of Material Culture Studies* (Oxford: Oxford University Press, 2010), pp. 25–98.

Hillaby, Joe, 'The London Jewry: William I to John', *Jewish Historical Studies*, 33 (1992–4), 1–44.

Hilton, Claire, 'St Bartholomew's hospital, London, and its Jewish connections', *Jewish Historical Studies*, 30 (1987–8), 21–50.

Hobsbawm, Eric, 'Introduction: inventing tradition', in Eric Hobsbawm and Terence Ranger (eds), *The Invention of Tradition* (Cambridge: Cambridge University Press, 1983), pp. 1–14.

Holsinger, Bruce, 'Lollard ekphrasis: situated aesthetics and literary history', *Journal of Medieval and Early Modern Studies*, 35:1 (2005), 67–89.

Hornbeck II, J. Patrick, *What is a Lollard?: Dissent and Belief in Late Medieval England* (Oxford: Oxford University Press, 2010).

Hornbeck II, J. Patrick, 'Barn of unity or the devil's church? Salvation and ecclesiology in Langland and the Wycliffites', in Seeta Chaganti and Penn R. Szittya (eds), *Medieval Poetics and Social Practice: Responding to the Work of Penn R. Szittya* (New York: Fordham University Press, 2012), pp. 33–52.

Hornstein, Shelley, *Losing Site: Architecture, Memory, and Place* (Farnham: Ashgate, 2011).

Hsy, Jonathan, 'City', in Marion Turner (ed.), *A Handbook of Middle English Studies* (Chichester: Wiley-Blackwell, 2013), pp. 315–29.

Hudson, Anne, *The Premature Reformation: Wycliffite Texts and Lollard History* (Oxford: Clarendon Press, 1988).

Jennings, Margaret, 'Tutivillus: the literary career of a recording demon', *Studies in Philology*, 74:5 (1977), 1–95.

Johnson, Holly, 'Fashioning devotion: the art of Good Friday preaching in Chaucerian England', in Georgiana Donavin, Cary J. Nederman,

Richard J. Utz(eds), *Speculum Sermonis: Interdisciplinary Reflections on the Medieval Sermon* (Turnhout: Brepols, 2004), pp. 315–34, pp. 316–17.

Jørgensen, Hans Henrik Lohfert, 'Cultic vision- seeing as ritual: visual and liturgical experience in the early Christian and medieval church', in Nils Holger Petersen, Mette Birkedal Bruun, Jeremy Llewellyn, and Mette Østrem (eds), *The Appearances of Medieval Rituals: The Play of Construction and Modification* (Turnhout: Brepols, 2004), pp. 173–97.

Katajala-Peltomaa, Sari, *Gender, Miracles, and Daily Life: The Evidence of Fourteenth Century Canonization Processes* (Turnhout: Brepols, 2009).

Kerling, Nellie J., *The Cartulary of St Bartholomew's Hospital* (London: Lund Humphries, 1973).

Kessler, Herbert, 'Gregory the Great and image theory in northern Europe during the twelfth and thirteenth centuries', in Conrad Rudolph (ed.), *A Companion to Medieval Art: Romanesque and Gothic in Northern Europe* (Oxford: Blackwell, 2006; paperback 2010), pp. 151–72.

Langin-Hooper, Stephanie M., 'Fascination with the tiny: social negotiation through miniatures in Hellenistic Babylonia', *World Archaeology*, 47:1 (2015), 60–79.

Lefebvre, Henri, *The Production of Space*, trans. Donald Nicholson Smith(Oxford: Blackwell, 1991).

Lilley, Keith, *City and Cosmos: The Medieval World in Urban Form* (London: Reaktion, 2009).

Lukes, Steven, 'Political ritual and social integration', *Sociology: Journal of the British Sociological Association*, 9 (1975), 289–308.

Lutton, Robert, *Lollardy and Orthodox Religious in Pre-Reformation England: Reconstructing Piety* (Woodbridge: Boydell, 2006).

Luxford, Julian, 'The idol of origins: retrospection in Augustinian art during the later middle ages', in Janet E. Burton and Karen Stöber (eds), *The Regular Canons in the Medieval British Isles* (Turnhout: Brepols, 2011), pp. 417–42.

Marks, Richard, *Stained Glass in England during the Middle Ages* (London: Routledge, 1993).

Marks, Richard, *Image and Devotion in Late Medieval England* (Stroud: Sutton Publishing, 2004).

Matthew, Gervase, *The Court of Richard II* (London: John Murray, 1968).

McFarlane, K. B., *England in the Fifteenth Century* (London: Hambledon, 1981).

McKisack, May, *The Oxford History of England: The Fourteenth Century, 1307–1399* (Oxford: Clarendon, 1959).

McNamer, Sarah, *Affective Meditation and the Invention of Compassion* (Philadelphia: University of Pennsylvania Press, 2010).

Moore, Norman, *The Church of St Bartholomew the Great, West Smithfield: Its Foundation, Present Condition and Funeral Monuments* (London: Adlard and son, 1908).

Moore, Norman, *The History of St Bartholomew's Hospital* (London: C. Arthur Pearson, 1918), vol. I.

Moore, Sally F., and Barbara Myerhoff, 'Secular ritual: forms and meanings' in Sally F. Moore and Barbara G. Myerhoff (eds), *Secular Ritual* (Assen, NL: Van Gorcum, 1977), pp. 3–24.

Morris, Colin, *The Sepulchre of Christ and the Medieval West: From the Beginning to 1600* (Oxford: Oxford University Press, 2005).

Morris, Richard, *Churches in the Landscape* (London: Dent, 1989).

Morrison, Susan Signe, *Women Pilgrims in Late Medieval England: Private Piety as Public Performance* (London: Routledge, 2000).

Muncey, R. W., *A History of the Consecration of Churches and Churchyards* (Cambridge: W. Heffer and Sons, 1930).

Nichols, Ann Eljenholm, *The Early Art of Norfolk: A Subject List of Extant and Lost Art including Items Relevant to Early Drama* (Kalamazoo: Medieval Institute Publications, 2002).

Nichols, Nick, 'The Augustinian canons and their parish churches: a key to their identity', in Janet E. Burton and Karen Stöber (eds), *The Regular Canons in the Medieval British Isles* (Turnhout: Brepols, 2011), pp. 313–37.

Owen, Dorothy, *The Making of King's Lynn: A Documentary Survey* (London: Oxford University Press for the British Academy, 1984).

Panofsky, Erwin, *Abbot Suger on the Abbey Church of St Denis and its Art Treasures* (Princeton: Princeton University Press, 1979).

Payne, Ann, 'Medieval heraldry', in Jonathan Alexander and Paul Binski (eds), *The Age of Chivalry: Art in Plantagenet England 1200–1400* (London: Royal Academy of Arts, 1987), pp. 55–9.

Peacock, Edward, 'Churchwardens' accounts of Saint Mary's, Sutterton', *Archaeological Journal*, 39 (1882), 53–63.

Pfister, Manfred, *The Theory and Analysis of Drama*, trans. John Halliday (Cambridge: Cambridge University Press, 1988).

Platt, Colin, *The Parish Churches of Medieval England* (London: Secker and Warburg, 1981).

Poole, Austin Lane, *From Domesday Book to Magna Carta, 1087–1216* (Oxford: Clarendon, 1955), vol. II.

Pratt, Mary Louise, *Imperial Eyes: Travel Writing and Transculturation* (London: Routledge, 1992).

Rawcliffe, Carole, *Medicine and Society in Later Medieval England* (Stroud: Alan Sutton, 1995).

Rentz, Ellen K., *Imagining the Parish in Late Medieval England* (Columbus: Ohio State University Press, 2015).

Repsher, Brian, *The Rite of Church Dedication in the Early Medieval Era* (Lewiston, NY: The Edwin Mellen Press, 1998).

Roger, Euan C., 'Blakberd's treasure: a study in fifteenth-century administration at St Bartholomew's hospital, London', in Linda Clark (ed.), *The Fifteenth Century, XIII: Exploring the Evidence. Commemoration, Administration, and the Economy* (Woodbridge: Boydell, 2014), pp. 81–107.

Rose, Adrian, 'Angel musicians in the medieval stained glass of Norfolk churches', *Early Music*, 29:2 (2001), 186–217.

Rosewell, Roger, *Medieval Wall Paintings in English and Welsh Churches* (Woodbridge: Boydell, 2008).

Rubin, Miri, 'Small groups: identity and solidarity in the late middle ages', in Jennifer Kermode (ed.), *Enterprise and Individuals in Fifteenth Century Europe* (Stroud: Alan Sutton, 1991), pp. 132–50.

Sargent, Michael G., 'Censorship or cultural change? Reformation and renaissance in the spirituality of late medieval England', in Vincent Gillespie and Kantik Ghosh (eds), *After Arundel: Religious Writing in Fifteenth-Century England* (Turnhout: Brepols, 2011), pp. 55–72.

Saul, Nigel, 'Richard II and the city of York', in Sarah Rees Jones (ed.), *The Government of Medieval York: Essays in Commemoration of the 1396 Royal Charter* (York: University of York, 1997), pp. 1–13.

Saul, Nigel, *Richard II* (London: Yale University Press, 1997; paperback 1999).

Saul, Nigel, *English Church Monuments in the Middle Ages: History and Representation* (Oxford: Oxford University Press, 2009).

Saunders, Corinne J., *The Forest in Medieval Romance* (Cambridge: Brewer, 1993).

Schechner, Richard, *Performance Theory* (London: Routledge, 2003).

Smith, Jonathan Z., *To Take Place: Toward Theory in Ritual* (Chicago: University of Chicago Press, 1987).

Somerset, Fiona, *Feeling like Saints: Lollard Writings after Wyclif* (London: Cornell University Press, 2014).

Spicer, Andrew, '"To show that the place is divine": consecration crosses revisited', in Krista Kodres and Anu Mänd (eds), *Images and Objects in Ritual Practices in Medieval* and *Early Modern Northern* and *Central Europe* (Newcastle-upon-Tyne: Cambridge Scholars Publishing, 2013), pp. 34–52.

Stanbury, Sarah, *The Visual Object of Desire in Late Medieval England* (Philadelphia: University of Pennsylvania Press, 2008).

Steel, Antony, *Richard II* (Cambridge: Cambridge University Press, 1962).

Strohm, Paul, 'The trouble with Richard: the reburial of Richard II and the Lancastrian symbolic strategy', *Speculum*, 71 (1996), 87–111.

Strohm, Paul, *England's Empty Throne: Usurpation and the Language of Legitimation 1399–1422* (London: Yale University Press, 1998).

Strohm, Paul, *Theory and the Premodern Text* (Minneapolis: University of Minnesota Press, 2000).

Sturges, Robert, 'The pardoner in Canterbury: class, gender, and urban space in "The prologue to the tale of Beryn"', *College Literature*, 33 (2006), 52–76.

Sullivan, Lawrence, 'Sound and senses: towards a hermeneutics of performance', *History of Religion*, 26 (1986), 1–33.

Szittya, Penn R., *The Antifraternal Tradition in Medieval Literature* (Princeton: Princeton University Press, 1986).

Tanner, Norman, *The Church in Late Medieval Norwich, 1370–1532* (Toronto: Pontifical Institute of Medieval Studies, 1984).

Thiery, Daniel, 'Welcome to the parish: remove your cap and stop assaulting your neighbour', in Douglas L. Biggs, Sharon D. Michalove, and Albert Compton Reeves (eds), *Reputation and Representation in Fifteenth Century Europe* (Leiden: Brill, 2004), pp. 235–65.

Tilley, Christopher, *Material Culture and Text: The Art of Ambiguity* (London: Routledge, 1991).

Trapp, J. B., 'Verses by Lydgate at Long Melford', *Review of English Studies*, n.s. 6:21 (1955), 1–11.

Tuan, Yi-Fu, *Space and Place: The Perspective of Experience* (Minneapolis: University of Minnesota Press, 1977).

Turner, Marion, 'Introduction', in Marion Turner (ed.), *A Handbook of Middle English Studies* (Chichester: Wiley-Blackwell, 2013), pp. 1–11.

Turner, Victor, 'Frame, flow, and reflection: ritual and drama as public liminality', in Michel Benamou and Charles Caramelo (eds), *Performance in Postmodern Culture* (Milwaukee: Center for Twentieth Century Studies, University of Wisconsin-Milwaukee, 1977), pp. 33–55.

Varnam, Laura, 'The Howse of God on Erthe: Constructions of Sacred Space in Late Middle English Religious Literature' (DPhil thesis, Oxford University, 2007).

Varnam, Laura, 'Sanctity and the city: sacred space in *The Life of St Werburgh*', in Catherine A. M. Clarke (ed.), *Mapping the Medieval City: Space, Place, and Identity in Chester c.1200–1500* (Cardiff: University of Wales Press, 2010), pp. 114–30.

Varnam, Laura, '*The Book of the Foundation of St Bartholomew's Church*: consecration, restoration, and translation', in Joseph Sterrett and Peter W. Thomas (eds), *Sacred Text, Sacred Space: Architectural, Spiritual, and Literary Convergences in England and Wales* (Brill: Leiden, 2011), pp. 57–75.

Varnam, Laura, 'Church', in Marion Turner (ed.), *A Handbook of Middle English Studies* (Chichester: Wiley-Blackwell, 2013), pp. 299–314.

Varnam, Laura, 'The crucifix, the pietà, and the female mystic: devotional objects and performative identity in *The Book of Margery Kempe*', *Journal of Medieval Religious Cultures*, 41:2 (2015), 208–37.

Varnam, Laura, 'The importance of St Margaret's church in *The Book of Margery Kempe*: a sacred place and an exemplary parishioner', *Nottingham Medieval Studies* (forthcoming 2017).

Walsham, Alexandra, *The Reformation of the Landscape: Religion, Identity, and Memory in Early Modern Britain and Ireland* (Oxford: Oxford University Press, 2011).

Ward, Graham, 'Introduction', in Graham Ward (ed.), *The Certeau Reader* (Oxford: Blackwell, 2000), pp. 1–14.

Watson, Nicholas, 'Vernacular apocalyptic: on *The Lanterne of Liȝt*', *Revista Canaria de Estudios Ingleses*, 47 (2003), 115–17.

Webb, E. A., *The Records of St Bartholomew's Priory and of the Church and Parish of St Bartholomew the Great, West Smithfield* (Oxford: Oxford University Press, 1921), 2 vols.

West-Pavlov, Russell, *Spaces of Fiction / Fictions of Space: Postcolonial Place and Literary DeiXis* (Basingstoke: Palgrave Macmillan, 2010).

Whitehead, Christiania, *Castles of the Mind: A Study of Medieval Architectural Allegory* (Cardiff: University of Wales Press, 2003).

Woodforde, Christopher, 'The medieval glass in Elsing church, Norfolk', *Journal of the British Society of Master Glass-Painters*, 4:3 (1932), 134–36.

Woodforde, Christopher, *Norwich School of Glass-Painting in the Fifteenth Century* (London: Oxford University Press, 1950).

Wylie, J. H., *The History of England under Henry IV: Volume III, 1407–1410* (London: Longmans, Green, and co, 1896).

Zuesse, Evan M., 'Ritual' in Mircea Eliade (ed.), *The Encyclopedia of Religion* (New York: Macmillan, 1987), vol. 12, pp. 405–22.

Online Resources

Corpus Vitrearum Medii Aevi: http://www.cvma.ac.uk/index.html.

Durham cathedral Lego project: www.durhamcathedral.co.uk/visit/what-to-visit/durham-cathedral-lego-build.

Great St Barts: http://greatstbarts.com/index.html.

Mapping Medieval Chester: www.medievalchester.ac.uk.

Medieval Wall Painting in the English Parish Church: www.paintedchurch.org.

The Middle English Dictionary: http://quod.lib.umich.edu/m/med/.

Oxford Dictionary of National Biography: www.oxforddnb.com.

St Mary's, Ashwell: www.stmarysashwell.org.uk/church/graffiti_pillars.htm.

Woolly Spires project: www.facebook.com/woollyspires and www.artsnk.org/news/2016/06/woolly-spires-exhibition-coming-soon-to-st-mary-st-nicolas-spalding/.

Index

Note: 'n.' after a page reference indicates the number of a note on that page. Page numbers in italics refer to figures.